THIRD EDITION

The Art of Integrative Counseling

Gerald Corey

California State University, Fullerton
Diplomate in Counseling Psychology
American Board of Professional Psychology

BROOKS/COLE
CENGAGE Learning

Australia • Brazil • Japan • Korea • Mexico • Singapore • Spain • United Kingdom • United States

BROOKS/COLE
CENGAGE Learning

The Art of Integrative Counseling, Third Edition
Gerald Corey

Acquisitions Editor: Seth Dobrin

Assistant Editor: Naomi Dreyer

Editorial Assistant: Suzanna Kincaid

Media Editor: Elizabeth Momb

Marketing Communications Manager: Tami Strang

Content Project Manager: Rita Jaramillo

Design Director: Rob Hugel

Art Director: Caryl Gorska

Print Buyer: Judy Inouye

Rights Acquisitions Specialist: Don Schlotman

Production Service: Cenveo Publisher Services

Cover Designer: Tom Ingalls Design

Cover Image: AKIRA/amanaimagesRF / Getty Images

Compositor: Cenveo Publisher Services

International Edition:
ISBN-13: 978-1-133-30875-1
ISBN-10: 1-133-30875-9

Cengage Learning International Offices

Asia
www.cengageasia.com
tel: (65) 6410 1200

Australia/New Zealand
www.cengage.com.au
tel: (61) 3 9685 4111

Brazil
www.cengage.com.br
tel: (55) 11 3665 9900

India
www.cengage.co.in
tel: (91) 11 4364 1111

Latin America
www.cengage.com.mx
tel: (52) 55 1500 6000

UK/Europe/Middle East/Africa
www.cengage.co.uk
tel: (44) 0 1264 332 424

Represented in Canada by Nelson Education, Ltd
www.nelson.com
tel: (416) 752 9100 / (800) 668 0671

Cengage Learning is a leading provider of customized learning solutions with office locations around the globe, including Singapore, the United Kingdom, Australia, Mexico, Brazil, and Japan. Locate your local office at: **www.cengage.com/global**

For product information and free companion resources: www.cengage.com/international Visit your local office: **www.cengage.com/global**
Visit our corporate website: **www.cengage.com**

Printed in the United States of America
1 2 3 4 5 6 7 15 14 13 12 11

To Kay Mikel, our long-time manuscript editor, for her tireless efforts on behalf of our readers.

ABOUT THE AUTHOR

GERALD COREY is Professor Emeritus of Human Services and Counseling at California State University at Fullerton. He received his doctorate in counseling from the University of Southern California. He is a Diplomate in Counseling Psychology, American Board of Professional Psychology; a licensed psychologist; a National Certified Counselor; a Fellow of the American Psychological Association (Counseling Psychology); a Fellow of the American Counseling Association; and a Fellow of the Association for Specialists in Group Work (ASGW). Along with Marianne Schneider Corey, Jerry received the Lifetime Achievement Award from the American Mental Health Counselors Association in 2011 and the Eminent Career Award from ASGW in 2001. He also received the Outstanding Professor of the Year Award from California State University at Fullerton in 1991. He regularly teaches both undergraduate and graduate courses in group counseling and ethics in counseling. He is the author or coauthor of 16 textbooks in counseling currently in print, along with numerous journal articles. His book, *Theory and Practice of Counseling and Psychotherapy*, has been translated into Arabic, Indonesian, Portuguese, Turkish, Korean, and Chinese. *Theory and Practice of Group Counseling* has been translated into Korean, Chinese, Spanish, and Russian.

Jerry and Marianne Schneider Corey often present workshops on the topic of group counseling. In the past 35 years the Coreys have conducted group counseling training workshops for mental health professionals at many universities in the United States as well as in Canada, Mexico, China, Hong Kong, Korea, Germany, Belgium, Scotland, England, and Ireland. In his leisure time, Jerry likes to travel, hike and bicycle, and drive his 1931 Model A Ford. The Coreys have been married for 48 years; they have two adult daughters and three grandchildren.

He holds memberships in the American Counseling Association; the American Psychological Association; the Association for Specialists in Group Work; the American Group Psychotherapy Association; the American Mental Health Counselors Association; the Association for Spiritual, Ethical, and Religious Values in Counseling; the Association for Counselor Education and Supervision; and the Western Association for Counselor Education and Supervision.

Recent publications by Jerry Corey, all with Brooks/Cole, Cengage Learning, include:

- *Theory and Practice of Counseling and Psychotherapy*, Ninth Edition (and *Student Manual*) (2013)
- *Case Approach to Counseling and Psychotherapy*, Eighth Edition (2013)
- *Theory and Practice of Group Counseling*, Eighth Edition (and *Student Manual*) (2012)
- *Becoming a Helper*, Sixth Edition (2011, with Marianne Schneider Corey)
- *Issues in Ethics in the Helping Professions*, Eighth Edition (2011, with Marianne Schneider Corey and Patrick Callanan)
- *Groups: Process and Practice*, Eighth Edition (2010, with Marianne Schneider Corey and Cindy Corey)
- *I Never Knew I Had a Choice*, Ninth Edition (2010, with Marianne Schneider Corey)
- *Group Techniques*, Third Edition (2004, with Marianne Schneider Corey, Patrick Callanan, and J. Michael Russell)

Jerry is coauthor (with Barbara Herlihy) of *Boundary Issues in Counseling: Multiple Roles and Responsibilities*, Second Edition (2006) and *ACA Ethical Standards Casebook*,

Sixth Edition (2006); he is coauthor (with Robert Haynes, Patrice Moulton, and Michelle Muratori) of *Clinical Supervision in the Helping Professions: A Practical Guide,* Second Edition (2010); he is the author of *Creating Your Professional Path: Lessons From My Journey* (2010). All four of these books are published by the American Counseling Association.

He has also made several educational DVD and video programs on various aspects of counseling practice: (1) *DVD for Theory and Practice of Counseling and Psychotherapy: The Case of Stan and Lecturettes* (2013); (2) *DVD for Integrative Counseling: The Case of Ruth and Lecturettes* (2013, with Robert Haynes); (3) *DVD for Theory and Practice of Group Counseling* (2012); (4) *Groups in Action: Evolution and Challenges—DVD and Workbook* (2006, with Marianne Schneider Corey and Robert Haynes); and (5) *Ethics in Action: CD-ROM* (2003, with Marianne Schneider Corey and Robert Haynes). All of these programs are available through Brooks/Cole, Cengage Learning.

CONTENTS

10   Working With Transference and Countertransference   124

11   Understanding How the Past Influences the Present and the Future   138

PREFACE

In my books dealing with the theory and practice of counseling, I devote specific chapters to presenting an integrative approach to counseling practice and a case example of the application of my integrative perspective. *The Art of Integrative Counseling* is basically an extension of these chapters and is aimed at helping readers conceptualize the various dimensions of an integrative perspective.

About This Book

The Art of Integrative Counseling is designed as a supplementary book for those who have had a basic course in counseling theory and practice. Unless you have had a course in counseling theory or have at least read a standard textbook covering the range of counseling theories, you may have trouble understanding and applying the ideas in this book. This book is not designed as a substitute for a text surveying the counseling theories. Instead, it is aimed primarily for courses in advanced counseling practice, counseling techniques, therapeutic procedures, practicum, and internship. I am assuming that you are familiar with the basic concepts associated with some of the major theoretical systems underlying counseling practice, such as psychoanalytic therapy, Adlerian therapy, existential therapy, person-centered therapy, Gestalt therapy, psychodrama, reality therapy, behavior therapy, cognitive behavior therapy, solution-focused brief therapy, motivational interviewing, narrative therapy, feminist therapy, redecision therapy, and family systems therapy.

One of the trends in the counseling field is the move toward integration of various theoretical systems and approaches to counseling. I believe an integrative approach is a more useful guide to practice. In this book I strive to do several things: (1) describe the concepts and techniques that I most draw from in my own integrative approach to counseling practice; (2) demonstrate how concepts and techniques can be borrowed from a variety of theoretical models and applied to the counseling process from the initial to termination stages through discussions of my work with two clients, "Ruth" and, to a lesser extent, "Stan";

(3) invite you to imagine that you are a client in counseling with me as I describe my approach to integrative counseling; and (4) suggest ways for you to think about designing your own integrative approach that will serve as a foundation for what you do in your counseling practice. To encourage active learning, I ask you to put yourself in the role of a therapist at times and to assume the role of a client at other times as you reflect these topics.

It is not possible for me to tell you how to develop a personal integrative style that will fit best for you. I can, however, provide some guidelines to assist you in the task of considering which key concepts and techniques you might incorporate in your personal therapeutic style. In writing about my own personal synthesis, I am in no way suggesting that there is "one right way" to formulate an integrative perspective. Indeed, what I hope you will get from reading and studying this book (along with using the *DVD for Integrative Counseling: The Case of Ruth and Lecturettes* and the *DVD for Theory and Practice of Counseling and Psychotherapy: The Case of Stan and Lecturettes*) is a framework that will assist you in systematically constructing an integrative counseling approach that works best for the person you are and for the clients you will serve.

About the DVD for Integrative Counseling: The Case of Ruth and Lecturettes

The *DVD for Integrative Counseling: The Case of Ruth and Lecturettes* serves as an ideal companion to this book. The chapter titles in this book and the sessions in the video program are the same. This video program illustrates my integrative perspective in working with one client, Ruth, and there are many references to the video program throughout the book. In each chapter the central case example is Ruth, which I use to illustrate the concepts and techniques that are a part of my integrative perspective. The program—structured within the framework of 13 counseling sessions from the initial to termination phase—is designed to involve you in learning about an integrative approach through the use of interactive exercises and questions. I strongly recommend that you incorporate the video program into your study to receive the maximum benefit from reading and studying this book.

The format of the 13 sessions consists of a lecturette on specific dimensions of my integrative approach, a counseling demonstration with Ruth, and a running process commentary of Ruth's and my work together. Many of my comments in this book are directed to how I would apply a range of selected concepts and techniques in working with Ruth over the course of short-term counseling. It will be important for you to interpret and apply what I write in this book to your own client population, as well as to the setting in which you work. Viewing the counseling sessions and the process commentaries—along with reading each of the chapters in this book—will assist you in designing your own personal integrative approach.

The videos from the DVD are available on the *Premium Website for Integrative Counseling* for students and faculty who prefer to access the material online. A printed access code can be bundled with the textbook, or an instant access code can be purchased online at CengageBrain.com.

About the DVD for Theory and Practice of Counseling and Psychotherapy: The Case of Stan and Lecturettes

In the *DVD for Theory and Practice of Counseling and Psychotherapy: The Case of Stan and Lecturettes* and a companion home-study program (also available online) I demonstrate counseling Stan from various theoretical perspectives. Like the DVD program in which I counsel Ruth, this program consists of 13 sessions, each beginning with brief introductory comments, followed by a counseling session with Stan from a specific theoretical orientation, and ending with a process commentary. One of the new features of this third edition is the extent to which I have tied the case of Stan into this book as a second case example presented in each chapter.

This program also is available on the *Premium Website for Theory and Practice of Counseling and Psychotherapy* for students and faculty who prefer to access the videos online. A printed access code can be bundled with the textbook, or an instant access code can be purchased online at CengageBrain.com.

A Complete Teaching/Learning Package

Case Approach to Counseling and Psychotherapy, Eighth Edition (Corey, 2013b) reflects my increasing emphasis on the use of demonstrations and the case approach method to bridge the gap between the theory and practice of counseling. This book highlights a variety of contemporary counseling approaches, and demonstrates how each of the various therapeutic approaches is applied to the same client, Ruth, who is followed throughout this book. A feature of the text is an assessment of Ruth's case by one or more guest consultants from each of the various theoretical perspectives. Twenty-six highly competent practitioners assess and treat Ruth from their particular theoretical orientation; they also provide sample dialogues to illustrate their style of working with Ruth. Practitioners who contributed their perspective on counseling Ruth are well-known figures representing the theories they are demonstrating. Among them are Albert Ellis, Arnold Lazarus, Frank Dattilio, David Cain, Sherry Cormier, William Glasser, Robert Wubbolding, John Murphy, and John Winslade.

In addition, in *The Art of Integrative Counseling* I make frequent reference to my main textbook, *Theory and Practice of Counseling and Psychotherapy*, which is accompanied by the *Student Manual for Theory and Practice of Counseling and Psychotherapy*. Whether you have used this book in a previous course, or another theories text, I encourage you to review the relevant chapters.

What's New in the Third Edition of The Art of Integrative Counseling?

In this Third Edition of *The Art of Integrative Counseling*, chapters have been revised to bring the discussions up to date and to refine existing ideas while retaining the informal, personal style of writing that characterized previous editions. The popular case example of Ruth is augmented in this edition by inclusion of a second case study (Stan). I have incorporated key findings from recent research on topics such as the central role of the therapeutic relationship (Chapter 2), the role of client feedback on therapy outcomes (Chapter 3), and the future of psychotherapy integration and the role of evidence-based practice (Chapter 13). Other material new to this edition includes a section on emotion-focused therapy (Chapter 3); an expanded treatment of diversity issues, especially the role of spirituality in counseling practice, and a new section on tailoring psychotherapy to individuals from diverse cultural backgrounds (Chapter 4); a broadened discussion of the dynamics of resistance, along with the importance of respecting and reframing resistance, and more on the stages of change (Chapter 5); new material on Meichenbaum's cognitive behavior modification approach (Chapter 6); a discussion of empathy fatigue (Chapter 7); a section on using mindfulness as a behavioral strategy (Chapter 8); an emphasis on flexibility and tailoring treatment to individuals and using motivational interviewing in an integrative approach (Chapter 9); understanding the dynamics of transference and countertransference (Chapter 10); understanding the role of the past, present, and future as it pertains to counseling individuals (Chapter 11); new material on solution-focused brief therapy and narrative therapy (Chapter 12); an expanded discussion on termination including the use of therapist's letters, and relapse prevention strategies to help clients deal with setbacks that occur after the end of therapy sessions (Chapter 13). All of the chapters have been carefully examined to determine how the topics fit with contemporary integrative approaches, and I have given particular attention to trends in the psychotherapy integration movement. Many new references update the discussion of key topics and provide avenues for further exploration.

Acknowledgments

I am indebted to the professors and students who reviewed this book and provided me with constructive input for this revised edition: I especially want to recognize two of my former students who provided many suggestions that were incorporated in the final manuscript: Amanda Connell and Susan Halim, both graduate students in the counseling program at California State University, Fullerton. Other reviewers included Jamie Bludworth, private practice, Phoenix, Arizona; Lori Bruch, University of Scranton; David Carter, University of Nebraska, Omaha; Pornthip Chalungsooth, University of Scranton; Robert Haynes, Borderline Productions; Amanda Healey, Sam Houston State University; Susan Marcus-Mendoza, University of Oklahoma; Patrice Moulton, Northwestern State University, Louisiana; and John Norcross, University of Scranton.

I want to acknowledge those on the Brooks/Cole, Cengage Learning team who are involved with our projects. These people include Seth Dobrin, editor of counseling, social work, and human services; Julie Martinez, consulting editor, who monitored the review process; Caryl Gorska, for her work on the interior design and the cover; Elizabeth Momb, media editor; Naomi Dreyer, assistant editor, who worked on supplemental materials; Michelle Muratori, Johns Hopkins University, for updating the *Instructor's Resource Manual* and assisting in the development of other supplements; and Rita Jaramillo, project manager. I thank Ben Kolstad of Cenveo Publisher Services, who coordinated the production of this book. Special appreciation goes to Kay Mikel, the manuscript editor, whose sensitivity and editorial skills contributed in important ways to the readability and interest of this text.

— GERALD COREY

CHAPTER ONE

Beginning of Counseling

Introduction

If you have applied to a graduate program in the helping professions, you are certain to have been asked these questions: "What is your approach to counseling?" "How does your theoretical orientation influence the manner in which you practice?" You will revisit these questions throughout your career—in job interviews and self-evaluations.

This book will assist you in conceptualizing what you do as a counseling practitioner and help you clarify your theoretical orientation. I want to stimulate your thinking about the importance of developing an integrative approach to counseling practice that pays attention to what your clients are *thinking, feeling,* and *doing.* Combining these three dimensions is the basis for a powerful and comprehensive approach to counseling practice. If any of these dimensions is excluded, the therapeutic approach is incomplete because no single theoretical model is comprehensive enough to explain all facets of the human experience.

It is important to examine the contemporary theories of counseling to determine which concepts and techniques you can incorporate in your approach to practice. Creating your own integrative stance is truly a challenge. You cannot simply pick bits and pieces from theories in a random and fragmented manner. Each theory represents a different vantage point from which to look at human behavior. Study all the major theories, resist embracing too quickly any single point of view, and look for a basis for an integrative perspective that will guide your practice.

Wampold (2010) describes theory as a good road map for understanding how therapy unfolds, but no one theory is best for all clients. Research has clearly established that psychotherapy works and is remarkably effective, but no particular theory or technique has proved to be superior to all others (Wampold, 2010). Although no one theory has "the truth," each may have something unique to offer you. In addition, evidence increasingly supports the idea that the working alliance and the therapist as a person are critical factors in determining therapy outcomes.

The aim of this book is to assist you in acquiring your own unique perspective on counseling, which will aid you in eventually developing your integrative approach to counseling practice. To develop this kind of integration, you need to be well grounded in a number of theories, be open to the idea that some aspects of these theories can be unified in different ways, be familiar with the research literature in the field of psychotherapy, and be willing to continually test your hypotheses to determine how well they are working. In developing and conceptualizing this integrative counseling approach, you need to consider your own personality. You also must think about what concepts and techniques work best with a range of clients. Choosing techniques that are suitable for particular problems and for different clients requires knowledge, skill, art, and clinical experience. It is also an art to know *when* and *how* to use a particular therapeutic intervention.

To be an effective counselor it is essential that you be willing to take an honest look at your own life. Are you willing to do for yourself what you ask clients to do? It will be hard to inspire clients to seek help when they need it if you are not open to change in your own life. Your own self-exploration likely will be one of the most important factors in learning how to use many of the techniques in this book. You can get many ideas of ways to creatively intervene with your clients by experiencing what it is like to be a client. (See Chapter 10 for more on the value of personal therapy for counselors in training.) As much as possible, I will ask you to put yourself in the shoes of the client. The "Becoming a Client" sections in this book can be useful sources of self-exploration and can offer you strategies for intervening with your own clients.

Examples of applications of techniques are provided in every chapter when I discuss my particular approach with two different clients, "Ruth" and "Stan." These clients are composite characters created to enhance your learning experience, and you will get to know both Ruth and Stan well in the remaining chapters. In many of the chapters I will be speaking to you as a counselor, especially when I discuss suggestions for developing your integrative approach to counseling.

If you have not read the preface, let me encourage you to do so before continuing with the text. The preface includes a number of specific suggestions on how to make the best use of this book in conjunction with the *DVD for Integrative Counseling: The Case of Ruth and Lecturettes*. This program consists of 13 counseling sessions with Ruth that parallel the 13 chapters in this book. The *DVD for Theory and Practice of Counseling and Psychotherapy: The Case of Stan and Lecturettes* also fits within the structure of this book. In this program, I demonstrate ways of counseling Stan from different theoretical perspectives. In the video program each session focuses on a singular therapy approach, but in this book my discussions on the case of Stan address ways of blending therapeutic modalities and showing how integration is possible. I frequently refer to highlights from specific theories in working with Stan in the various chapters.

An Integrative Theoretical Approach: An Overview

This book represents my own integrative approach to counseling. I define an *integrative approach* to counseling as being rooted in a theory, with techniques systematically borrowed from other approaches and tailored to a client's unique needs. I am not suggesting that you adopt my conceptualization of theory applied to practice. You will develop your own integrative style based on your personality and the kinds of clients you expect to counsel. By describing my personal orientation to counseling, I hope to provide a framework to assist you in designing a theoretical orientation that makes sense to you.

The early history of counseling was full of theoretical wars as practitioners argued over the "best" way to bring about personality change. Many practitioners and scholars were resistant to psychotherapy integration, often to the point of being blind to alternative theories and ignoring effective methods from other theoretical schools. However, since the 1980s most therapists have seriously considered integrating the best from the various schools. Therapists now acknowledge the limitations inherent in specific theories and the potential value of other theoretical systems. Most practitioners use some form of integration today, and research supports the efficacy of an integrative approach (Norcross, 2005).

As a student, you can begin the process of developing a style tailored to your own personality by familiarizing yourself with the major approaches to therapeutic practice. Then choose one theory to study in some depth and branch out from there in your search for an integrative style. I recommend that you study in depth the one theory that comes closest to your worldview, and use this theory as a foundation for developing your personal orientation. Being grounded in a theory provides an anchor for making sense of what you are doing as a counselor. Without a theoretical foundation you are liable to flounder, and neither you nor your client is likely to experience productive results.

Attempting to practice without having an explicit theoretical rationale is like trying to build a house without a set of blueprints. The foundation of a house needs to be sturdy and strong to support the structure. If you operate in a theoretical vacuum and are unable to draw on theory to support your interventions, your attempts to help people change will have uncertain outcomes. Theory is not a rigid set of structures; rather, it provides a general framework that enables you to make sense of the many facets of the counseling process and gives direction to what you do and say.

You need to believe in the basic philosophy of the theory you embrace and that the treatment you are delivering will be effective. Therapists providing a treatment that they find interesting and fits for them are likely to be more effective than therapists who deliver a treatment not to their liking (Wampold, 2010). The treatment needs to be consistent with your beliefs, values, and personality. Ask yourself: "Which treatment delivered by me will be most effective?" (p. 49).

I draw on concepts and techniques from most of the contemporary counseling models. I then adapt them to a style that fits me personally, taking into account the universal thinking, feeling, and behaving dimensions of human experience. I typically ask clients to think about the decisions they have made about themselves. Some of these decisions may have been necessary for their psychological survival as children but may now be ineffective.

I encourage clients to pay attention to their "self-talk" and to ask themselves these questions:

- How do your problems reflect the assumptions you make about yourself, about others, and about life?
- How do you create your problems by the thoughts and beliefs to which you cling?
- How can you begin to free yourself by critically evaluating the statements you repeat to yourself?

These interventions help clients think about events in their lives, how they have interpreted those events, and what they need to do cognitively to change their belief systems.

Once clients begin thinking about their problems, they often feel stuck due to unexpressed and unresolved emotional concerns. I encourage clients to experience the range of their feelings and to talk about how certain events have affected them. The healing process is facilitated by using techniques that tap feelings and allow individuals to feel listened to and understood.

Thinking and feeling are vital components in the helping process, but eventually clients must express themselves in the behaving or acting dimension. Clients can spend countless hours gaining insights and venting pent-up feelings, but at some point they need to get involved in a program of change. Their feelings and thoughts can then be tested and adapted to real-life situations. If the helping process includes a focus on what people are doing, there is a greater chance that clients also will be able to change their thinking and feeling. Using an integrative counseling style, interaction among these three dimensions occurs throughout the counseling process.

I help clients consolidate what they are learning by encouraging them to apply new behaviors to situations they encounter every day. Some strategies I use are contracts, homework assignments, action programs, self-monitoring techniques, support systems, and self-directed programs of change. (These strategies are discussed in some detail in Chapters 8, 9, and 12). These approaches all stress the role of commitment on the part of clients to practice new behaviors, to follow through with a realistic plan for change, and to develop practical methods of carrying out this plan in everyday life.

Ultimately, the most meaningful counseling perspective for you to use is one that is an extension of your values and personality. As your philosophy of life evolves, so will your philosophy of counseling. Having a clearly defined and articulated philosophy of counseling is essential to your professional practice. Developing a personalized approach that guides your practice is an ongoing process, and your personal approach to counseling will continuously undergo revision. Reflecting on your own values, life experiences, and philosophy of life is a good starting point.

Put Yourself in the Shoes of the Client

The Initial Counseling Session

One of my goals in writing this book is to include you experientially in the process of deciding which aspects you might incorporate into your own philosophy of counseling, based upon the existing theories. I ask you to "become the client" and reflect on integration from that perspective. Imagine that you are the client and we are about to have our first session. As a therapist, I realize that the first few minutes are critical in setting the tone. I begin by explaining to you the confidential nature of our work together, including the limitations of confidentiality. By explaining a few of the basic rules of therapy, I hope to provide a sense of safety that will encourage you to talk freely. To promote trust and rapport, I ask you what you expected of today.

What I most want to be able to do is listen to your story. Meeting and valuing you as a person is essential to positive change. To create a working therapeutic relationship, I try to make a good connection with you. My aim is to establish a positive relationship by listening, responding, demonstrating respect for your capacity to understand yourself, and exhibiting faith, hope, and caring. Here are some questions I am likely to ask you during the first session. Reflect on your responses to each of these questions.

- What brings you here? What has been going on in your life recently that prompted you to seek professional help at this time?
- What expectations do you have of therapy? Of me? What are your hopes, fears, and reservations? What goals do you have for yourself through therapy?
- Could you give me a picture of some significant turning points in your life? Who have been the important people in your life? What significant decisions have you made? What are some of the struggles you've dealt with, and what are some of the issues that are current for you?

To the extent possible, I avoid preconceived notions about what our dialogue will consist of or how the therapy process will unfold. My hope is that you will share your present thoughts and feelings as they arise in this session. You may not be sure what you want from counseling, and you may have ambivalent feelings about being with me. You may be uncertain about how being in counseling will change your relationships at home. This lack of certainty is a good place to begin. I want to give you a chance to express your expectations, hopes, concerns, and doubts about making a commitment to the counseling process. This is one way I get to know you and connect with you.

Informed Consent

Educating you (the client) about the counseling process, addressing your questions, and clarifying your expectations are routes to ethical and effective counseling practice. The challenge is to create a balance between giving you too much or too little information. A well-written informed consent document can provide much of this information without overwhelming the client in the first session. The main agenda is to provide you with the opportunity to talk about what you hope to gain from being in counseling. For you to feel safe enough to meaningfully express yourself, you need to have at least some minimal information about the nature of the therapeutic relationship. What would you want to know about how counseling works as you begin as my client? What do you consider essential to know before you make a commitment to this professional relationship? Here are some topics we might explore as part of the therapeutic contract during our early sessions:

- Why is confidentiality essential to our work together, and what are the limits of confidentiality?
- How does the therapeutic process work?
- What is my primary role as a therapist?
- What is expected of you as a client, both during the sessions and outside of sessions?
- How can you and I become collaborators?
- What is the approximate length of the counseling process? How long will it take for you to begin feeling and acting better?
- How will we know when it is time to end our work? Who has the right and the responsibility to terminate?
- What are your rights and responsibilities as the client?
- What are some of the benefits and risks of therapy that you can expect?

Let's assume, during this first session, that you say this to me: "One of the troubles I have is trusting myself. I always think about what others expect of me. I've tried to please others for so long that I don't know who I am most of the time." This is a good opportunity for me to briefly educate you about a key task of therapy: challenging you to begin to examine the ways in which you think, feel, and act.

I want to establish a collaborative working relationship with you. (In Chapter 2, I discuss in detail how I strive to create an effective therapeutic alliance.) I spend time explaining my view of the therapy process and how it works. By demystifying the therapeutic process, I am conveying the message that you are largely in charge of the direction your therapy will take. I operate on the assumption that you are the expert on your own life. I will encourage you to look within to find your own answers, but I won't try to provide easy solutions or answers. I will provide guidance and support as you strive to develop your own answers. As an outcome of our work together, I hope to help you increase your awareness of your choices and come to realize any ways that you limit or restrict yourself.

By this time, we have talked about the nature of counseling, the purpose and limitations of confidentiality, the procedures that we may employ, and the benefits and risks of the process. What questions and reactions do you have? In later sessions we will discuss specific therapy procedures I believe may be appropriate as we uncover your particular problems. You may help choose the techniques used in dealing with your problems.

Informing you about the counseling process is an important professional responsibility and an ethical requirement of all the major mental health professions. To what extent has this discussion helped you feel informed and a partner in the therapeutic venture?

Initial Assessment

Next, I begin the process of conducting an assessment of your circumstances and sharing my impressions with you. Assessment consists of evaluating the relevant factors in your life to identify themes for further exploration in therapy. I am likely to employ an Adlerian technique as part of your assessment, which is presented in the form of *The Question*: "How would your life be different if you did not have this problem? What would you do differently if you did not have this symptom or problem?" "How would your life be different if you didn't have these issues or concerns?" When the answer is: "Nothing would be different, except the symptoms would be gone," I suspect the problem is probably physiological or organic, even if it manifests itself as a psychological complaint. However, if you say that "if it weren't for this depression, I would get out more and see my friends," I would suspect that your problem serves the purpose of helping you to avoid something you perceive as necessary, but from which you would like to retreat. Such a statement may reveal your concern about the possibility of being a good friend or being welcomed by your friends. Raising such questions can be a good catalyst to stimulate your reflection on what it might be like for you if you were able to change some problematic area in your life.

I am also interested in learning something about your family of origin during the initial assessment. Understanding and assessing your family of origin will reveal patterns of interpersonal behavior and communication you learned in your family that are likely to be repeated in other interactions outside your family. As a way of learning about the influence of your family on the person you are, I may ask you to identify what you learned from interacting with your parents, from observing your parents' interactions with each other, and from observing how your parents interacted with each sibling.

I favor a collaborative approach to assessment, one that includes you, the client, as a therapeutic partner. Assessment is an ongoing process. It will not be completed during the intake interview, nor will fixed judgments be made. Assessment can be linked directly to the therapeutic process, forming a basis for developing methods of evaluating how well my interventions are working to achieve your goals. At this time I encourage you to tell your story. As you do, I listen not only to the content but to the manner in which you present the story of your life. I am interested in learning about strengths and resources you have to draw on in addressing your life concerns. This kind of assessment goes beyond simply understanding your problems. Together we can build on the positive patterns your life story reveals.

Therapy Is a Time-Limited Process

If you are my client in a setting in which brief therapy is the standard, it is especially important for me to be clear about the number of sessions the agency allows or that your insurance will pay for. If an agency policy specifies that you can be seen for only six sessions, you have a right to know this from the onset. If we are working from a short-term therapy approach, I will always keep in mind the short duration of our work together. The goal is to help you learn, as quickly and efficiently as possible, the coping skills you need to live in self-directed ways.

The limitation of time can assist us in establishing short-term, realistic goals. Toward the end of each session, I will ask you the degree to which you see yourself reaching the goals you have established, and I will also ask you to take a few moments to fill out a rating scale of the session. (This written rating scale is described by Duncan, Miller, and Sparks [2004] in *The Heroic Client*.) I will ask you to rate four areas:

Relationship: To what degree did you feel heard, understood, and respected?

Goals and topics: To what degree did we work on and talk about what you wanted to work on and talk about?

Approach or method: To what degree is the therapist's approach a good fit for you?

Overall: To what degree was the session right for you today?

By reviewing the course of treatment, you are in a position to identify what is and is not working for you in the counseling process. I will include you by asking for your feedback on the progress of treatment and your experience in the therapeutic process. If I listen to feedback from you, together we can modify what we are doing in our therapy sessions, making the therapeutic process a collaborative endeavor.

My overriding goal is to increase the chances that you will not continue to need a therapist. If I do my work well, eventually I hope to put myself out of business. Thus, I am open to exploring termination issues with you at any point during the counseling process. As my client, would you want to know about these matters from the start? To what extent do you think discussing termination early on could be helpful to you?

Introduction to the Case of Ruth

See Session 1 (Beginning of Counseling) on the *DVD*
for Integrative Counseling: *The Case of Ruth and Lecturettes.*

Let's switch perspectives now and talk about how the case of Ruth can inform your process of developing your integrative approach to therapy. Ruth's case is the primary example throughout this book, and she is the client in the video. She is a 39-year-old married woman with four teenagers, coming to therapy for the first time with some anxiety and a host of somatic complaints. She lives with her husband (John, 45) and their children (Rob, 19; Jennifer, 18; Susan, 17; and Adam, 16). Here is a brief summary of data taken from Ruth's intake form.

☙ Psychosocial History   Ruth is the oldest of four children. Her father is a fundamentalist Christian minister, and her mother is a housewife. She describes her father as distant, authoritarian, and rigid; as a child, her relationship with him was one of unquestioning, fearful adherence to his rules and standards. She remembers her mother as being critical, and Ruth thought she could never do enough to please her mother. At other times her mother was supportive. The family demonstrated little affection. In many ways she took on the role of caring for her younger brother and sisters, largely in the hope of winning the approval of her parents. When she attempted to have any kind of fun, she encountered her father's disapproval and outright scorn. To a large extent, this pattern of taking care of others has extended throughout her life.

Presenting Problem   Ruth reports general dissatisfaction with her life, seeing it as rather uneventful and predictable. She feels some panic over reaching the age of 39, wondering where the years have gone. For 2 years she has been troubled with a range of psychosomatic complaints, including sleep disturbances, anxiety, dizziness, heart palpitations, and headaches. At times she must push herself to leave the house. Ruth complains that she cries easily over trivial matters, often feels depressed, and does not like her body.

Ruth has recently become aware that she lives for others. Living this way leads her to overlook many of her own needs and desires. She has not cultivated healthy interdependence in her relationships and realizes that she plays a role of "superwoman" in all aspects of her life. She feels that she gives and gives in all of her relationships, to the point that she feels empty. She has a difficult time asking others to attend to her needs. She tries to be the good wife and good mother that her family expects her to be—and that she expects herself to be. In most respects, Ruth does not like herself. She does not like her looks or her body, and she worries about what her family of origin expects of her. She goes to church every Sunday, but she has left her father's church, which is a source of some guilt for her. Although her parents have not disowned her, it sometimes feels that they have.

History of Presenting Problem   Ruth's major career was as homemaker and mother until her children became adolescents. She then entered college part-time and obtained a bachelor's degree in child development. She recently graduated from college as an elementary education major, and she is now working on her teaching credential. She looks forward to becoming an elementary school teacher, yet she often feels so overwhelmed that she wonders if she will ever reach her career goals.

Through her contacts with others at the university, she became aware of how she has limited herself, how she has fostered her family's dependence on her, and how frightened she is of branching out from her secure roles as mother and wife. She completed an introductory course in counseling that encouraged her to look at the direction of her own life. This course and her experiences with fellow students acted as a catalyst in getting her to take an honest look at her life. Ruth is not clear at this point who she is, apart from being a mother, a wife, and a student. She realizes that she does not have a good sense of what she wants for herself and that she typically lives up to what others in her life want for her.

Drawing on Theories Applied to the Case of Ruth

Let's shift perspectives again and discuss how I would draw on different theories to work with Ruth. I will tap into five general theoretical models of counseling. First are the *psychodynamic approaches*, which include psychoanalytic therapy, object-relations approaches, and Adlerian therapy. Although Adlerian theory differs from psychoanalytic theory in many respects, it can broadly be considered a psychodynamic perspective. The second category comprises the *experiential* and *relationship-oriented therapies,* which include the existential approach, the person-centered approach, Gestalt therapy, and psychodrama. Third are the *action-oriented therapies,* which include behavior therapy, rational emotive behavior therapy, cognitive therapy, reality therapy, and redecision therapy (or transactional analysis). These are sometimes known generally as cognitive behavioral approaches. Fourth are the *postmodern approaches,* which include solution-focused brief therapy and narrative therapy. The fifth general approach is the *systems perspective,* of which feminist therapy and family therapy are a part, as are some of the emerging culture-specific counseling approaches. The systems orientation stresses the importance of understanding individuals in the context of the surroundings that influence their development.

Theories During the Early Stage   At the beginning of the counseling relationship, my concern is to establish a foundation that will provide safety for clients to be able to undertake the risks necessary in making fundamental life changes. The concepts that I find particularly useful at this time come from the experiential therapies, especially person-centered and existential therapy.

I incorporate many constructs from the person-centered approach in my therapeutic style. For example, I believe Ruth will tell me a great deal about what she wants from life if I can really listen with deep understanding. Although I see my overall style as being active and directive, I first and foremost want to see the world from Ruth's vantage point. She will offer rich clues and provide me with leads if only I care enough to deeply listen and observe. From the person-centered approach, I value the emphasis on striving to experience Ruth's world from her subjective perspective and trusting in her basic wisdom. This approach gives priority to the quality of our relationship, which I believe is the curative factor that brings about healing and change. I want to approach meeting Ruth with as much presence, openness, and interest as I am able to bring to the initial encounter. What I most want to do is assist her in creating her own agenda rather than being too quick to present my agenda to her.

Let me share my thoughts about Ruth's first counseling session. Early in the session, she lets me know that she is anxious about coming to her first counseling session. She does not know what to expect. She lets me know that she feels confused about what she really wants for herself and what kind of life she most wants. Her hope is that I will tell her what to do so that she can go and do it and then feel better. She expects that I will give her guidance, at the very least, and would like it if I were to give her advice and tell her what to do with her life. Ruth is putting me in the place of the expert and, in doing so, is minimizing her personal power to make meaningful decisions herself. Although I can appreciate her anxiety and lack of faith in her own ability to take an active stance toward life, I do not serve her well if I make decisions about her life for her. I believe she is the expert on her own life. Consistent with the philosophies of person-centered therapy, feminist therapy, and the postmodern approaches,

I believe that Ruth, with good support, has the capacity to identify what she wants in her life and that she will be able to chart her own course.

🎋 Questions to Facilitate the Initial Session   At our initial meeting I do not have a clear idea of where our journey together will take us, for much depends on how far Ruth wants to go and what she is willing to explore. I start by giving her a chance to say how she feels about coming to the initial session, and I ask some of these questions, giving her time to respond to each one:

- What prompted you to call and come in for this appointment?
- What do you want me to know about you?
- In what areas is your life going well?
- What do you wish were different?
- What were you experiencing as you were getting ready to come to this session?
- What is going on in your life that you particularly like?

These questions open the discussion of what Ruth is experiencing as she makes her first contact with me. They are central to the assessment process, which begins during the initial session. A guiding question in the back of my mind during this assessment is, "What does this client most need to understand about herself to grow and to deal more effectively with her present relationships?"

From our initial session, I learn that Ruth has decided to seek individual counseling to explore several areas of her life.

- Ruth describes some of these major symptoms: "I sometimes feel very panicky, especially at night when I'm trying to sleep. Sometimes I wake up and find it difficult to breathe, my heart will be pounding, and I break out in a cold sweat. I toss and turn trying to relax, and instead I feel tense and worry a lot about many things. It's hard for me to turn off these thoughts. Then during the day I'm so tired I can hardly function, and I find that lately I cry very easily if even minor things go wrong." A physician whom she consulted could find no organic or medical basis for her physical symptoms and recommended personal therapy.
- Ruth's four children range in age from 16 to 19, and all of them are now finding more of their satisfactions outside the family and the home and are spending increasing time with their friends. She sees these changes and is concerned about "losing" them. She is having particular problems with her daughter Jennifer, and she is at a loss as to how to deal with Jennifer's rebellion manifested by staying out late at night, drinking excessively at parties, and showing no interest in school. Ruth feels very much unappreciated by her children.
- Ruth is not really sure who or what she wants to become in the future. She would like to develop a sense of herself apart from the expectations of others. She does not find her relationship with her husband, John, at all satisfactory. He appears to be resisting her attempts to make changes and prefers that she remain as she was. Ruth is anxious over the prospect of challenging this relationship, fearing that she might end up alone.
- Ruth is experiencing increasing concern over aging and losing her "looks."

These factors have provided the motivation for her to take the necessary steps to initiate individual therapy. Perhaps the greatest catalyst that triggered her to come for therapy is the increase in her physical symptoms and her anxiety.

❧ Anxiety Over Beginning Counseling
It is to be expected that Ruth has some anxiety about initiating therapy. I want to provide her with the opportunity to talk about what it is like for her to come to the office today. That in itself provides the direction for much of our session. I surely want to get an idea of what has brought her to therapy. What is going on in her life that motivates her to seek therapy? What does she most hope for as a result of this venture? I structure the initial session so that she can talk about her expectations and about her fears, hopes, and ambivalent feelings.

Because Ruth's trust in me will be an important part of the therapy process, I give her the chance to ask questions about how counseling generally works. I believe in demystifying the treatment process. Ruth will get more from her therapy if she knows how it works, the nature of her responsibilities and mine, and what she wants from this process. (These basic concepts are all derived from several theoretical approaches, especially from models such as Adlerian therapy, behavior therapy, cognitive behavior therapy, reality therapy, and feminist therapy.) As a way for Ruth to establish trust with me, she might ask personal information about me, such as my beliefs, values, and life circumstances. Depending on what she asks, I am likely to directly answer her questions. However, I will probably also explore with her why this information is important to her. While I strive to be appropriately open and self-disclosing, I also want to establish appropriate therapeutic boundaries.

Feminist therapy offers a number of key concepts that can be incorporated in the early phases of the therapeutic endeavor. The feminist perspective assumes that the client is an expert in her own life, and I want to reinforce this idea with Ruth. This is not to minimize my expertise as a healer, but my interventions must be guided by what Ruth wants for herself, not what I think Ruth should want or my vision of her ideal life. To help her sort out conflicting beliefs about the roles she plays, her therapy might include a gender-role analysis so that she can come to a fuller understanding of the limiting roles she has uncritically accepted. With this expanded awareness, she can assume more power to make choices about the roles she wants to accept or modify.

I must truly secure Ruth's informed consent, and in doing so convey to her the expectation that she will be in charge of much of what we do in the sessions. She will be an active agent and make decisions at every juncture. I will not keep Ruth in the dark about how therapy works or about my interventions. Ultimately, my hope is that Ruth will be empowered to become her own counselor. My role will be to help her acquire the tools necessary to actively shape the events of her life and to actively engage in directing her own life.

❧ Letting Ruth Tell Her Story
Counselors often receive information about clients through the intake or referral process before meeting them for the first time. Although I think life-history information is important, I begin by making

person-to-person contact with Ruth. Even if her concerns surface in therapy rather quickly, my initial attention is on Ruth as a whole person, not on the presenting problem. I see value in first letting her tell her story in the way she chooses. How she walks into the office, her tone of voice, postures, facial expressions, gestures, hesitations in speech, nonverbal language, mannerisms, and style of speech are all of interest to me. The details she chooses to go into, and what she decides to reveal, provide me with a valuable perspective from which to understand her. I am interested in how she perceives the events in her life and how she feels in her subjective world. (This concept of understanding the phenomenological world of the client is especially important in the existential, person-centered, Adlerian, and narrative models.)

Ruth has generated stories to make sense of herself and the world. One of my tasks as a counselor is to assist Ruth in freeing herself from problem-saturated stories and to help her reauthor her story about herself and her relationships. Drawing upon the narrative approach involves a shift in the focus of most traditional psychotherapy approaches. Being influenced by narrative therapy, I will strive to establish a collaborative approach with special interest in listening to Ruth's story, searching for times in her life when she was resourceful, and assisting her in separating herself from identifying herself with her problem. From the very beginning of our work together, I will be listening for times when Ruth was not bogged down with her problems and when she was able to draw upon some strength. Granted, there will be limited time for Ruth to share her story during the first session. This process can begin, yet it will take several sessions for her to reveal key themes in her life.

As I begin to understand Ruth's experiential world, I have a basis for making interventions. Most of what I will do in my therapeutic work with Ruth is based on the assumption that she can exercise her freedom to change situations, even though the range of this freedom may be restricted by external factors.

I assume that Ruth cannot be understood without considering the various systems that affect her—family, social groups, community, church, and other cultural forces. For the counseling process to be effective, it is critical to understand how Ruth influences and is influenced by her social world. (As multicultural, feminist, and family therapists have emphasized, the human condition needs to be understood within the context of a system, which includes the social and cultural framework.) Ignoring either the internal or the external perspectives in understanding Ruth's life experience will restrict my effectiveness with her.

As I work with Ruth, I am not consciously thinking about what set of techniques I am about to use. I adapt the interventions to fit her needs rather than attempting to fit her to my techniques. In deciding on techniques to introduce, I take into account an array of factors about Ruth. Some of the areas I consider include her readiness to confront an issue, her stage in the change process, her cultural background, her value system, and her trust in me. My concern is to help her identify and experience whatever she is feeling, identify ways in which her assumptions influence how she feels and behaves, and experiment with new behaviors.

Introduction to the Case of Stan

See Session 1 (Intake and Assessment) on the *DVD for Theory and Practice of Counseling and Psychotherapy: The Case of Stan and Lecturettes.*

A number of themes appear to represent core struggles in Stan's life. Here are some statements Stan may make at various points in his therapy and themes that will be addressed from an integrative perspective:

- I'd like to have people in my life, but I feel awkward being with people.
- I'd like to make some changes, but I don't have a clue of how to begin.
- I want to make a difference in this world.
- I often feel stupid, and I am sure that people will discover this about me.
- There are times when I get overwhelmed and don't know what to do next.
- I would like a relationship with a woman, but I am afraid of reaching out.
- Sometimes at night I feel a terrible anxiety and feel as if I'm dying.
- I often feel guilty that I've wasted my life, that I've failed, and that I've let people down.
- There are times when I get depressed and don't know how to get out of this slump.
- I doubt myself a great deal.
- I've never really felt loved or wanted by my parents.
- I'd like to get rid of my self-destructive tendencies and learn to trust people more.
- I put myself down a lot, but I'd like to feel better about myself.
- There are times when I wonder if I want to live.

Drawing on Theories Applied to the Case of Stan

❧ Beginning Concerns   I begin by asking Stan what it was like for him to come to this first therapy session. I am particularly interested in why Stan is seeking counseling at this particular time and what he most hopes to get from our work together. At the initial session Stan asks what good talking will do. One of his expectations is that he will reveal his problems and that I will then give him advice that will help him feel better. He admits to feeling anxious about approaching his first counseling session, but he adds that he is generally very anxious in most social situations. In response to my question about what he expects to get from counseling, he replies, "I just want to feel better about myself. I feel nervous about everything."

❧ Establishing a Therapeutic Relationship   From the beginning, I want Stan to understand as much as possible about our mutual responsibilities as partners in this therapeutic endeavor. Informing Stan about how the therapeutic process works, obtaining his informed consent, and establishing a therapeutic alliance are key matters to attend to early in our sessions. Because the therapeutic relationship is central to the outcome of therapy, this is something I begin to establish at our first meeting. This relationship is critical at the initial stages of therapy, but it must be maintained during all stages if therapy is to be effective.

In establishing the therapeutic relationship, I am influenced by the assumption that therapy is a joint venture, not something that I *do* to a passive client. I tend to ask myself questions such as these: "To what degree am I able to listen to and hear Stan in a nonjudgmental way?" "Am I able to empathize and care for him?" "Do I have the capacity to enter his subjective world without losing my own identity?" I begin by being as honest as I can be with Stan as the basis for creating this relationship. I invite Stan to raise any questions that will help build our working alliance.

❧ The Therapeutic Contract

To establish a therapeutic alliance with Stan, I begin formulating a working contract that will give some direction to Stan's sessions. I discuss with him what I see as my primary responsibilities and functions, as well as Stan's responsibilities in the process. I want him to know at the outset that I expect him to be an active party in this relationship, and I tell him that I function in an active and directive way. (This is characteristic of most of the cognitive behavioral and action-oriented therapies.)

Early in the counseling process it is essential that I get some sense of what Stan wants from counseling and from life. Although his responses may be vague at first, I work with Stan to be as specific and concrete as possible regarding how he views his life situation and what he expects from the therapy process. (This process is especially important in Adlerian therapy, behavior therapy, cognitive behavior therapy, reality therapy, and feminist therapy. Goals are discussed further in Chapter 3.)

Establishing a therapeutic contract, which is a part of informed consent, is critical at the beginning of the counseling process, but timing must be considered. Educating Stan about how he can get the most from his therapy is important, but I need to be careful not to overwhelm him with too much information or interfere with his typical style of presenting himself. I strive to listen carefully and to let Stan know what I am hearing without talking too much. Being fully present in the therapy session and giving Stan my sincere attention will yield dividends in our subsequent work together. If I listen well, I will get a good sense of why Stan has come to therapy. If I fail to listen accurately and sensitively, there is a risk of going with the first problem he states and being too eager to help resolve his presenting problem. Patience is critical in learning to listen before designing and implementing an intervention.

❧ Initial Assessment

During the first two sessions, I conduct an assessment of Stan, which helps me to conceptualize his case and implement a treatment plan. I develop hypotheses about Stan, and the two of us discuss them. Diagnosis is often a part of this assessment process, and viewed broadly, diagnosis consists of describing behavior and thinking about its meaning. In this way, diagnosis becomes a process of thinking *about* Stan *with* him. I think of diagnosis as a general descriptive statement identifying Stan's style of functioning. Based on the process of assessment over a period of time, I develop hunches about Stan's behavioral style, and I may share these observations with him as part of the therapeutic process. Accurate diagnosis is important in some clinical settings, but it is not the defining point of therapy in general, nor the goal of the initial session.

From the first couple of sessions, I encourage Stan to spend time reflecting on what he would like to change in his life and what he wants from therapy. My main message is that change will come about to the degree that he becomes an active participant in the therapy sessions. I reinforce the importance of taking small steps that will result in the changes he desires.

Existential Themes
Some existential themes surface even in our initial session. Although Stan feels that he has made bad choices in the past, I want him to realize that he does not have to be the victim of his past experiences and that he has the capacity to redesign his future. Stan's anxiety is a vital part of living with uncertainty and freedom. Because there are no guarantees in life, Stan can expect to experience some degree of healthy anxiety, aloneness, and guilt. These conditions are not self-destructive in themselves, but the way in which Stan copes with these existential conditions is critical.

Suicidal Thoughts
Stan sometimes talks about his suicidal feelings. Certainly, I investigate further to determine whether he poses an immediate threat to himself. In addition to this assessment to determine lethality, I view his thoughts of "being better off dead" as symbolic. Could it be that Stan feels he is dying as a person? Is he choosing a way of merely existing instead of affirming life? In later sessions I will ask Stan to explore the meaning and purpose in his life. I will likely raise questions such as these: "Is there any reason you want to continue living?" "What are some of the projects that enrich your life?" "What can you do to find a sense of purpose that will help you feel more significant and alive?"

Personal Resources and Strengths
During the early phases of Stan's therapy, I do not dwell exclusively on his problems. I believe Stan can create an identity that is different from his current problem-saturated identity. Stan has many personal resources and strengths to help him make fundamental changes in his life. Thus, I will draw on the strength-based approaches to counseling that will assist Stan in recognizing his personal competencies. As will become evident in the chapters that follow, Stan is far more than a set of problems. Working together, Stan will discover and come to appreciate his personal resources and how to draw from them as he faces the task of re-creating his life story.

Concluding Comments

I am convinced that an integrative perspective is needed to effectively counsel the diverse range of clients who seek counseling. Each therapeutic approach has useful dimensions, and accepting the validity of one model does not necessarily imply a rejection of seemingly divergent models. It is not a matter of a theory being "right" or "wrong," for every theory offers a unique contribution to understanding human behavior and has unique implications for counseling practice. Pluralism in society necessitates choosing an integrative approach to counseling practice.

Of necessity, discussion of the theoretical orientations mentioned in this chapter has been brief. For a more elaborate discussion of the various theoretical approaches, see *Theory and Practice of Counseling and Psychotherapy* (Corey, 2013d). If you are using the *DVD for Integrative Counseling: The Case of Ruth and Lecturettes* (Corey, 2013b), Session 1 (The Beginning of Counseling) illustrates some of the principles I've developed in this chapter. The first session of the program *DVD for Theory and Practice of Counseling and Psychotherapy: The Case of Stan and Lecturettes* (Corey, 2013c) demonstrates setting the foundation for assessment and treatment. Also, Chapter 1 of *Case Approach to Counseling and Psychotherapy* (Corey, 2013a) provides an overview of 11 counseling models and a comprehensive picture of the case of Ruth, including various practitioners' views regarding her diagnosis.

After reading this chapter on the beginning of counseling, take time to reflect on the following questions as a way of clarifying your thoughts:

- At this point, what is the main theory you would choose as a framework for practice?
- What are the main challenges you face in developing your personalized approach to counseling?
- What aspects of informed consent would you want to be sure to address with a client during the initial counseling session?
- What do you consider to be the main advantages and disadvantages of time-limited therapy?
- What experiences of being a client provided you with the most valuable lessons about counseling others?
- Do you think it is essential to arrive at a diagnosis of a client during the initial session? Why or why not?
- Do you believe assessment and diagnosis should be a collaborative endeavor?
- What are some advantages and disadvantages of designing your integrative approach based on the thinking, feeling, and doing dimensions?

CHAPTER TWO

The Therapeutic Relationship

Introduction

It is essential to use skills and techniques effectively—and to have a theoretical base from which to draw a range of techniques—but these abilities are meaningless in the absence of a therapeutic connection that is characterized by mutual respect and trust. The quality of this person-to-person encounter is what leads to positive change. Because therapy is a deeply personal relationship, I place central emphasis on the client–counselor relationship. My attitude toward the client and my personal characteristics of honesty, integrity, and courage are what I have to offer.

The existential approach is primarily concerned with the basic conditions of being human and views therapy as a shared journey. This approach to therapy provides the foundation upon which I conceptualize the therapeutic relationship. Both existential and person-centered approaches emphasize the personal characteristics and attitudes of the therapist. Existential therapists strive to be authentic and self-disclosing in their therapy work. Although existential therapists can be creative in developing techniques and may apply techniques from many other theoretical orientations, practitioners are not bound by specific techniques. Their interventions are guided by a philosophical framework about what it means to be human. Therapy is a journey taken by counselor and client, a journey that delves deeply into the world as perceived and experienced by the client. This type of quest demands that the therapist be in contact with his or her own phenomenological world as well.

Developing a Working Alliance

The importance of the client–therapist relationship is a common factor among all approaches to counseling, yet some models place more emphasis on the quality of the relationship than do others. This is especially true of the existential, person-centered, and Gestalt approaches, and it is also true of feminist therapy and the postmodern approaches (solution-focused therapy and narrative therapy).

These relationship-oriented approaches (sometimes referred to as experiential approaches) are all based on the premise that the quality of the client–therapist relationship is primary, with techniques being secondary. Other therapeutic approaches acknowledge that a working alliance is necessary, but may place more emphasis on the effective use of research-based techniques or other factors.

The quality of the therapeutic relationship, or therapeutic alliance, is of critical importance to therapy outcomes (Duncan, Miller, & Sparks, 2004; Hubble, Duncan, Miller, & Wampold, 2010). Norcross (2010) reports that hundreds upon hundreds of research studies convincingly demonstrate that the therapeutic relationship makes a substantial contribution to psychotherapy outcome. Researchers have repeatedly discovered that a positive alliance and a collaborative therapeutic relationship are the best predictors of therapy outcome (Hubble et al., 2010). An effective therapeutic relationship fosters a creative spirit that focuses on developing techniques aimed at increasing awareness, which enables clients to change their thinking, feeling, and behaving.

Part of the therapeutic relationship involves listening to client feedback about the therapy process. It is essential to use formal client feedback to inform, guide, and evaluate the treatment process (Duncan, Miller, Wampold, & Hubble, 2010). The active participation of clients in their therapy, along with their experience of meaningful change in the early stage of treatment, are the most potent contributors to positive outcome. One of the best ways to improve the effectiveness of psychotherapy is by taking direction from clients through client-directed, outcome-informed therapy (Duncan et al., 2004; Miller, Hubble, Duncan, & Wampold, 2010).

Here are some assumptions I hold and some key notions that are central to my definition of effective therapy. This is an example of my personal metatheory.

- The quality of the person-to-person encounter in the therapeutic situation is the catalyst for positive change.
- The therapist's role is rooted in his or her way of being; attitudes are more important than the techniques employed.
- The counselor's chief role is to be present with the client, both physically and emotionally, during the therapeutic hour.
- The basic work of therapy is done by the client; the therapist's job is to create a climate in which the client is likely to try out new ways of being.
- The therapist can best invite the client to change by modeling authentic behavior.
- The therapist's attitudes and values are at least as critical as his or her knowledge, theory, or techniques.
- To function optimally, the therapist must have a good connection with the client and be centered within him- or herself.
- A therapist who is not sensitively tuned in to his or her own reactions to a client runs the risk of becoming a technician and is likely to miss key pieces of information.
- An effective alliance enables the client to experience the safety necessary for risk-taking behavior.
- Awareness emerges within the context of authentic engagement between therapist and client.

These somewhat overlapping notions give a sense of the paramount importance of the therapeutic relationship. If you operate within a relationship-oriented framework, you will be much less anxious about using the right technique or about stimulating clients to think, feel, or act in a specific manner. Of course, you will most likely utilize a wide range of techniques designed to enhance clients' capacity to savor their experience.

As a therapist, you might conceive of your role as that of a consultant. This role is stressed in both behavioral and solution-focused approaches. Your clients tell you what they want, and you then serve as a resource person, helping them explore ways to achieve their goals. As a consultant, you will teach your clients specific strategies they can use in a variety of situations.

The person of the therapist is a critical ingredient in the therapy process (Hubble et al., 2010; Wampold, 2010). Who you are as a person will influence clients' progress in therapy. We invite our clients to grow by modeling authentic behavior. The therapist who possesses wide knowledge, both theoretical and practical, yet lacks human qualities of compassion, caring, good faith, honesty, authenticity, and sensitivity, will have difficulty making a significant difference in the lives of clients.

Self-disclosure is one avenue for both letting clients know you better and of being "real" in your work. If you keep yourself hidden during the therapeutic session or if you engage in inauthentic behavior, clients will remain guarded and persist in their own inauthentic ways. You can help clients become more trusting and open by selectively disclosing your own responses at appropriate times. Of course, this disclosure does not mean an uncensored sharing of every fleeting feeling or thought. Rather, it entails a willingness to share persistent reactions with clients, especially when this sharing is likely to be facilitative. Therapist self-disclosure is a value shared by a number of theoretical orientations including existential therapy, the person-centered approach, Gestalt therapy, reality therapy, and feminist therapy.

The person-centered approach has contributed greatly to an understanding of the central role of the therapeutic relationship in the healing process. Carl Rogers (1957, 1961, 1980) did pioneering work on three personal characteristics of the therapist that form the essence of the therapeutic relationship: (1) congruence or genuineness, (2) unconditional positive regard and acceptance, and (3) accurate empathic understanding. Known as the therapeutic core conditions, these factors are a basic part of all theoretical orientations.

Congruence means that as a therapist you are real; that is, you are genuine, integrated, and authentic during the therapy hour. You are without a false front; your inner experience and outer expression of that experience match; and you can openly express feelings, thoughts, reactions, and attitudes that are present in the relationship with your client.

In your therapeutic work, you need to communicate your genuine caring for your client. This caring is unconditional in that you do not judge your client's feelings, thoughts, and behavior as good or bad. You value and accept the client without placing stipulations on this acceptance. Acceptance recognizes a client's right to have her or his own beliefs and feelings. One of your main tasks is to understand your client's experiences and feelings with sensitivity and accuracy as they are revealed in the moment-to-moment interaction during the therapy session.

It is imperative that you strive to sense your client's subjective experience, particularly in the here and now. Empathy requires a subjective understanding of the internal world of the client and a sense of personal identification with the client's experience. By tuning in to your own feelings, you are able to share the client's subjective world. Empathic understanding implies that you will sense your client's feelings as if they were your own without becoming lost in those feelings. This empathy on your part deepens the client's self-understanding and helps the client clarify his or her beliefs and worldview.

Even the action-oriented approaches (such as behavior therapy, cognitive behavior therapy, rational emotive behavior therapy, reality therapy, and solution-focused brief therapy) view the quality of the client–therapist relationship as a core element of effective therapy. Unlike a person-centered therapist who is not particularly concerned about techniques, action-oriented therapists draw upon techniques designed to produce specific changes. For example, behavior therapists believe clients are mainly helped by the skillful application of specific behavioral interventions that have been validated by evidence-based research. However, the successful application of these research-supported techniques requires a good working alliance. Beyond a working relationship, which is monitored throughout the duration of counseling, the behavior therapist is expected to be skilled in making interventions that will help clients change in the direction they choose. A more extensive discussion of the role of techniques for assisting clients to change the ways they are thinking, feeling, and behaving is presented in Chapters 6, 7, and 8.

Becoming the Client: Sharing in a Collaborative Partnership

Therapy as a Collaborative Venture

Throughout this book I invite you to assume the role of a client from time to time, so this book contains three client cases: Ruth, Stan, and you. The aim of asking you to become the client is to personalize the material and provide you with an experiential sense of how integrative therapy can be applied.

Assume that you and I are beginning a therapeutic relationship. Let's expand on the idea that therapy is a collaborative effort. Although research supports the value of the client as an active agent, Bohart and Tallman (2010) have noted that the client is often the neglected common factor in psychotherapy. I see many advantages to your assuming an active role as a client, and I encourage you to participate as fully as possible in all phases of assessment and treatment. Therapy at its best is an active collaborative process of working with the client as an active self-healer. Bohart's (2006) integrative approach is based on the assumption that the client is the most important common factor in making therapy work. He points to research findings that postulate the client as an active agent. Bohart describes his role as creating a supportive, empathic relationship with clients that enables them to go beyond a defensive stance.

A number of therapeutic approaches stress this notion of collaboration between client and therapist, including feminist therapists, Adlerians, cognitive
behavior therapists, behavior therapists, solution-focused therapists, and narrative therapists. Therapy as a collaborative venture involves client and therapist working together toward common goals. How can you best be encouraged
to assume an active stance in your treatment?

If you appear to be getting little from the therapeutic relationship, I examine
my part in this outcome by asking myself about my involvement and willingness
to risk with you as your therapist. In addition, I explore with you how you might
be contributing in part to your lack of progress. I recognize that I cannot make
you want to change, but I can create a climate in which together we are able to
look at the advantages and disadvantages of making changes. Both of us share
the responsibility for creating an environment that is supportive of change.

The Relationship During the Early Stage of Counseling

During the first few sessions my main task is helping you define and clarify
your problems. My aim is to build a relationship with you that will encourage
you to reveal your story, focus more clearly on what you want to change, and
attain a new perspective in dealing with your problems. What do you feel your
role should be in this process?

You might be seeking professional assistance because you realize you are
not dealing with problem situations satisfactorily. You may seek counseling because you struggle with self-doubt, feel trapped by your fears, or suffer from
some form of loss. You may need to heal from psychological wounds. And you
might seek help not because you feel plagued by major problems but because
you are not coping with daily challenges as effectively as you would like. You
may find yourself in a meaningless job, experience frustration because you are
not living up to your own goals and ideals, or feel dissatisfied in your interpersonal life. You realize that you are not managing your life as well as you might.
Why have you come for counseling?

Creating a Therapeutic Climate   How open are you to self-exploration?
The kind of climate I am able to create during the initial sessions is crucial to
a good therapeutic relationship. I can make the mistake of working too hard,
asking too many questions, or offering quick solutions. If we can create a collaborative partnership together, I can assist you greatly by teaching you how
to assess your own problems and search for your own solutions. How much
responsibility are you willing to assume, both inside and outside the sessions?
(These aspects are central to both behavior therapy and reality therapy.) You
will learn to identify and clarify problem areas and how to acquire problem-
solving skills that you can use in a variety of difficult situations in everyday
living. In a sense, from the very first meeting I can be most helpful to you by
encouraging you to look within yourself for resources and strengths you can
draw on to better manage your life.

Considering the Cultural Context   You may be frustrated and angry due
to societal factors such as being discriminated against in your workplace because

of your age, gender, disability, race, religion, or sexual orientation. It would be a disservice if I were to encourage you to settle for injustices in an oppressive environment. Instead of merely solving your presenting problem, I can begin supporting you in your efforts to take action within your community to bring about change. To accomplish this, I may need to be prepared to assume a variety of helping roles—educator, advocate, social change agent, and influencer of policymakers.

I must respect the purpose for which you initiated therapy. If I pay careful attention to what you tell me about what you want, this can be the foundation of our work. My task then is to encourage you to weigh the alternatives and to explore the consequences of what you are doing with your life. Even though oppressive forces may be severely limiting the quality of your life, you are not merely the victim of circumstances beyond your control. What can you do to improve your situation? Together we may be able to discover new courses of action that will lead to a change in your situation.

As I engage you in identifying and assessing your problems, I must avoid a stance of "blaming the victim." (As both feminist and family systems therapy stress, the source of your problems may be within your environment rather than due to an internal conflict on your part.) It may be that you come to me not to resolve internal conflicts but to better understand and deal with external stressors in your environment. I am aware that self-reliance and independence may not be a part of your worldview, and interdependence may be a core value in your life. It can be useful to put you in contact with external resources within the community that you can utilize in meeting the demands of daily living. You may need my services and my guidance to establish links to resources within your community. Some of these resources include arranging for legal assistance or assisting you in coping with day-to-day survival issues such as getting a job, arranging for child care, or taking care of an elderly parent. This is a vital part of the community approach to change.

Treating all clients in the same manner and using the same basic interventions will most likely restrict the effectiveness of therapy. The "one size fits all" notion hampers creativity and can lead to your feeling misunderstood. What can you tell me about your basic values and beliefs? Understanding your cultural background helps me establish a therapeutic working relationship. Although it is not necessary that I always have an in-depth understanding of your culture and worldview, I must know some of your basic beliefs and values if I hope to make a significant contribution to your change. If I am not aware of the central values that guide your behavior and decisions, you will soon pick up on this and will not likely return for further sessions.

I am open to a discussion with you regarding some of the similarities and differences in our background (such as ethnicity, age, disability, and gender, to mention a few). This allows us to be alert to the ways that our differences might influence our work together.

⚜ Understanding the Family Context   From a family systems perspective, individuals are best understood within the context of their relationships and by assessing their interactions within an entire family. I cannot fully understand you by viewing you only from an individual frame of reference. It is necessary to work with you from a person-in-environment context, which includes having some appreciation of your family's past and present influence on you. What can you tell me about your family history and patterns?

From the family systems models, your problems are viewed as an expression of a dysfunction within a family, and these dysfunctional patterns often can be identified across several generations. The central principle of family systems therapy is that the client is connected to living interpersonal systems and that change in one part of the system reverberates throughout other parts. Actions by any individual family member will influence all the others in the family, and their reactions will have a reciprocal effect on the individual. Therefore, as your counselor, it is not possible for me to accurately assess your concern without observing the interaction with and mutual influence among other family members, including the broader contexts in which you and your family live. To focus primarily on studying your internal dynamics without adequately considering interpersonal dynamics yields an incomplete picture of you. Your family provides a primary context for understanding how you function in relationship to others and how you behave.

Your Role as a Counselor in Creating a Working Relationship

In this section, reflect on the attitudes you think would be conducive to establishing good rapport with your clients and think about behavior that you would want to model to your clients.

Establishing the Relationship

If your clients are to feel free to talk about their problems, you must provide attention, active listening, and empathy. Clients must sense your respect for them, which you demonstrate by your attitudes and behaviors. You reveal an attitude of respect when you are concerned about your clients' best interests, view them as being able to exercise control of their own destiny, and treat them as unique individuals rather than as stereotypes. Your clients will benefit greatly by your acknowledgment that their concerns are important and that it takes courage to talk about themselves. You demonstrate your attitudes toward your clients through your behavior in a session. Some of these behaviors include the following:

- Actively listening to and understanding clients
- Acknowledging their desire to change
- Suspending critical judgment
- Expressing appropriate warmth and acceptance
- Communicating that you have an understanding of their world as they experience it
- Providing a combination of support and challenge
- Assisting clients in cultivating their inner resources for change
- Helping clients take the specific steps needed to bring about change

Ask yourself how well you are able to pay attention to others, to fully listen to them, and to empathize with their situation. Assess the qualities you possess that will either help or hinder you in assuming the internal and subjective frame of reference of clients. Because these qualities exist on a continuum, it is best to think about the degree to which you see yourself possessing these attitudinal and behavioral characteristics. Consider how you would rate yourself on these questions:

- How do you attend to what clients are telling you both verbally and non-verbally? Do you pay attention mainly to what clients disclose, or do you also notice the way they deliver their messages?
- How do you let others tell their story? Do you get impatient and want to interrupt? Do you encourage clients to tell stories in great detail to satisfy your own curiosity? Do you have a tendency to get lost in the details of their story and miss the essence of their struggle?
- How often are you able to detect the core messages when clients speak? How do you check with clients to make certain you are understanding them?
- How do you keep clients focused on issues they want to explore? Can you keep your own centeredness, even when clients may seem very fragmented or are making demands on you?
- To what degree can you set aside your own biases for a time and attempt to enter the client's world? For example, if you consider yourself a self-sufficient or independent woman or man, are you willing to accept the client who tells you she is willing to be subservient to her husband?
- How do you communicate your understanding and acceptance to clients?
- To what extent do you work nondefensively when you detect signs of resistance from clients? How do you use this resistance as a way of helping clients explore their issues more deeply?

Although it may seem deceptively simple to merely listen to others, the attempt to understand the world as others see it is demanding. Respect, genuineness, and empathy are best considered "states of being," not techniques to be used on clients. Establishing a working relationship with clients implies that you are genuine and respectful in observable ways and that the relationship is a two-way process in which clients' interests assume priority.

Helping Clients Gain a Focus

People who seek assistance are often overwhelmed by their problems. By trying to talk about everything that is troubling them in one session, they may also manage to overwhelm you. A focusing process is necessary to provide direction for the therapeutic efforts. To achieve this focus, make an assessment of the major concerns of the client. You could say to a client who presents you with a long list of problems: "Unfortunately, we won't be able to deal with all your problems in one session. What was going on in your life when you finally decided to call for help?" Other focusing questions are "At this time in your life, what seems most pressing and troublesome to you?" and "If you could address only one problem today, which one would you pick?"

Once clients determine what concerns they are willing to explore, you can collaborate with them in designing a treatment contract. By focusing on what is salient in the present, you assist clients in clarifying their own problems and establish a direction for you to design other interventions. Your power to heal others is the result of a process of genuine dialogue with your clients.

Developing a Therapeutic Alliance With Ruth

See Session 2 (The Therapeutic Relationship) of the *DVD for Integrative Counseling: The Case of Ruth and Lecturettes.*

🦋 **Our Second Session**   I ask Ruth to reflect on any thoughts she might have about our first session. She lets me know that she is not accustomed to looking at herself, nor is she comfortable being the focus of attention. We'll need to explore this further because much of the therapeutic process depends on clients paying increased attention to what they are experiencing and doing. Together we explore how Ruth can assume an active role by thinking about topics she wants to bring up in her sessions and by deciding on some ways she wants to be different in her daily life. Rather than assume total responsibility for the direction of her therapy, I look for ways to collaborate with Ruth on the direction of our work. As a teacher and a consultant, I am helping her learn about her own therapeutic process so that she can continue personal growth on her own after therapy has ended.

🦋 **Listening to Ruth's Story**   I make the assumption that many of Ruth's problems have been created by her restricted and self-defeating vision of herself and her world. Part of our work together will be to look for inner resources that will enable her to create a new story for herself. From the narrative perspective, my commitment is to help her rewrite the story of her life. Through this collaboration, she can review and reframe events from her past and write a new story for her future. At this phase of our work, I am also influenced by the feminist therapy notion that our collaboration will be aimed at freeing Ruth from the influence of oppressive elements in her social environment and empowering her to become an active agent who is directing her own life.

Although I did not begin the initial session by asking Ruth a series of questions pertaining to her life history, in this session I will ask questions to fill in the gaps in her story. This method gives a more comprehensive picture of how she views her life now, as well as events that she considers significant in her past. Through the use of questions that challenge her to separate herself from an identity that is linked to problems, I assist her in the process of reauthoring her life story. As a homework assignment, I may suggest an autobiographical approach and ask Ruth to write about the critical turning points in her life. This will include events from her childhood and adolescent years, relationships with parents and siblings, school experiences, current struggles, and future goals and aspirations. I ask her what she thinks would be useful for her to recall and focus on, and what she imagines would be useful to me in gaining a better picture of her subjective world. In this way, Ruth does some reflecting on her life experiences outside of the session, she takes an active role in deciding what her personal goals will be for therapy, and I have a sense of where and how to proceed with her.

🍃**Helping Ruth Externalize Her Problem** Ruth's autobiography provides me with significant clues to the unfolding of the story of her life. During the early sessions, I encourage her to separate her identity as a person from her problems. I am influenced by narrative therapy in understanding the value of externalizing a client's problem. Narrative therapy insists that the person is not the problem, and I view Ruth's problems as something separate from her. She presents many problems that are of concern to her, yet we cannot address all of them at once. When I ask her what one problem most concerns her right now, she replies, "Guilt. I feel guilty so often over so many things that I don't do. No matter how hard I work at what is important to me, I generally fall short of what I expect of myself, and then I feel guilty."

From reading Ruth's autobiography and from listening to her story, it becomes clear that her problem-saturated story contains a theme of "guilt." She feels guilty because she is not an adequate daughter, because she is not the mother she thinks she should be, and because she is not as accomplished a student as she demands of herself. When she falls short of "perfect performances" in these and other areas, guilt is the result.

To help Ruth view her problem of guilt as being separate from who she is as a person, I ask questions about how her guilt occurs and ask her to give examples of situations where she experiences guilt. I am interested in charting the influence of the problem of guilt. Using elements of solution-focused therapy and the framework of narrative therapy, I ask Ruth questions aimed at finding exceptions to her feeling guilty:

- Has there ever been a time when guilt could have taken control of your relationship, but didn't? What was it like for you? How did you do it? What does it say about you that you were able to do that?
- How do you imagine your life would be different if you didn't have the problem of guilt?
- Can you think of ways that you can begin to take even small steps to divorce yourself from unnecessary guilt?

My questioning is aimed at discovering moments when Ruth hasn't been dominated or discouraged by the problem of guilt. This provides a basis for considering how life would be different if guilt were not in control. I assure her that there may be times when feeling some guilt is appropriate and can alert us that it is time to change our actions. However, we want to work together so that she can let go of unnecessary or overly burdensome guilt.

As our therapy proceeds, I expect that Ruth will gradually come to see that she has more control over her problem of guilt than she believed. As she is able to distance herself from these problematic themes (such as guilt), she will be less burdened by her problem-saturated story and will discover a range of options. She will likely focus more on the resources within herself to construct the life she wants.

Developing a Therapeutic Alliance With Stan

See Session 5 (Person-Centered Therapy) on the *DVD for Theory and Practice of Counseling and Psychotherapy: The Case of Stan and Lecturettes.*

For much of this session, I demonstrate how I work with Stan when he presses me for more direction and for giving him answers to his problems. He has many doubts about his capacity to make good choices, and he is hoping that I will have advice for him. I demonstrate *immediacy*, in which I share with Stan how I perceive him and how he affects me. I also affirm that I believe Stan has the capacity to find answers within himself and that he does not need to rely on me to give him answers.

Building the Therapeutic Relationship   I am convinced that one of the most significant factors determining the degree to which Stan will attain his goals is the quality of the therapeutic relationship that he and I can create. I believe Stan will get the most from his therapy if he knows how the therapeutic process works. I am mindful of the potentially harmful effects of the power differential in my relationship with Stan and strive to build mutuality and a sense of partnership in the therapeutic endeavor. Although Stan does not have a great deal of confidence in making decisions about his life, I will not serve him well if I short-circuit the process of assisting him in finding resources within himself.

One way of deepening the therapeutic relationship is to demonstrate my interest in Stan's story. I began listening to his story during the first session, but more time is needed for him to share the many significant events and turning points in his life. In subsequent sessions Stan fleshes out his story. I hope he will begin thinking about the kind of life he would like and what he can do to make this happen. Narrative therapy emphasizes the value of devoting time to listening to clients' stories and to looking for past events that clients can interpret in new ways. Stan's life story influences both what he notices and what he remembers. In this sense, his story influences how he will perceive the future.

I am most influenced by the person-centered approach, which places primary value on the power of the client–therapist relationship. My main focus during our early work together is on being real, on accepting Stan's feelings and thoughts, on demonstrating my unconditional positive regard for him, and on respecting him as a person. Because I trust Stan's ability to find his own direction, I encourage him to participate with me in planning and structuring the sessions. If I am able to listen carefully and reflect what I am hearing, and if I am able to deeply empathize with his life situation, I believe that eventually Stan will begin to clarify his struggles and work out his own solutions to his problems. Although he is only somewhat aware of his feelings at the initial phase of therapy, he will move toward increased clarity as I accept him fully, without conditions and without judgments. My main aim is to create a climate of openness, trust, caring, understanding, and acceptance. Then he can use this relationship to move forward and grow.

Stan wonders what I think of him and is convinced that I must be frustrated with his slow progress. Most of this session addresses what is going on in the here and now of the therapy office as we talk about our relationship.

Reflect on how you might intervene with Stan to enhance your therapeutic relationship with him. Consider these questions:

- Stan doubts his ability to make good decisions. He tells you that he never makes good decisions. How might you work with him when he says this?
- If Stan were to ask what you think of him, how would you be inclined to answer him?
- Would you want to give Stan answers to his problems? Why or why not? How do you think your answers might either help or hinder Stan in finding his own way?
- What aspects of Stan's experience might you emphasize to deepen your therapeutic relationship with him?

Concluding Comments

The single most important element in becoming a competent counselor is your way of being. If you can be fully present and be yourself, you can be a catalyst for clients to engage in introspection, relevant self-disclosure, and risk-taking. Knowing who you are is the starting point for developing your own view of counseling. Techniques are always secondary to your personal vitality and your ability to establish and maintain a growth-producing therapeutic relationship. Although skills and techniques are useful, they must be sensitively adapted to the particular client and context. The outcome of a technique is influenced by the relationship between you and your client. Techniques are merely tools to amplify emerging material that is present and to encourage exploration of issues that have personal relevance to clients. More important than the techniques you use are the attitudes you have toward clients. As a therapist, one of your main functions is to provide encouragement to clients in making decisions regarding how they want to live.

After reading this chapter about the therapeutic relationship, take time to reflect on the following questions as a way of clarifying your thoughts on the kinds of relationships you want to create with your clients:

- How do you view the role of techniques in the counseling process?
- What emphasis do you place on the client–therapist relationship? If you had to describe in a few words what you consider a "working relationship" to be, what would you tell your client?
- How important do you consider your self-disclosure to be in your work as a counselor? How do you assess when it might be helpful to your client for you to self-disclose? What kinds of disclosures are you most likely to make? Are there some disclosures you are not likely to make to clients?
- To what degree do you agree that counseling is a collaborative venture? What are some specific things you are likely to say and do as a counselor during the initial session to establish a collaborative relationship? What are some things you might say to clients about what they can expect of you as their counselor? What would you most expect of them as clients?

- If you were a client in counseling, what kind of relationship would you want and expect from your counselor?
- Carl Rogers identified three therapeutic factors that contribute to successful therapy outcomes: congruence, unconditional positive regard, and empathy. In what ways are these core conditions basic to all theoretical models?
- Are you able to be empathic and respectful of clients? What work do you need to do to improve in these areas?
- Are you a good listener? Do you sometimes find yourself starting to think about your response when you are listening to a person (or a client)? In a conversation, are you able to devote your full attention to what the other person is saying?
- What things would you most want to attend to during the early stage of counseling to created a safe environment for clients to explore their concerns?

CHAPTER THREE

Establishing
Therapeutic Goals

Introduction

All theoretical orientations address the central role of goals as a factor in successful outcomes. Some therapies focus on expressing feelings, whereas others stress identifying cognitive patterns, and still others concentrate on changes in behavior. I believe combining a thinking, feeling, and acting approach is most useful when integrating theory and technique.

In working with clients, you will establish target goals in each of the areas of their functioning, especially those that the client views as problematic. Even with the same client, you will at times be focusing on different dimensions of functioning such as changing beliefs, exploring a range of feelings, or implementing behavioral changes. It is essential that you be flexible in defining with your clients a variety of goals that provide direction to their therapy. Without clear goals, the counseling sessions will most likely not be productive.

At its best, therapeutic goal setting is a collaborative process. As a therapist, you may have goals for treatment outcomes, but your clients set specific, measurable, manageable goals with your assistance. In discussing counseling goals with your clients, it is a good practice to address goals pertaining to the therapeutic process, especially general goals that influence the way you work as a counselor. For example, you would probably agree that it is desirable for clients to strive to know themselves and to make choices about the way they want to live. Many process-oriented goals are part of the therapeutic endeavor, such as clients engaging in personal reflection, self-disclosure, risk-taking, and doing work outside the therapy sessions to bring about change. It is useful to articulate these process goals early in the counseling relationship.

Overview of Goals From Various Theoretical Perspectives

The goals of counseling are almost as diverse as are the theoretical approaches. Goals include restructuring the personality, uncovering the unconscious, finding meaning in life, curing an emotional disturbance, examining old decisions and making new ones, developing trust in oneself, increasing social interest, becoming more self-actualizing, reducing anxiety, shedding maladaptive behavior and learning adaptive patterns, gaining more effective control of one's life, designing creative solutions to life's challenges, reauthoring one's life story, finding exceptions to problems, finding inner resources, acquiring emotional competence, reducing ambivalence to change, becoming aware of and reducing the influence of gender-role socialization, acquiring personal empowerment, and creating new patterns of relationships within a family system. Given this broad range of goals, the perspectives of the client and the therapist on goals will have an impact on the therapeutic interventions chosen. A brief overview follows that describes some key goals associated with each of the various theoretical perspectives that have the potential for developing an integrative approach to counseling practice.

Therapeutic Goals of Psychoanalytic Therapy   A primary goal is to make the unconscious conscious. Successful outcomes of psychoanalytic therapy result in significant modification of an individual's personality and character structure. This goal is accomplished through interventions such as maintaining the analytic framework, free association, interpretation, dream analysis, analysis of resistance, and analysis of transference.

Therapeutic Goals of Adlerian Counseling   Counseling is a collaborative effort, with the client and therapist working on mutually accepted goals. A major goal is to increase the client's social interest, which leads to courage, finding happiness, and achieving a true sense of belonging in the world. Change is aimed at both the cognitive and behavioral levels. Adlerians are mainly concerned with challenging clients' mistaken notions and faulty assumptions.

Therapeutic Goals of Existential Therapy   The principal goal is to challenge clients to recognize and accept the freedom they have to become the authors of their own lives. Therapists encourage clients to examine the ways in which they are avoiding their freedom and the responsibility that accompanies it.

Therapeutic Goals of Person-Centered Therapy   A major goal is to provide a climate of safety and trust in the therapeutic setting so that the client, by using the therapeutic relationship for self-exploration, can become aware of blocks to growth. Because this approach stresses the client–therapist relationship as a necessary and sufficient condition leading to change, it minimizes directive techniques, interpretation, questioning, probing, diagnosis, and collecting history.

Therapeutic Goals of Gestalt Therapy   The goal is to attain awareness so clients can expand their choices. Awareness includes knowing the environment and knowing oneself, accepting oneself, and being able to make contact. Clients are helped to pay attention to their own awareness process so they can be responsible and can selectively and discriminatingly make choices.

❧ **Therapeutic Goals of Behavior Therapy**   The cornerstone of behavior therapy is the identification of specific goals at the outset of the therapeutic process. The general goals are to increase personal choice and to create new conditions for learning. An aim is to eliminate maladaptive behaviors and to replace them with more constructive patterns. The client and therapist collaboratively specify treatment goals in concrete, measurable, and objective terms.

❧ **Therapeutic Goals of Cognitive Behavior Therapy**   The goal of cognitive behavior therapy is to change the way clients think by identifying their automatic thoughts and introducing the idea of cognitive restructuring. Changes in beliefs and thought processes tend to result in changes in the way people feel and how they behave. Through the collaborative therapeutic effort, clients learn to discriminate between their own thoughts and the events that occur in reality. Clients learn practical ways to identify their underlying faulty beliefs, to critically evaluate those beliefs, and to replace them with constructive beliefs.

❧ **Therapeutic Goals of Reality Therapy**   The overall goal is to help people find better ways to meet their needs for survival, love and belonging, power, freedom, and fun. Changes in behavior tend to result in the satisfaction of basic needs. Clients are assisted in examining what they are doing, thinking, and feeling to assess whether this is getting them what they want.

❧ **Therapeutic Goals of Solution-Focused Brief Therapy**   Clients establish their own goals and preferences in a climate of mutual respect, dialogue, inquiry, and affirmation. Much of the therapeutic process involves clients thinking about their future and what they want to be different in their lives.

❧ **Therapeutic Goals of Narrative Therapy**   The goal is for clients to experience a heightened sense of personal agency to act in the world. Narrative therapists invite clients to describe their experience in fresh language, which tends to open new vistas of what is possible. The heart of the therapeutic process involves identifying how societal standards and expectations are internalized in ways that constrain and narrow the kind of life clients are capable of living.

❧ **Therapeutic Goals of Feminist Therapy**   The main goals of feminist therapy include equality, balancing independence and interdependence, self-nurturance, empowerment, social change, and valuing and affirming diversity. Feminist therapists believe gender is central to therapeutic practice and that understanding a client's problems requires adopting a sociocultural perspective.

Goals From an Integrative Perspective

Despite the diversity of therapy goals, most approaches share some common features even though they differ in their assumptions about the best way to achieve these goals. To some degree, they have the goal of identifying what clients want and then helping them modify their thoughts, feelings, and behaviors. As can be seen in the overview of diverse approaches, each theory focuses on a particular dimension of human experience as a way to change other facets of personality. In my own integrative approach, there is room to incorporate most of these goals. At different stages in therapy, different goals assume prominence. You can work with clients by helping them identify a range of specific goals that will provide a framework for their work. The priority of the client's goals will influence the current direction of therapy, but all of the goals will continue to be relevant throughout the course of the client's therapy.

The main goal of therapy endorsed by most theoretical orientations is to assist the client in bringing about changes within an individual in the realms of thinking, feeling, and behaving. These changes, however, often have repercussions on the systems of which the individual is a part. Family systems approaches have a broader goal than merely bringing about change within the individual. In family therapy, and in feminist therapy as well, the goal is to bring about change within systems. When therapy is successful, the family often learns about patterns that have been transmitted from generation to generation or learns ways to detect and solve problems that keep members stuck in dysfunctional relational patterns. Incorporating concepts from systems models into an integrative approach broadens counseling to deal with changing individuals and systems.

Becoming the Client: Establishing Counseling Goals

In this section, I identify basic considerations in the process of formulating meaningful counseling goals by asking you to become the client again. Keep in mind that goal setting for your therapy will be a collaborative process. How can I work with you to identify clear and personal goals to guide the sessions? What are some of the obstacles to formulating concrete goals, and how can we best deal with these obstacles?

To begin with, I have some general goals that are congruent with my philosophy of counseling that will influence the direction of our sessions. One major goal is to establish a therapeutic relationship that will serve as a foundation for all of our work together. Another goal is to operate from a guiding philosophy that will allow for systematic exploration of the personal goals you identify as being central to you. I want to teach you a framework for resolving the problems you bring to counseling, with special emphasis on teaching you how to deal successfully with future problems. What goals do *you* have for our work together?

It is up to you to identify personal goals that will determine what we talk about in our sessions. Perhaps you have given a good deal of thought to what you want out of life, yet you could still benefit from identifying, clarifying, and discovering better ways of reaching your goals. It is possible that you have a generalized notion of what you want to get from your counseling. For example, you might tell me that "I'd just like to feel better about myself. I don't like myself very much." It probably would not be of much help to you if I simply asked you to be more concrete. By asking self-reflective questions such as those that follow, we may be able to clarify what you want for yourself.

- If you were feeling better about yourself, what would you be feeling?
- Imagine that you felt better about yourself. What would you be telling me about who you are and how your life is?

- Can you give me some idea of what goes on in your head when you feel bad about yourself?
- Tell me about a particular area in your life that you'd like to feel better about. Is there one special area that you wish could be different?

By following your lead and gently asking you to say more about specific times that you have felt good or what situations in particular you most struggle with, both you and I will gradually get a clearer picture of what you want.

Your goals for counseling will be much more meaningful if you define them for yourself. As I listen to you, my interventions are aimed at getting you to state your goals in such a manner that we both know what you want and have a frame of reference to understand the degree to which you are attaining your goals.

The action-oriented therapies (behavior therapy, cognitive behavior therapy, rational emotive behavior therapy, reality therapy, and solution-focused brief therapy) provide very useful concepts for identifying specific goals at the outset of the therapeutic process. In helping you to achieve your goals, I assume an active and directive role. Although you generally determine what behavior will be changed, I typically suggest ideas of how this behavior can best be modified. In designing a treatment plan, I will borrow techniques from a variety of therapeutic systems and apply them to your unique situation. Therapeutic flexibility and versatility are required to effectively achieve a diverse range of goals.

Drawing on the behavioral approaches, reality therapy, and solution-focused brief therapy, you and I identify goals that can be measured or monitored. The goals of reality therapy include behavioral change, better decision making, improving significant relationships, enhanced living, living more mindfully, and more effective satisfaction of psychological needs. These action-oriented therapies provide a specific focus of directional change that enable us to evaluate our work together. Can you think of a personal goal that fits one of these categories?

I also ask you to consider long-range goals. What would you most like to be able to say about yourself or your life situation one year from now? Five years from now? The art of developing goals consists of breaking these long-term goals into relatively short-term objectives that lead you in the direction you want to move. The category of goals we might discuss would encompass the full spectrum of your thinking, feeling, and behaving—with a particular focus on specific areas within each of these domains that you most want to change. Together we will continue this process of delineating personal goals by identifying specific steps you are willing to take, both in the session and outside the office, to get what you want from life. Indeed, I expect that your goals will change as counseling progresses. As you learn how to best use the counseling sessions, other concerns may become evident.

Various Types of Therapeutic Goals

Because counseling is a collaborative partnership, I do not accept full responsibility for deciding what the focus of our therapy sessions will be. It is not my job to decide for you how you should live your life. My job is to help you formulate workable goals and to provide you with the tools you'll need to achieve your goals. There are three general categories of goals: the cognitive realm, the emotional dimension, and the behavioral realm.

Cognitive Goals First, let's examine some possible goals in the cognitive realm that you'd be interested in exploring in your counseling sessions. I operate on the assumption that your thinking influences how you feel and act. If you want to change your emotions and certain behaviors, one route is to identify problematic cognitions and change these. My aim is to listen for some of your underlying beliefs, especially thought patterns that seem to present difficulty for you. I would not identify what I think are faulty beliefs; rather, I would ask you to identify beliefs that you hold that do not serve you well or that lead to problematic behavior. Because you are likely preparing to become a counselor, or are already engaged in some type of counseling practice, reflect on these statements to determine the degree to which you hold similar beliefs pertaining to yourself as a counselor in training:

- I must always function competently and perfectly. There is no room for making mistakes.
- I really need the continual affirmation from my clients if I am to feel worthwhile as a professional.
- It is essential that I have the right technique for every problem situation a client presents or else I will look incompetent.
- I am fully responsible for the progress or lack of progress that my clients make.
- If a client does not turn up for a second session, it is most likely due to my ineptness in making good contact with this person at the first meeting.

In listening to self-statements such as these, I strive to focus on core beliefs that potentially result in problematic emotional and behavioral consequences for you. For instance, are you convinced that you are completely responsible for your clients' therapeutic outcomes? Your core beliefs have a number of consequences. You may worry excessively about your clients and experience a great deal of stress in your work. Not only does the belief that you are totally responsible for client outcomes cause you anxiety, this belief can actually contribute to client dependency. Working together it is important that you and I determine specific cognitive goals that will guide your work in therapy. For example, you may decide that you want to challenge your beliefs about the need to assume total responsibility for those with whom you work.

Affective Goals I invite you to be as specific as possible in identifying emotional concerns. You might say that you are frightened of intimacy. First of all, I want to know what intimacy means to you. I also want to know if this is a situation that you want to change. You may shy away from getting too close to people because of a host of fears, yet keeping distant could well be acceptable to you. It is not my job to urge you to take risks in this area if you do not want to be different. However, if you'd like to be able to experience closeness with a few people and not flee from intimacy, this could become a target goal for our work.

As my client, I ask you about the realm of emotions you are experiencing, especially feelings that you view as problematic. I tend to notice any bodily changes that may indicate emergent feelings. Rather than interpret what you are feeling, my tendency is to ask you what you are experiencing. As you are talking, what did you just become aware of? I notice that you just teared up. Can you say what that is about? What are you experiencing right now? I find that it is most useful to begin work with the affective realm and then move to an exploration of thoughts and behaviors.

I draw heavily from emotion-focused therapy to assist you in getting closer to your moment-by-moment experiencing. I encourage you to identify and experience your feelings. By asking you to notice what you are aware of in the present moment, you are better able to move into whatever realm is salient for you—be it awareness of a thought, a bodily state, or feelings. You need to come into contact with your feelings and to intensify them in order to find a pathway to personal change. You will not change by simply talking about your feelings, or by trying to understand the origins of problematic feelings, or by changing the way you think. If it is appropriate, we might use a range of experiential techniques to identify and deal with affective goals that are important to you.

Behavioral Goals   In addition to setting cognitive and affective goals, it is essential that we identify concrete behavioral goals. Let's assume that you let me know that you would like to take better care of yourself. You realize that too often you feel driven by outside forces rather than feeling in charge of yourself. You contribute to this sense of constant pressure by telling yourself that you don't have time for yourself. Using elements of behavior therapy, reality therapy, and rational emotive behavior therapy, I invite you to examine the choices you are making about your body and your overall wellness. I ask you to examine your present level of physical and psychological well-being. What balance do you want to achieve in areas such as rest, exercise, diet, and ways you spend time? Which of the following behavioral goals might fit for you as a client?

- I am willing to keep a record of what I do in my work to determine whether there are some patterns that I want to change.
- I am willing to make more time for rest and sleep.
- I want to create a better balance between work and leisure.
- I am willing to ask for help when I feel overwhelmed.
- I want to find an exercise program I would profit from and enjoy.
- I want to change my diet. I am willing to start by monitoring what and how much I eat and drink to determine if there are areas I want to change.

Identifying counseling goals may seem like a simple matter, but counseling is not a linear process of resolving a single problem. You are a complex and integrated being, and any one problem you have is best seen as one aspect of the larger picture. Counseling is a more complex and interesting process than simply resolving problems.

Goal-Directed Behavior and Goal Setting

I find the Adlerian approach particularly valuable in establishing therapeutic goals. Several key Adlerian concepts have special relevance for the process of establishing goals, both for therapy and for life: the goal-directedness of behavior, struggling with feelings of inferiority, striving for superiority, and social interest. Alfred Adler's system emphasizes the social determinants of behavior. This "socioteleological" approach implies that we are primarily motivated by social forces and strive to achieve specific goals. Adler's view is that we create both short- and long-term goals that motivate our behavior and influence our personality development. It is our long-term goals, in particular, that guide our movement toward what we perceive as completion and perfection.

Another key concept from the Adlerian approach that is directly related to the process of forming goals is the notion of social interest. This concept embodies the feeling of being connected to all of humanity—past, present, and future—and to being involved in making the world a better place. Social interest is the individual's positive attitude toward other people in the world that involves a sense of identification and empathy with others. As an antidote to social isolation and self-absorption, social interest leads to courage, optimism, and a true sense of belonging. Our happiness and success are largely related to social connectedness. As social beings, we have a need to be of use to others and to establish meaningful relationships in a community. We cannot be understood in isolation from our social context. We are primarily motivated by a desire to belong. Only within the group can we actualize our potential.

Clarifying Counseling Goals With Ruth

See Session 3 (Establishing Therapeutic Goals) on the *DVD for Integrative Counseling: The Case of Ruth and Lecturettes.*

During the beginning stages, I assist Ruth in getting a clearer grasp of what she most wants from therapy as well as seeing some steps she can begin to take to attain her objectives. Like most clients, Ruth's stated goals in her autobiography are overly broad, so I work with her on describing her goals in more concrete terms. When she looks in the mirror, she says she does not like what she sees. She would like to have a better self-image and be more confident. In general, she says that she is dissatisfied with her body. I am interested in knowing specifically what she does not like, the ways in which she now lacks confidence, and what it feels like for her to confront herself by looking at herself and talking to me about what she sees.

I suggest that Ruth use a journal to keep track of how she is doing in meeting her goals. Journal writing can bring clarity to her work in the therapy sessions, and this practice is a good way to extend the influence of what we do together into her daily life. If Ruth experiences difficulties in applying what she is learning in therapy to daily life, writing about it will be an excellent way to figure out alternative strategies. She can bring to her sessions the essence of some of what she writes in her journal.

Ruth will be able to make progress toward her self-defined goals because she is willing to become actively involved in challenging her assumptions and in carrying out behavioral exercises, both in the sessions and in her daily life. For instance, Ruth establishes a number of goals that she is interested in pursuing in the counseling sessions. She does not like her appearance, she is experiencing considerable difficulty with her daughter (Jennifer), and she would like to improve her relationship with her husband. In a later session, Ruth decides that she wants to enroll in a fitness class as part of her exercise program. The class is full, however, which gives her an opportunity to practice her assertive behavior skills. She is successful and is able to attend the class. Previously it would not even have occurred to Ruth to seek out the instructor and ask to be admitted to a class that was already full. She learns early on the importance of making specific plans aimed at translating what she is learning in the therapy sessions to various segments in her daily life. Although my job is to help her learn how to change, she is the one who actually chooses to apply these skills, making change possible.

At the beginning of most sessions, Ruth and I will discuss at least briefly what she wants from this particular session. I tend to ask these questions:

- What are you aware of as you approach this session?
- How do you want to use your time in here today? What is it that you want to talk about?
- What are you hesitating to explore yet think it would be important for you to talk about?

With these focusing questions, the responsibility is with Ruth to determine what her therapy goals are for each session. In short, I see goal setting as an ongoing process that is best defined with the client. It is my job to teach her how to become a collaborator in selecting both short- and long-term goals as well as being a partner in deciding how she wants to use her therapy hour.

For a further discussion of counseling goals with Ruth, see the different practitioners' perspectives presented in Chapters 2 through 14 of *Case Approach to Counseling and Psychotherapy* (Corey, 2013a).

Clarifying Counseling Goals With Stan

See Session 1 (Intake and Assessment) on the *DVD for Theory and Practice of Counseling and Psychotherapy: The Case of Stan and Lecturettes.*

I let Stan know that determining goals is a joint project that we will work on together. I won't be making decisions for him about what we will explore. I like the Adlerian notion of goal alignment, which means that goal setting involves a mutual, collaborative process. In addition, I value the cognitive behavioral approaches that emphasize collaboration between therapist and client in determining goals. It is Stan's responsibility to define the target areas for us to explore in our sessions, and it is my responsibility to guide him in narrowing his goals so we both have a clear picture of how to proceed. Establishing and refining goals takes time, effort, and thoughtful reflection on Stan's part. The goals he chooses to explore highlight the areas Stan is most interested in changing and provide direction for the counseling process.

Stan reports that he would like to make himself known more in his classes. He does not ask for time from his professors. He would like to ask more questions in his classes, but he lacks confidence in being able to ask "good" questions. Although he would like to participate more actively in class discussions, he is hesitant to state his thoughts on topics. When he says this, I help him pinpoint specific instances in which he tends to fade into the background. We consistently move from the general to the specific. The more concrete he is, the greater are his chances of attaining what he wants.

In the process of assisting Stan in establishing personal goals, I borrow from reality therapy by asking him to look at the direction of his life. What is his life like at this time? What seems to be working for him? What feelings, thoughts, and actions are not moving him in the direction he would like to evolve? I might well ask Stan to project his life one year into the future and describe what he would like to say that he has become or achieved. My aim in doing this is to invite him to evaluate what he is presently doing to determine whether his actions are getting him what he wants. To help him pinpoint what he wants, I ask him these questions:

- If you were already the person you wish to be, what kind of person would you be?
- What would you be doing if you were living your life more fully?
- Is what you are doing at this time taking you closer to or farther from your goals?

This line of questioning focuses Stan on the process of critically thinking about where he is now and where he would like to go in the immediate future. Self-evaluation is at the heart of reality therapy.

One of the aspects of reality therapy that I especially value is the emphasis placed on guiding clients in the self-evaluation process. By consistently expecting Stan to engage in a self-evaluation process, I help him create his own agenda based on an inner inventory of his own actions, cognitions, and feelings. When he decides for himself that his present behavior is not working, he will be much more open to participating collaboratively in designing goals that will meet his needs. Once clear goals are established in a collaborative fashion, meaningful evaluation of the progress of therapy can be charted. At each session, it will be critical that Stan and I spend a brief amount of time assessing the degree to which counseling is helping him attain his goals. If his goals seem to lose vitality, this is a sign that we need to take another look at what he most wants to explore in our sessions.

Concluding Comments

It is important to be flexible in defining with your clients meaningful goals that provide direction to therapy. Carefully consider the purposes for which your clients seek counseling and then collaboratively design specific, clear, and realistic goals to guide the therapeutic process. Your job is to assist your clients in getting a better grasp of what they want to accomplish in therapy with you. It is not your role as a therapist to identify goals for your clients. If clients do not seem to be making progress toward a given goal or goals, perhaps the goals are not personally meaningful because they have been prescribed to them by others. Developing a collaborative partnership is of the utmost importance when clients struggle with defining their own goals.

In reflecting on the construction of your own integrative approach to counseling, develop a systematic way of incorporating cognitive, affective, and behavioral goals as a starting point for therapy. After reading this chapter on establishing therapeutic goals, take time to reflect on the following questions as a way of clarifying your thoughts on the kinds of goals you want to establish with your clients.

- As a counselor, how could you make establishing therapeutic goals a collaborative process?
- How does your theoretical orientation influence your view of therapy goals?
- What are your goals for the therapeutic process?
- What would you do if your goals for therapy conflicted with your client's goals?
- What challenges do you expect to face in assisting your clients in the development of specific goals for the therapeutic process?
- How could a client's therapy goals be used as a way to evaluate therapy outcomes?
- What importance do you place on expecting your clients to develop both short- and long-range goals?
- How could you help clients who have ill-defined goals formulate meaningful and clear goals for their therapy sessions?

CHAPTER FOUR

Understanding and Addressing Diversity

Introduction

In this chapter I examine the role of diversity in an integrative counseling model. There are many types of diversity to consider, but perhaps the ones that come to mind most readily revolve around ethnicity and culture. In this discussion I include integrating spirituality into counseling as an aspect of culture. As you read, think about how open you are to learning about diversity as it pertains to your counseling practice. What is required for you to become a diversity competent counselor?

Being able to draw on techniques from various theoretical models seems especially necessary in working with a diverse range of cultural backgrounds. Harm can come to clients who are expected to fit all the specifications of a given theory, whether or not the values espoused by the theory are consistent with their own cultural values. Rather than stretching your client to fit the dimensions of a single theory, it is best to make your theory and practice fit the unique needs of the client. Norcross and Wampold (2011b) emphasize tailoring psychotherapy to the person, creating a new and responsive psychotherapy for each client that considers client characteristics, including contextual factors. To adapt your therapy to each client implies that you understand your client on a deep level. It also calls for you to possess knowledge of various cultures, awareness of your own cultural heritage, and skills to assist diverse clients in meeting their needs within the realities of their culture.

Multicultural Concerns

Multiculturalism cannot be ignored by practitioners if they hope to meet the needs of their increasingly diverse client groups. Traditional theories of counseling have been criticized by some practitioners for have major limitations with respect to working with culturally diverse clients (Sue & Sue, 2008). I believe that the contemporary theories can be expanded to incorporate a multicultural component. Many of the key concepts of these theories can be adapted to a cultural framework that has meaning for diverse client groups. Multicultural theory is based on the premise that assessment and treatment must take into account the cultural experiences and contexts that shape clients' identities. Multicultural counseling utilizes techniques drawn from various therapeutic approaches, yet it is essential to adapt these methods to the cultural values and expectations of individual clients.

Let me add a word of caution about generalizing to a particular racial, ethnic, or cultural group. Individuals within a particular group may differ more than individuals from various groups. I like the perspective taken by Vontress (2008), who suggests a conceptual approach to counseling in which the proper focus is on the individual rather than on the individual's race, ethnicity, or cultural background. Vontress maintains that we need to recognize that people are more alike than different. He encourages counselors in training to pay attention to the universal commonalities of clients first and then to address areas of differences. Cultural differences can be very important, but counselors need to recognize the ways we are alike as well as the ways we are different.

Vontress (2008) emphasizes basic human conditions that transcend culture, such as existential concerns about living, loving, and dying. A human-to-human encounter is therapeutic for all clients, regardless of their cultural background. How this encounter occurs, however, is culturally determined. Keep in mind that different cultures ascribe varying meanings and definitions to the universal existential concerns. Although mental health problems are best understood in a cultural context, it is essential to remember that each client is a unique individual. The central challenge we face working with clients who differ from us is to find a way to pay attention to what is significant to them and to get into their world. We can accomplish this goal by listening to what our clients are expressing and respecting what we hear.

Diversity as Central in the Counseling Process

According to Paul Pedersen (2008), the multicultural perspective seeks to provide a conceptual framework that both recognizes the complex diversity of a pluralistic society and suggests bridges of shared concern that link all people, regardless of their differences. This perspective looks at both the unique dimensions of a person and how this person shares themes with those who are different. Mere knowledge of certain cultural groups is not enough; it is important to understand the variability within groups. Each individual must be seen against the backdrop of his or her cultural group, the degree to which he or she has become acculturated, and the level of development of racial identity.

According to Pedersen (2008), it is no longer possible for therapists to ignore their own cultural context or the cultural context of their clients. Whether practitioners pay attention to cultural variables or ignore them, culture will continue to influence both the client's and the therapist's behavior, and the counseling process as well. Counselors who ignore culture will provide less effective services. Understanding the role that diversity plays in the therapeutic process is essential to successful outcomes.

Pedersen (2008) calls for a culture-centered approach to counseling, maintaining that accurate assessment, meaningful understanding, and effective intervention demand that the client's cultural context be central to the counseling process. He believes culture-centered interventions depend on an inclusive definition of culture as well as a broad definition of the counseling process. Pedersen defines culture broadly to include variables such as race/ethnicity, gender, age, socioeconomic status, religion, sexual orientation, and disability. Using this framework, all counseling can be considered multicultural. He contends that by defining culture broadly it is possible to view culture as the "thousand persons" we all have collected from various sources who follow us wherever we go and who influence all our decisions. To have a sense of cultural self-awareness, it is necessary for us to have access to and dialogue with those inner voices.

As a counselor, you need to be able to assess the special needs of your clients. Depending on the individual client's ethnicity and culture and on the concerns that bring this person to counseling, you will have to show flexibility in utilizing diverse therapeutic strategies. Some clients will need more direction and guidance; others will be very hesitant in talking about themselves in personal ways, especially early in the counseling process. What may appear to be resistance is very likely to be the client's response to years of cultural conditioning and respect for certain values and traditions. It is important to be familiar with a variety of theoretical approaches and to have the ability to adapt your techniques and relational style to fit the person-in-environment. Working from an integrative perspective enhances your ability to be flexible and adapt to different circumstances, which is useful in working with a diverse set of clients (Stricker, 2010).

Ivey and Brooks-Harris (2005, p. 332) identify a number of key multicultural strategies for bringing about individual and social change. These practical strategies include viewing clients culturally, clarifying the impact of culture, celebrating diversity, facilitating identity development, recognizing the impact of identity, appreciating multiple identities, highlighting oppression and privilege, creating an egalitarian collaboration, exploring societal expectations, integrating spiritual awareness, understanding the psychotherapist's worldview, reducing biases, and supporting social action. As a counselor, if you are able to implement practical strategies such as these, your clients will then be able to make decisions about what facets of their existence they want to keep and what they would like to change.

Being an effective counselor involves reflecting on how your own culture influences you and your interventions in your counseling practice. This awareness is a critical factor in your becoming more sensitive to the cultural backgrounds of the clients who seek your help. Various writers suggest that understanding and addressing diversity evolves from three primary practices. First, as a counselor, you must be aware of your own assumptions, biases, and values about human behavior, and of your own worldview as well. Second, you need to become increasingly aware of the cultural values, biases, and assumptions of diverse groups in our society, and come to an understanding of the worldview of culturally different clients in nonjudgmental ways. Third, you need to begin developing culturally appropriate, relevant, and sensitive strategies for intervening with individuals and with systems (Sue & Sue, 2008).

Lum (2011) believes cultural competence is a relational and dialogical process between counselor and client, between cultures, and between people and contexts. He calls for a paradigm shift away from an exclusive focus on the competence of the practitioner to an inclusive relationship between the practitioner and the client that is based on the cultural competence of both parties in the helping relationship. Regardless of your viewpoint, becoming culturally competent is a continuing process, not a destination that you reach once and for all. It is possible to carry our biases around with us and yet not fully recognize how they influence our view of the therapeutic process. It takes consistent effort, honesty, and vigilance to monitor our biases and values so they do not interfere with establishing and maintaining effective working relationships with our clients.

At this point I recommend that you take an inventory of your current level of awareness, knowledge, and skills that have a bearing on your ability to function effectively in multicultural situations by reflecting on these questions:

- To what extent are you aware of how your own culture influences the way you think, feel, and act?
- What could you do to broaden your understanding of both your own culture and other cultures?
- To what degree are you able to identify your basic assumptions, especially as they apply to diversity in culture, race/ethnicity, gender, class, religion, disability, language, and sexual identity?
- How are your assumptions likely to affect the manner in which you function in your professional work?
- How flexible are you in applying the techniques you use to the specific needs of your clients?
- How prepared are you to understand and work with individuals from different cultural backgrounds?
- What life experiences have you had that will help you to understand and make contact with individuals who have a different worldview from yours?
- Can you identify any areas of cultural bias that could inhibit your ability to work effectively with people who are different from you? If so, what steps might you take to challenge your biases?

Theories Applied to Understanding Diversity Perspectives

In this section I summarize a number of theoretical systems from the vantage point of their contributions to understanding diversity. I have included key concepts that I find most useful in understanding and working with clients from a multicultural perspective and some main points that I incorporate in my integrative counseling practice.

❧ **Contributions of Brief Psychodynamic Therapy**   Therapists assist clients in identifying and dealing with the influence of environmental situations on their personality development. The goals of brief psychodynamic therapy can provide a new understanding for current problems. With this briefer form of psychoanalytically oriented therapy, clients can relinquish old patterns and establish new patterns in their present behavior.

❧ **Contributions of Adlerian Therapy**   The Adlerians' focus on social interest, on belonging, and on the collective spirit fits well with the value systems of many client populations. Collectivist cultures that stress the welfare of the social group and that emphasize the role of the family will find the Adlerian focus on social interest to be congruent with their values. Adlerian practitioners are flexible in adapting their interventions to each client's unique life situation. Adlerian therapy has a psychoeducational focus, a present and future orientation, and is a brief, time-limited approach. All of these characteristics make the Adlerian approach suitable for working with a wide range of client problems.

If culture is defined broadly to include age, roles, disability, sexual orientation, and gender differences, there will be cultural differences even within a family. The Adlerian approach emphasizes the value of subjectively understanding the unique world of the individual. Culture is one significant dimension for grasping the subjective and experiential perspective of an individual.

❧ **Contributions of Existential Therapy**   Vontress (2008) contends that the existential approach is perhaps the most applicable of all approaches for working with culturally diverse clients because of its focus on universal themes, or the common ground that we all share. We are all multicultural in the sense that we are the product of many cultures.

The existential approach emphasizes presence, the I/Thou relationship, and courage, qualities that demonstrate a great deal of respect for the client and an interest in deeply understanding the client's world. This approach can be effectively applied with diverse client populations with a range of specific problems and in a wide array of settings (Schneider, 2008; Schneider & Krug, 2010). Existential therapists assist clients in critically evaluating the source of their values and making a choice, rather than uncritically accepting the values of their culture and family. Clients in existential therapy are encouraged to examine the ways their present existence is being influenced by social and cultural factors.

❧ **Contribution of Person-Centered Therapy**   An emphasis on core conditions provides the person-centered approach with a framework for understanding diverse worldviews. Empathy, being present, and respecting the values of clients are essential attitudes and skills in counseling culturally diverse clients. Person-centered counselors convey a deep respect for all forms of diversity and value understanding the client's subjective world in an accepting and open way. These characteristics fit well with understanding the worldview of diverse clients.

❧ Contributions of Gestalt Therapy   There are many opportunities to apply Gestalt experiments in creative ways with diverse client populations. Gestalt experiments can be tailored to fit the unique way in which an individual perceives and interprets his or her culture. Experiments are done with the collaboration of the client and with an attempt to understand the background of the client's culture. Gestalt therapists strive to approach each client in an open way without preconceptions. They check their understanding of the client in dialogue with the client. Gestalt practitioners who have truly integrated their approach are able to apply their skills in a flexible way by adapting their methods to each individual. They are concerned about how and which aspects of the client's background become central, or figural, and what meaning the client places on these figures.

❧ Contributions of Behavior Therapy   Behavioral approaches can be appropriately integrated into counseling with culturally diverse client populations when culture-specific procedures are developed. The approach emphasizes teaching clients about the therapeutic process and stresses changing specific behaviors. In designing a change program for clients from diverse cultures, effective practitioners conduct a functional analysis of the problem situation. This assessment includes the cultural context in which the problem behavior occurs, the consequences both to the client and to the client's sociocultural environment, the resources within the environment that can facilitate change, and the impact that change may have on others in the client's surroundings. By developing their problem-solving skills, clients learn concrete methods for dealing with practical problems within their cultural framework.

❧ Contributions of Cognitive Behavioral Therapy   In the cognitive behavioral approaches therapists function as teachers who encourage clients to learn skills to deal with the problems of living. The emphasis is on changing specific behaviors and developing problem-solving skills rather than on expressing feelings. Clients who appreciate the educational dimensions of a helping relationship and who are looking for action plans and behavioral change will be receptive to this therapy because it offers concrete methods for dealing with their problems.

One aspect of the cognitive behavioral approaches that I especially appreciate is providing clients with a framework to think about their thinking. Within the framework of their cultural values and worldview, clients can explore their beliefs and provide their own reinterpretations of significant life events. This allows therapists to guide clients in a manner that respects clients' underlying values. This dimension is especially important when counselors do not share the same worldview and cultural background as their clients.

❧ Contributions of Reality Therapy   Many of the key concepts of reality therapy can be applied when working with a diverse range of clients. I especially value the straightforward approach of asking clients to look at what they are doing to determine the degree to which their actions are satisfactory to them. Once clients decide what thoughts, feelings, and behaviors they want to target for change, reality therapy offers practical procedures in designing action plans to bring about these changes.

Wubbolding (2000, 2011) believes the confrontational style used with Western clients must be modified to fit the cultural context of people other than North Americans. In Japanese culture, for example, assertive language is not appropriate, and communication is less direct. The reality therapist's tendency to ask direct questions may need to be softened, with questions being raised more elaborately and indirectly. It may be a mistake, for example, to ask individualistic questions built around whether specific behaviors meet clients' needs. Flexibility in using techniques is a foremost requirement in working with culturally diverse clients, and key concepts and procedures must be tailored to fit each individual.

Contributions of Solution-Focused Brief Therapy Solution-focused brief therapists learn from their clients about their experiential world rather than approaching clients with a preconceived notion about their worldview. The therapist-as-expert is replaced by the client-as-expert, especially when it comes to what the client wants in life and in therapy. This nonpathologizing stance moves away from dwelling on what is wrong with a person and emphasizes creative possibilities. Clients become actively involved in resolving their problems, which makes this a very empowering approach. The therapist attempts to create an atmosphere of understanding and acceptance that enables individuals from a wide variety of cultures to utilize their resources to make constructive changes.

Contributions of Narrative Therapy With its emphasis on multiple realities and the assumption that what is perceived to be true is the product of social construction, narrative therapy is a good fit for individuals with diverse worldviews. Narrative therapists operate on the premise that problems are identified within social, cultural, political, and relational contexts rather than existing within individuals, which makes this approach especially relevant for counseling culturally diverse clients. Narrative practitioners are concerned with considering the specifications of gender, ethnicity, race, disability, sexual orientation, social class, and spirituality and religion as therapeutic issues. The sociopolitical conceptualization of problems offers understanding of cultural notions and practices that produce dominant and oppressive narratives. Practitioners deconstruct, or take apart, the cultural assumptions that are a part of a client's problem situation. Clients are able to understand how oppressive social practices affect them, which allows for the possibility of creating alternative stories.

Contributions of Feminist Therapy Feminist therapy is intentionally multicultural, which makes this approach ideally suited to responding to the needs of diverse individuals. The emphasis in feminist therapy is on tailoring treatment to the individual client, collaboration on the goals of therapy, and creating a strong working alliance. All of these factors are central to working in a diversity context and all are empirically linked to positive treatment outcomes (Brown, 2010).

Feminist therapy demands recognition of the role oppressive environmental forces have played in keeping women subjugated to men in cultures throughout the world. The feminist perspective of understanding the use of power in relationships can be applied to understanding power inequities due to racial and cultural factors as well. Unwilling to settle for adjustment to the status quo, feminist therapists demand direct action for social change as part of the role of therapists. Many of the social action and political strategies that call attention to oppressed groups have equal relevance for women and for ethnic minorities. Therapists who subscribe to the assumptions underlying feminist therapy demonstrate their belief that therapy should free individuals and increase their range of choices.

Recognizing the Spiritual Domain

Effective counseling addresses the body, mind, and spirit. Today there is widespread interest in the role of spirituality in both assessment and treatment. Evidence for this interest is found in the many books and articles written on spiritual and religious values in counseling, including those published by the American Counseling Association (ACA) and the American Psychological Association (APA). Part of being culturally competent involves possessing competence to work with clients' spiritual and religious concerns. The Association for Spiritual, Ethical and Religious Values in Counseling (ASERVIC) has developed a set of 14 spiritual competencies to provide a framework for training counselors in learning to address spiritual concerns in an ethical and effective manner (Robertson & Young, 2011). The ASERVIC spiritual competencies can serve as a useful checklist to assess your ability to work effectively with clients' spiritual and religious concerns.

There is also a growing interest in *positive psychology*, which considers topics such as humility, virtue, forgiveness, gratefulness, altruism, and hope. Psychologists have given more attention to negative emotions than to positive emotions, and there has been a historical focus on studying pathology, weaknesses, and suffering. The advocates of positive psychology call for increased attention and research on positive emotions, health, hope, courage, contentment, happiness, well-being, perseverance, resilience, tolerance, and human strengths (Weiten, Dunn, & Hammer, 2012). According to Weiten and colleagues, the humanistic emphasis on optimism, growth, and health laid the foundation for the development of the positive psychology movement, which is increasingly influencing the field of contemporary psychology. Both humanistic psychology and positive psychology are based on common principles. Humanistic psychology focuses on a set of philosophical assumptions about what makes life meaningful. Positive psychologists explore factors that make people happy, focusing on human strengths and how people can flourish in daily life.

Many of the themes stressed in both of these approaches are grounded in spiritual values. Spirituality, like the cultural dimension, might very well be at the center of an integrative approach. Spirituality and religion are critical sources of strength for many clients, are the bedrock for finding meaning in life, and can be instrumental in promoting healing and well-being. Spirituality is an important component of mental health, and integrating spirituality into counseling can be important for many clients. In your work with culturally diverse client populations, you will need to be prepared to address your clients' spiritual concerns.

Religion and spirituality are often part of the client's problem, but these values can also be part of the client's solution. You will be challenged to address spiritual and religious beliefs in both assessment and treatment practices, if these beliefs are important to the client. Many therapists and researchers now consider spiritual beliefs and behaviors as potentially powerful resources for promoting therapeutic change (Cashwell & Young, 2011).

Religious faith, or some form of personal spirituality, can be a powerful source of meaning and purpose. For some, religion does not occupy a key place, yet a personal spirituality may be a central force. Spiritual values help many people make sense out of the universe and the purpose of our lives on this earth. Spirituality can help us get in touch with our own powers of thinking, feeling, deciding, willing, and acting. Like any other potential source of meaning, religious faith or spirituality seems most authentic and valuable when it enables us to become as fully human as possible.

Your clients may sometimes discover that they need to reexamine their values. It is essential that you remain open and nonjudgmental, and recognize that there are multiple paths toward fulfilling spiritual needs. It is not your role as a counselor to prescribe any particular pathway. It is unethical to attempt to convert clients to a particular religious or spiritual set of values. You can, however, assist clients in exploring their own values to determine the degree to which they are living within the framework of this value system. It is important that you monitor yourself for subtle ways you might be inclined to push certain values in your counseling practice, either toward embracing a particular spiritual perspective or abandoning it. It is critical to keep in mind that it is the client's role to determine what specific values to retain or modify.

There are some common denominators that both religion and counseling share. Both religion and counseling help people ponder questions such as: "Who am I?" "What is the meaning of my life?" "Who decides the direction of my life?" At their best, both counseling and religion foster healing through self-exploration. Some of the ways spirituality can influence successful treatment outcomes include learning to accept oneself, forgiving others and oneself, admitting one's shortcomings, accepting personal responsibility, letting go of hurts and resentments, dealing with guilt, and learning to let go of self-destructive patterns of thinking, feeling, and acting. To be able to address these values with clients without imposing your spiritual views is part of ethical and effective practice, which implies that you are aware of your own spiritual and religious values.

Assessing Your Own Spirituality

Your own value system influences every facet of your counseling practice, including your assessment strategies, your views of goals of treatment, the interventions used, the topics explored during the sessions, and evaluations of therapy outcomes. You have an ethical responsibility to be aware of how your beliefs affect your work and make sure you do not unduly influence your clients. If you hope to assist your clients with their spiritual concerns, you must both acknowledge and be comfortable with your own spiritual and religious beliefs. Take a moment to reflect on these questions:

- What role does spirituality or religion play in your life?
- To what extent does religion or spirituality provide you with a source of meaning?
- What connection, if any, do you see between spirituality and religion?
- What are your views concerning established, organized religions?
- Has religion been a positive, negative, or neutral force in your life?

Even if spiritual and religious issues are not the focus of a client's concern, these values may enter into the sessions indirectly as your client explores moral conflicts or grapples with questions of meaning in life. Can you maintain objectivity when spiritual and religious values are explored in counseling sessions? How do you think your values will influence the way you counsel? How would you answer direct questions from your clients about your religious/spiritual beliefs? Can you maintain a healthy awareness of the similarities and differences between your worldview and that of your client? If you have little belief in spirituality, are negative with respect to organized religions, or identify yourself as a secular humanist, can you empathize with clients who view themselves as being deeply spiritual or who feel committed to the teachings of a particular religion? If you are convinced that having a meaning in life hinges on accepting certain religious beliefs, can you be of help to clients who do not share your conviction?

Understanding Ruth From a Diversity Perspective

See Session 4 (Understanding and Addressing Diversity) on the
DVD for Integrative Counseling: The Case of Ruth and Lecturettes.

Ruth brings up the point that she and I are different. When I inquire about *how* we are different and what this means to her, she mentions that she is a woman and I am a man and implies that we have experienced a different type of socialization. As I mentioned earlier, some differences between client and counselor cannot be ignored. Yet more important than the specific ways that she and I differ is the matter of which differences are salient for Ruth. I cannot assume that I automatically know the meaning of our differences, even if they seem obvious. I ask her what differences particularly stand out to her and what meaning these differences hold for her. My aim is to make it easier for Ruth to talk about whatever differences she is aware of and how these differences affect her in our relationship.

Ruth wonders if I can really empathize with her experience as a woman. In many ways she has been socialized to obediently follow traditional roles and behave in ways that others expect of her. Although she does not identify herself as being an oppressed person, she does seem to be oppressed in some respects.

Because of our differences in gender and socialization, Ruth wonders if I am able to understand her and if we can work together. I let her know that it might be difficult for me to understand some aspects of her life, and also let her know that I will tell her when I am having trouble grasping her subjective perspective. For instance, I may have trouble in fully understanding the power of the socialization she has experienced and how difficult it is for her to change certain roles that she has been playing for most of her life. I also invite her to tell me whenever she feels that our differences are getting in her way. I do not want to make assumptions about my ability to work effectively with Ruth until we have had an opportunity to work together for at least a short time.

Principles of feminist therapy can provide useful guidelines in understanding the therapeutic implications of ways that Ruth and I have unique life experiences. In the therapy sessions, I can assist her in evaluating how oppression may be operating in her life today. As a woman, she has learned to put her personal needs on the back burner and to focus on her role as caretaker for her family. This makes it difficult for her to identify and honor what she wants out of therapy. I need to monitor my own perceptions, which are filtered through the lens of my experiences and which may not be the same as Ruth's. Because oppression profoundly influences her beliefs, choices, and perceptions, we will examine the cultural context of how her gender-role socialization is influencing her behavior now.

🪷 Ruth Brings Up Her Spirituality

Although I do not have an agenda to impose religious or spiritual values on Ruth, I do see it as my function to assess the role spirituality plays in her life currently—and to assess beliefs, attitudes, and practices from her earlier years. Ruth grew up attending a fundamentalist religious group, and she very much hopes I will be able to understand this aspect of her upbringing. Several times she initiated a discussion about the void she feels in the area of religion. When she does bring up this topic, I want to honor her request to seriously consider the personal meaning religious themes have for her.

Ruth was taught that she should never question the religious and moral values that were "right." Eventually, she rejected much of the guilt-oriented aspects of her religion, but on an emotional level she still felt a sense of unease and has yet to find what she considers a viable alternative to the religion of her parents. At this time, I do not have a vested interest in having Ruth return to her former beliefs or to find a new religion to replace the one she rejected. The focus of our work is on Ruth's agenda for herself, not my agenda for her. When it comes to religion, I will pay attention to where she appears to be stuck, or where she is conflicted, or what she most hopes she could change about the role of religion in her life.

Ruth lets me know that mainly what she remembers from her church experiences is feeling a sense of guilt that she was not good enough and that she always fell short of being the person her church and parents thought she should be. Not only was she not enough in the eyes of her parents, but she was also not enough in the eyes of God. Guilt is a natural response when we fail to meet our own standards or when we are not living in accordance with our core values.

However, guilt that results in self-criticism and self-condemnation needs to be explored. I work with Ruth to examine the role guilt serves in her life.

Ruth is engaged in a struggle to find spiritual values that will help her find meaning in her life. Although formal religion does not seem to play a key role for her now, she is struggling to find her place in the world. She is seeking spiritual avenues that provide her with purpose, but she is floundering somewhat and realizes that this is a missing dimension in her current life. I see my role as encouraging her to remain open to pursuing a variety of spiritual pathways.

Ruth lets me know that she is pleasantly surprised that I am even mentioning religion and spirituality. She was not sure whether it was appropriate to bring such matters into counseling. She lets me know that it was good for her to be able to initiate a discussion about her past experiences with religion and her present quest to find a spiritual path that has meaning to her. She informs me of her intention to further explore in her sessions ways that she can enhance her spiritual life. I will remain open to these discussions as they are introduced by Ruth.

Understanding Stan From a Diversity Perspective

See Session 10 (Feminist Therapy) on the *DVD*
for Theory and Practice of Counseling and Psychotherapy:
The Case of Stan and Lecturettes.

Stan and I explore how gender-role socialization is inhibiting Stan's ability to experience a rich life. Stan becomes aware of many of the messages that he has internalized from society about what it means to be a man. From his father he learned the message of numbing himself to emotional pain. His father's advice was "Suck it up and be a man." Stan feels that he has never measured up to the expectations of his father and his brother, who both seem never to allow problems to derail them. Stan describes his brother and his father as being confident, strong, and like a rock. When I asked Stan if he wants to be like either of these men, this caused him to pause and reflect on the values he has received from his family and culture about what men are supposed to be like. We spend considerable time exploring his attitudes about gender roles and about decisions he has made regarding his gender identity. As a homework assignment, I suggest to Stan that he read a book on masculine identify and gender-role socialization. In several following sessions, we discuss many of the ideas in this book that seem to have a profound effect on Stan's way of thinking about modifying some of his views of what kind of man he would like to become.

Merely talking about gender-role messages will not bring about changes in Stan's established behavior patterns, but these discussions may result in a shift in Stan's thinking about the self-limiting roles he has accepted without question. Stan begins to increasingly see how these messages were reinforced by expectations from his parents, and he becomes aware of how the damaging self-statements he makes now are related to his early experiences. These conversations may eventually result in shifts in how Stan feels about himself as a man and the ways he allows himself to respond in many different social situations.

Concluding Comments

Diversity is a reality that must be factored into an integrative approach to counseling. Regardless of theoretical orientation, both clients' and therapists' underlying values must be taken into account. Some of the values implicit in contemporary counseling theories include an emphasis on individualism, the separate existence of the self, and individuation as the foundation for maturity. But these values may not be equally relevant to all people, and therapists must recognize that contemporary counseling theories are not value-neutral.

Spiritual or religious values can be considered a dimension of a client's culture. Research has indicated that spirituality is a key component of mental health, so integrating spirituality into the therapy process is appropriate for some clients. Counselors need to be prepared to address spiritual and religious concerns that a client might raise. "If spirituality and religion are important aspects of a client's culture and sense of well-being, the counselor is not practicing competently if he or she summarily dismisses this part of the client's life. A wealth of information is simply being dismissed" (Young & Cashwell, 2011b, p. 285). However, the key is to include a consideration of a client's spiritual and religious background to determine how these factors may play a role in the individual's treatment. Young and Cashwell make it clear that a thorough assessment makes it quite possible to explore a client's spiritual and religious values without imposing the counselor's values.

The psychoanalytic, behavioral, cognitive behavioral, and existential approaches originated in Euro-American culture and are grounded on a core set of values. There is a danger of seeing these values as having universal applicability. The relationship-oriented therapies—such as person-centered theory, existential therapy, and Gestalt therapy—emphasize freedom of choice and self-actualization. If you base your practice on these orientations, you will likely focus on individual responsibility for making internal changes as a way to cope with problems, and you will view individuation as the foundation for healthy functioning. Listen to your clients and determine why they are seeking help and how best to deliver the help that is appropriate for them in their unique context.

After reading this chapter on understanding and addressing diversity, take time to reflect on the following questions as a way of clarifying your thoughts on these issues in counseling practice.

- To what extent do you think contemporary counseling theories can incorporate a multicultural perspective?
- In what ways should diversity be a central part of the counseling process?
- What do you think it will take for you to become a culturally competent counselor?
- Do you agree with Lum that cultural competence is a joint venture and dialogue between client and counselor? If so, what implications are there for the way you will practice?
- To what extent do you believe that spiritual and religious issues have a place in counseling? Would you be comfortable talking with a client about these topics?

- How can spiritual or religious values of a client be best addressed in the counseling process?
- What questions might you ask a client during the assessment process regarding his or her spiritual and religious beliefs and experience?
- Would you tend to initiate a discussion of a client's spiritual or religious beliefs, or would you wait for the client to bring up this topic?
- How is gender a key facet of diversity? What importance do you place on exploring the ways gender-role socialization has affected the views your clients have about what it means to be a woman or a man?

CHAPTER FIVE

Understanding and Working With Resistance

Introduction

One of your biggest fears as a counselor in training may be working with highly resistant behavior in a client. Many beginning counselors take any signs of resistance in those with whom they are counseling in personal ways. They may think, "If I were an effective counselor, I shouldn't have this resistance. I should be able to help anybody who comes to me." or "If clients reach an impasse, or are uncooperative, or don't come back for a second session, this is a sign that I am doing something wrong."

Your self-talk may not be quite so harsh, yet faced with a difficult client you might well blame yourself for what you've done or failed to do. In any event, you will probably not actually welcome resistance as the source of productive material for therapeutic work. Take a few moments to think about the meanings you attach to resistance. Is it a part of every counseling venture, regardless of how motivated your client is and how skillful you may be as a counselor? Is resistance a client's intention to sabotage your best efforts?

Most clients with whom you work will test you in some way to determine whether the relationship with you is safe for them. It is essential that you encourage openness on the part of your clients so that they are able to express their hesitations and anxieties. Your clients are likely to have mixed feelings regarding staying in a safe zone versus taking the risk of letting you know them. Both you and your clients need to understand the meaning of resistance and come to view it as something to explore in the counseling process rather than as an enemy to be defeated.

Understanding the Dynamics of Resistance

Some of my colleagues have trouble with the word "resistance," thinking of it as a negative term that implies something is wrong with the client. They have a good point because resistance is often equated with a stubborn refusal to cooperate with treatment, is viewed as something the client is doing wrong, or is perceived by counselors as a sign of their ineptness. Resistance is typically viewed as a phenomenon that resides within the client, and traditional therapy approaches often assume that clients who are "stuck" are resistant to change. If an impasse in therapy is reached, therapists frequently blame clients and label them as "unmotivated," and the clients sometimes judge or blame themselves as well. This way of viewing resistance is limiting and does not facilitate the therapeutic process.

Although resistance is often viewed as an impediment to therapeutic progress, in actuality it can be central to productive work. My view of resistance is that it is a normal phenomenon that is basic to the counseling process. Resistance is a fundamental part of therapy that must be recognized, accepted, and explored. Once resistance is identified, it can be addressed cognitively, affectively, and behaviorally in an integrative way. As I hope to illustrate, by coming to understand and deal with your own patterns of resistance, you open up possibilities for modifying your behavior and also for developing skills in managing resistance in clients. In understanding the dynamics of resistance, both clients' and therapists' contributions to the resistance must be considered. It is important that clients do not feel blamed or come to believe that something is inherently wrong with them for experiencing resistance. Nor should therapists feel that resistance always implies a lack of sensitivity or timing on their part. If you are engaged in intense work with a client, he or she might become frightened and stop the process as a form of self-protection against anxiety. Your client may have been psychologically and physically hurt in the past and resorted to defenses as a way to cope with an intolerable situation. Your client's guarded behavior might well be a defense against getting wounded again. Past experiences are often associated with negative experiences with significant others, and you may need to explore these fears for your client to learn to trust you. It is important that you and your client make a commitment to talk about your present relationship. If you show a willingness to address your client's defensive behavior, the chances are increased that your client will be willing to take a look at various forms of resistive behavior. If you consistently approach what appears to be resistance with respect, interest, compassion, and concern, you increase the chances your client will explore this behavior in counseling sessions.

Respecting and Reframing Resistance

Various Perspectives on Understanding Resistance

From a behavioral perspective I am reminded that what I identify as "resistance" might well be an excuse on my part for not doing a thorough assessment or for inadequately utilizing techniques. This perspective requires that I look at what I am doing to determine how I might be getting in my client's way. Chapter 3 emphasized the value of the therapist working with clients to establish clear and realistic personal goals as a framework for the direction of counseling. If I impose my vision of what I think the client should be working on, "resistance" is to be expected.

From a psychoanalytic perspective, resistance is typically defined as the individual's reluctance to bring into conscious awareness threatening material that has been previously repressed or denied. It also can be viewed as anything that prevents individuals from dealing with unconscious material. From a broader perspective, resistance can be viewed as behavior that keeps us from exploring personal conflicts or painful feelings. I agree with the psychoanalytic conceptualization of resistance as defensive strategies aimed at protecting us and preserving our inner core in the face of anxiety.

Levenson (2010) describes resistance from the perspective of time-limited dynamic psychotherapy (TLDP) as being best understood within the context of the client–therapist relationship. The assumption is that clients are doing the best they can considering how they view the world. Psychodynamic therapists work with clients to assist them in understanding and dealing with resistance as a form of self-protection, which helps them maintain their self-perception, personal integrity, and interpersonal connectedness. Levenson states that "when TLDP therapists feel as if they have hit a wall of resistance from the client, they can stand back, appreciate the attachment-based significance of the wall, and invite the client to look at possible 'good' reasons to have the wall. Such an approach often avoids power plays with hostile clients and helps to promote empathy and collaboration" (p. 84).

In understanding resistance from the perspective of existential-humanistic therapy, Schneider and Krug (2010) address resistance as a safety issue for clients. They believe it is crucial to respect resistance because it is a lifeline to many clients that represents a familiar path. Schneider and Krug urge therapists "to tread mindfully when it comes to resistance, acknowledging to clients both its life-giving and life-taking qualities" (p. 54). Before confronting clients on their defensive and protective patterns, it is necessary to have established a solid therapeutic alliance. If clients do not feel safe, a challenge from the therapist can exacerbate rather than alleviate the situation.

Teyber and McClure (2011) support an interpersonal perspective. They suggest that counselors honor clients' resistance as an outdated coping strategy that at one time served a self-preservative and adaptive function. When clients are able to appreciate the fact that a particular coping strategy was the best possible response to a difficult situation at an earlier time in their development, both counselors and clients can recognize that some resistance is normal and makes sense. When clients learn to identify present coping strategies that no longer serve a useful purpose, therapists can assist clients in reframing their resistance. Too often clients adopt a self-critical stance toward their resistance. They want to avoid talking about the topic because they are afraid of a therapist's critical judgment.

Therapists need to remain nondefensive and nonjudgmental if clients express any dissatisfaction or raise questions about their experience in therapy. It is a therapist's job to welcome any concerns that clients have so these matters can be discussed in a straightforward way. It is helpful for the counselor to explore with clients how they are experiencing each session, beginning at the initial meeting. Unless counselors ask clients about potential problems they experience with the counseling process, their concerns will likely remain unspoken (Teyber & McClure, 2011).

Resistance is not something that needs to be "gotten around quickly" or bypassed. Clients may demonstrate a variety of resistances, and these defenses need to be understood and therapeutically explored. Part of respecting resistance means that you understand the functions these defenses serve. There are times when people need their defensives in order to survive a crisis situation. At such times, you need to be supportive rather than insist that your clients surrender their protection.

Stages of Change

Prochaska and DiClemente (2005) view a client's unwillingness to recognize or own a problem not as an act of resisting the therapist but as resisting change. They emphasize the importance of a therapist appreciating how frightening the prospect of change is to many clients. Clients who are contemplating change often experience ambivalence, and the therapist needs to develop patience during this sometimes lengthy and frustrating stage of change. Although therapists are responsible for challenging clients to take action necessary to bring about desired changes, they must avoid instilling blame and guilt in their clients. Prochaska and DiClemente suggest that the therapist become an ally rather than a person attempting to coerce change.

It is helpful to consider a client's readiness for change. Norcross, Krebs, and Prochaska (2011) describe a transtheoretical model of change that involves clients progressing through a series of five identifiable stages in the counseling process:

Precontemplation stage: client has no intention of changing a behavior pattern in the foreseeable future

Contemplation stage: client is aware of a problem and considering overcoming it but has not yet made a commitment to take action

Preparation stage: client intends to take action in the near future and reports some small behavioral changes

Action stage: client takes steps to modify behavior, experiences, and/or environment to solve problem

Maintenance stage: client works to consolidate gains and prevent relapse

Clients do not pass neatly through these five stages in linear fashion, and if change is initially unsuccessful, individuals may return to an earlier stage. Effective therapy calls for matching specific interventions with whatever stage of change clients are experiencing. If there is a mismatch between process and stage, movement through the stage will be impeded and is likely to be manifested in reluctant behavior (Norcross, Krebs, & Prochaska, 2011; Prochaska & Norcross, 2010).

Working within the framework of the stages of change model has implications for the role a therapist assumes at the different stages. Norcross, Krebs, and Prochaska (2011) describe the relational stances taken by therapists. With clients in the precontemplation stage, the role assumed is that of a *nurturing parent.* With clients in the contemplation phase, therapists function as *Socratic teachers* who encourage clients to achieve their own insights. For clients who are in the preparation stage, therapists take the stance of *experienced coach.* With clients who are progressing into action and maintenance, therapists function in the role of *consultant*. As termination approaches, therapists are consulted less often as a way to foster client autonomy. Norcross, Krebs, and Prochaska claim that stage of change assessment is straightforward and takes but a few minutes during the initial session. They recommend the following research-supported therapist strategies to guide the course of treatment and enhance treatment outcomes:

- Take time to assess the client's stage of change.
- Do not assume all clients are in the action stage and motivated to change.
- Set realistic goals that are in keeping with the client's readiness to change.
- Deal with clients who are in precontemplation in a respectful manner.
- Tailor therapeutic interventions to the client's stage: insight and awareness interventions are useful during the early stages; action-oriented strategies are appropriate at later stages.
- Use stage-matched relationship style (or role) that will best help the client progress to the next stage of change.
- It is well to practice from an integrative perspective.
- Expect to recycle through the stages several times before achieving long-term maintenance.

These stages of change can be applied to many different therapeutic approaches. This model of client readiness for change has implications for all of the theories, and this assessment can help therapists better understanding their clients.

Understanding How Resistive Behavior Affects You as a Therapist

The key to understanding clients' various forms of defensive behavior is to pay attention to your own reactions that are triggered by this resistance. Many clients will replay their early history with significant others in their present relationship with you. Tune in to what you are feeling as you are working with your clients. If you respond to clients' resistance in a personal way, it will be difficult for you to work with their dynamics. If you respond in an aggressive or defensive way, a difficult situation is likely to worsen. Your task is to approach difficult clients in a different way and work cooperatively with them so that they might learn new and more effective ways of coping.

Clients whom you perceive as being difficult or resistant may contribute to your own feelings of self-doubt and incompetence and bring out your feelings of inadequacy and impatience. In dealing with difficult clients, monitor your responses and potential countertransference to their behavior. If you quickly become annoyed with clients you view as resistive, you are likely to cut off avenues of reaching them. Do your best to avoid labeling clients and instead describe the behaviors you are observing. When you view clients as being scared, overwhelmed with grief, cautious, or hurt, you can reframe any pattern of resistance they manifest. If you change the word "resistant" to more descriptive and nonjudgmental terminology, your own attitude toward clients who appear to be "difficult" may change. As you change the lens by which you perceive clients' behaviors, it will be easier for you to adopt an understanding and respectful stance. This stance will help your clients begin to explore the meaning of their reluctance. Instead of viewing their resistance as behavior that is designed to make your work impossible, approach such behavior with a genuine sense of interest.

Stricker (2010) cautions therapists to avoid attributing problems in the treatment process to the client's shortcomings because the interactive role between client and therapist often contributes to seeming barriers to treatment. Reflect on your own style of interacting with clients to better understand your part in creating or contributing to resistant or noncompliant client behavior. By viewing resistance as something that emerges from the interactions between clients and counselors, the functions resistance serves are illuminated. "Resistance then can be seen as the friend rather than the enemy of treatment, because it carries clues as to the client's typical means of functioning" (p. 41).

Becoming the Client: Experiencing Resistance in Yourself

I ask you again to assume the role of client and imagine that you and I are engaged in a therapeutic relationship. I am presenting some key ideas about the experience of resistance in this way because I believe you will come to appreciate the inevitable place of resistance in the therapeutic process if you allow yourself to consider ways you might resist when you are anxious.

I encourage you to involve yourself in personal counseling if you plan to become a professional counselor. You are apt to learn a great deal about helpful and unproductive interventions through your experiences as a client. If you and your therapist work well together, you also will learn quite a bit about how you present yourself to the world. You are bound to respect the courage it takes to forge ahead even though you are frightened, particularly at those times when you wonder if the gain is worth the pain you might be experiencing. In Chapter 10, when we consider the topics of transference and countertransference, I go into greater detail on the importance of opening yourself to some form of personal self-exploration—individual counseling, group counseling, family therapy, or some other pathway toward self-understanding such as spiritual direction. For now, let me encourage you to be as open as you can in imagining yourself in the role of a client in counseling with me as you deal with your own ways of resisting.

I will assign a variety of resistive behaviors to you in this section and show how I might intervene. Allow yourself to get into the role of actually experiencing the various forms of defensive behaviors. Some of these scenarios will not fit you, and you may have other creative ways of resisting that I do not describe. See what you can learn about yourself by placing yourself in the center of resistance.

If you and I are involved in a client–therapist relationship, my main endeavor is to create and maintain the kind of working relationship that will allow you to take significant risks. Part of this relationship means that I must recognize the signs of resistance, both in you and in myself. If you and I are not dealing well with resistance, it may be a sign that our relationship needs strengthening. (Refer to Chapter 2 on the therapeutic relationship as the foundation for effective counseling for more on this topic.)

The ways you might resist are many, some subtle and others more obvious. Ask yourself if you might engage in any of these resistive or defensive behaviors:

- Forgetting about your counseling appointment
- Frequently showing up late for your sessions
- Not having material to bring into the sessions
- Complaining that you are not being helped by counseling
- Being silent and expecting to be drawn out by the therapist
- Becoming defensive when you get feedback
- Engaging in long-winded stories and leaving out how you are feeling
- Doing a great deal of intellectualizing about why you feel the way you do
- Avoiding emotional expression
- Striving very hard to please the therapist
- Talking in the abstract and remaining global
- Depending on the therapist excessively

Some of these behaviors may be anchored in reality and be a realistic and appropriate response. For instance, your defensiveness regarding feedback from your therapist may be a function of how the therapist presents the feedback to you. Everything that looks like resistance may not actually be resistance. This is why resistance needs to be explored and its meaning sensitively discussed. What are some other ways that you might resist?

Imagine that you are coming for one of the early sessions of counseling with me. Are you experiencing any reluctance? Are you aware of ambivalence regarding changing versus staying as you are? How do you think you would deal with any anxiety you might be experiencing? What will you talk about at the first session? If you are like many in the helping professions, you might have trouble asking for help for yourself. Do you think you should be problem-free if you are going to be an effective counselor? Do you have some pressing problems but feel that you should be able to resolve them on your own without any assistance from anyone?

How open are you? How much do you want from counseling? Students enrolled in counseling programs often go for counseling because it is required as part of the program or because they have been encouraged by their professors (or authors of their textbooks). Some of the reluctance they might be experiencing can be summarized thusly:

> Well, I'm not really sure I need therapy, but I suppose I could learn something about myself from coming in here. To be truthful, though, it is sort of difficult for me to ask for help. In many ways I think I should be able to deal with my problems by myself. After all, everyone has problems, so maybe I could get along fine without counseling. Besides, I've got a lot going for me in my life, and things are great. If I start questioning, who knows what I might find out. Maybe it would be better to let good enough be!

Now I don't expect you or any client to say this much as an opening statement, but it does illustrate some of the ambivalence I see in counseling students when they present themselves for personal counseling. Reflect for a moment about some of the ambivalence you might be experiencing if you came to counseling because of the urging of your professors or mainly to meet a requirement of your program. If you do have feelings of ambivalence, or negative reactions, to the expectation of receiving personal therapy, how might this relate to your views of counseling in general?

It will be beneficial to spend time exploring some of your beliefs about seeking counseling for yourself. Do you think initiating counseling means that you are not in control of your life? Are you admitting that there is something wrong with you by going for counseling? We can certainly talk about these beliefs and how such beliefs might hinder your openness in this counseling relationship—and how these beliefs might hinder you as a counselor. Talk about what you are experiencing as you come into this session today. Are you feeling excited? Anxious? Hopeful? Frightened? Cautious? Eager? I will continue to center my questions around your feelings, especially if you are experiencing hesitation, to facilitate a deeper understanding of the meaning of your resistance.

Imagine we work well together and you decide there are some areas of your life in which you feel somewhat stuck and want to understand more fully. Assume this is the fifth session, and you bring up for discussion the gulf that you sense between you and your father:

> My Dad has never been emotionally available to me, and I still miss this. You'd think that by this time I should be over needing approval and affection from my father. The truth is there are times when I realize I'm still looking to others for what I've missed with him. I still remember when I was a child and how much I wanted him to notice me and tell me I was special. But I felt he never really knew me and wasn't too interested in spending time with me.

There is a great deal of rich material to pursue here. But let's assume that with every question I pose you draw a blank. You have little to say and seem emotionally reserved. There are long pauses, and many times you grow silent. You give only terse responses to my inquiries. Can you imagine any of this happening?

There are many reasons you might not be ready to work and why you may be hesitant. I want to know about these reasons, but I also want you to understand your own reluctance, and I will encourage you to talk about this. If you can remain nonjudgmental and can accept some ambivalence, there is much you can learn about yourself by exploring these feelings. Resistance typically occurs when a person begins to approach painful or threatening material that, if revealed, could result in feelings of vulnerability. It makes sense that you are not eager to experience feelings of shame, vulnerability, and uncertainty. At the same time, I want to be consistent in inviting you to address the ways you may be holding back. When you get close to painful experiences and become frightened, do you try to avoid these feelings by some kind of diversion? I will encourage you to challenge your tendency to avoid an uncomfortable state and to go deeper into the feeling or behavior you wish to avoid. In my view, facing and experiencing feelings takes courage. Your willingness to endure the pain or anxiety that is necessary for getting unstuck and making way for new growth is a reflection of that courage.

At this point I suggest that you participate in a Gestalt experiment. I ask you to bring what you are experiencing with your father into the room at this moment:

> There is an empty chair over here. Would you be that child who so much wanted to be noticed and wanted Dad's approval? Tell him that now. He is sitting in that chair and is ready to listen to you.

Your response is a flat refusal! Although I am not invested in forcing you to participate in any particular technique, I am interested in exploring your reluctance in seeing where this experiment might lead. Talking about what is holding you back seems crucial to me. You respond to my questioning in one of these ways:

- It seems stupid to talk to an empty chair. I would feel foolish doing that.
- I'm afraid of doing what you ask because just thinking about it brings tears to my eyes.
- I'd rather just tell you about my father because it would feel weird for me to talk to him when he is not really here.

Talking about what your reluctance means to you is one way to make this setting safer for you. If you'd feel foolish, I ask what it would be like for you to feel foolish in my presence. This could open up useful material. If you indicate you don't want to put your father in the empty chair and talk to him because just imagining this brings you to tears, I follow that lead more fully. What are you crying about? How is it for you to get close to sadness at this moment? If I am able to understand the purpose your resistance serves and respect your hesitation, you will be more likely to come to a new understanding of your defensiveness. I want to show you that I am willing to go as far as you are and that I will not push you to do what you say you do not want to do. Ultimately, you decide which topics you are willing to pursue and how far you will go. By exploring the anxiety underlying an apparent resistance, the soil is being prepared for you to engage in self-exploration in more depth.

In another session you provide the starting point for our discussion:

> Today I want to talk about the tough time I am having in getting over being rejected in a relationship. Some days I think I'm fine, and other days I really get depressed and start thinking all sorts of horrible things about myself.

There are many ways for us to work with this. Depending on the context of what you are describing, I might pursue a cognitive path with you, or encourage you to get more in contact with the feelings you are experiencing, or talk with you about actual courses of action you might take in doing something different. In fact, in one session it is very possible that we would work with what you are telling yourself about this breakup (cognitions and self-talk), I'd invite you to stay with feelings that are surfacing as you talk, and I'd suggest some behavioral steps you can take in moving in a different direction.

But what if you have mixed reactions about engaging in a dialogue on any level? What if your resistances are getting the best of you and you don't seem to be getting far in working cognitively, emotionally, or behaviorally? Put yourself in the following scenario and imagine these ways you might resist.

You feel greatly disappointed over this breakup. This is proof that you're unlovable. I suggest that you examine the validity of your conclusions. You reply that you should have been over this by now. As you reveal some of what you tell yourself about the breakup, I notice you tearing up, yet smiling at the same time. I describe what I'm noticing, and you withdraw. I suggest that you talk more about feeling rejected. Instead you provide an intellectual discussion about the tentative nature of interpersonal relationships and come up with a number of truisms such as "Life is difficult" and "Nothing ventured, nothing gained." I notice the ways I see you are defending yourself, and I invite you to say more. For instance, what might happen if you were to allow yourself to feel the intensity of what you are feeling about the loss of this relationship—without smiling and without giving intellectual explanations? Following your resistance in a gentle but insistent manner could free you of the impasse you are experiencing. I am not at all sure where your exploration will lead if I ask you to stay with whatever avoidances emerge, yet I have a hunch that doing so will be productive. I encourage you to let down some unnecessary defenses, but not to strip away all of your defenses. This process must be done respectfully and carefully, yet persistently.

There are many ways to approach resistance both in session and outside of the sessions. Reflect on some of the main ways you are likely to resist when your anxiety surfaces and write about this in your journal. Imagine all the ways you might resist when you are threatened psychologically. What are some defenses you rely on? What are examples of defenses you have used when you felt vulnerable? How did this work for you? To what extent do you think you would challenge your resistance by talking about it? I hope you don't think courage means that you are without any fear. Courage means being afraid yet going ahead nevertheless. At points in your therapy you may become hesitant because of fear of your emerging feelings. How could you remain in the moment longer when your initial tendency is to withdraw?

By putting yourself in the role of the client, I hope you have come to appreciate how complex the counseling process can be. I suspect that some of your most valuable lessons on how to recognize, understand, and deal with resistance in your clients will be learned from your own experience with personal counseling.

Understanding Ruth's Resistance

See Session 5 (Understanding and Working With Resistance) on the *DVD for Integrative Counseling: The Case of Ruth and Lecturettes.*

I want to do my best to respect Ruth's genuine concerns about moving forward, which will entail giving up some of her comfortable ways. If handled properly, resistance can be one of the most valuable tools that she can use in her quest for self-understanding. Rather than fighting her initial resistance, hesitation, and ambivalence, I view it as a positive sign of her strength. Originally, Ruth's defenses served her in adapting to very difficult life circumstances. Her defenses were her best attempt to deal with conflicting situations at an earlier period of development. It is important for her to realize that she is now capable of far more creative and healthy responses to the life tasks she faces.

Overall, Ruth is willing and motivated. She is insightful, courageous, able to make connections between current behavior and past influences, and is willing to try risky behaviors both in our sessions and in daily life. Even under such favorable and almost ideal circumstances, it is not uncommon for her to experience ambivalence about change and to entertain doubts about the value of counseling. I want to convey to her that it is healthy to experience ambivalence and to proceed cautiously; it shows that she is aware of the risks of changing and the anxiety that is associated with coming to terms with unknown parts of herself. In one of her sessions, Ruth discusses whether to continue therapy. She exhibits some resistance in the form of not wanting to be in the therapy session. She is realizing that many in her family do not like the changes she is making. She recalls me telling her that she might get worse before she gets better. From her vantage point, this is exactly what is happening at home. Things are getting worse, which is causing her to doubt the value of what she is doing in counseling.

꙳ Borrowing From a Psychoanalytic   View Ruth's resistance can be understood in the context of the intolerable anxiety that she fears might arise if she were to become aware of feelings locked up inside of her. Because her resistance blocks threatening material from entering awareness, I ask her to talk about what specific forms of resistive behavior mean to her. I am interested in her interpretation about how she is dealing with threatening situations, and perhaps later I will offer my hunches. I support her in facing her fears. At times I suggest an interpretation in the form of a hunch to help Ruth become aware of the reasons for her resistances. For example, "Let me share a hunch about what I see going on and see what you think of it. What we've been talking about is really frightening for you. Getting your family riled up over your changes is certainly not comfortable for you. It has temporarily overwhelmed you, and you seem to want to give up." Ruth can then reflect on the feedback I offer her and decide how accurate and useful my impressions of her are. By sharing a hunch with her about the possible meanings a certain behavior may hold, I hope to deal with signs of resistance in a collaborative, nonjudgmental, nonthreatening, respectful, straightforward, and therapeutic manner.

꙳ Drawing on Other Approaches   As a process concern, I inform Ruth that most clients are ambivalent, defensive, and hesitant at some point in the counseling process. This push-pull is occurring with Ruth and could result in premature termination of therapy if she does not discuss her fears and reservations about being in counseling. Although she is externalizing her concerns by focusing on her husband's displeasure over her changes and the negative reactions from her children, internal factors also may be affecting Ruth and contributing to her resistance. She is really split. Part of her wants to cling to the status quo, but another part of her wants to branch out and become more of the person she would like to be. I ask her to voice her doubts about the value of therapy. It is clear that she is ambivalent and is reluctant to make choices.

Talking about her reluctance to participate fully in therapy can be done in a gentle yet challenging way, along with providing support to face issues that she might otherwise avoid.

Later in the session I suggest we work with her ambivalence over wanting to change and resisting change, which is a central principle in motivational interviewing. I suggest a role play as a way of exploring her ambivalence. I ask Ruth to be the side of her that wants to remain the same because that is the feeling that seems to be the strongest in her now. I take on the role of the side of Ruth that wants to move forward. In this role play we debate the pros and cons of changing. I do my best to highlight the advantages of taking the risks involved in making significant life changes. She has an opportunity to express out loud what she tends to rehearse silently about the guarantees of sticking with the "old version" of her life. After engaging in this role play for a time, I ask her what she is experiencing. We then reverse roles so that she can deepen her experience of the ambivalent feelings within her. After switching roles for a time, she decides that she wants to stay in therapy, even though it is causing chaos at home.

Toward the end of the session Ruth admits that she had not realized how scared she was, yet she adds that preserving the status quo isn't working for her either. It has become clear to her that she is caught in a rut and experiences life as being limited. She wants more from her life, yet she is frightened when she considers what she might have to do or become to have a more satisfying existence. Because I accept the existential notion of the client's place in choosing how far to go, it is Ruth who decides whether she has sufficient motivation to face her reluctance in making some basic changes in her life.

The feminist therapy approach reminds me of how crucial it is for Ruth to be an active participant in her counseling and to make her own choices. I am committed to ensuring that our therapeutic relationship does not become another arena in which she stays in a passive, dependent role. It is important that she give voice to her experiencing now. Initially, she tended to look to me for answers or advice. As I continued to place the responsibility back on her, and to relate to her more as a person than as an "expert," she experienced glimpses of what it is like to trust more in her own power. She is beginning to get in touch with a range of feelings, including anger and other "prohibited" emotions she learned to deny to herself. Some of her self-doubts and anxiety over continuing in therapy relate to a host of feelings that she has kept in check but that are now emerging within her. I want her to feel that it is acceptable to talk openly about her anxiety over these "new" feelings.

At this point I attempt to pull together some of the conflicting themes we've talked about in the session and invite Ruth to reflect on where she wants to go from here. I suggest a homework assignment, as I frequently do, with the expectation that she will gain greater clarity of the options open to her and the choices she is willing to make. (Here I draw on behavior therapy, reality therapy, and rational emotive behavior therapy.) For one week I ask Ruth to write in her journal all the reasons for staying the same versus the reasons for making changes. I ask her to reflect, for one day, on what her life might be like if she quits therapy and to think about the kind of life she might have if she continues on the path she has pursued for much of her life. On another day I ask her to write in her journal about how she imagines her life could be if she continues with her therapy and makes some of the changes she desires. She agrees to follow through with this homework, which gives us a good place to continue in a subsequent session.

Understanding Stan's Resistance

See Session 2 (Psychoanalytic Therapy) on the *DVD* *for Theory and Practice of Counseling and Psychotherapy:* *The Case of Stan and Lecturettes.*

Although Stan has had several sessions with me, he is still reluctant to trust me as his therapist. In this session, I hope to explore his reasons for this resistance. Stan tends to be guarded and measures his responses, doing a great deal of internal rehearsing before he speaks or replies to any of my questions or comments. He appears to be censoring his thoughts and carefully editing what he verbally expresses. Stan and I talk about what his hesitation and guarded behavior might mean. He lets me know that he wants to "get it right" when he speaks, and he does not want to look foolish. He is concerned that I may be judging him, and he does not want to be criticized. To protect himself, Stan thinks carefully about what he wants to say and how to say it before he begins to speak to me.

I encourage Stan to say more about what is going on inside of him that he is not expressing with his long pauses, internal rehearsing, and short answers. I find what Stan is not saying to be very interesting, and this seems like a useful avenue for exploration. I might say any or all of these things to Stan: "I hope you will rehearse out loud." "You are quiet, yet it seems like a lot is going on in your head. Are you willing to put words to any of this?" "I'm noticing that you give short answers, that you think a long time before replying, and that you seem to be very cautious. What is it like to be in here now? How free do you feel to put into words what is on your mind and in your heart?"

Stan's silences may represent a sure sign of resistance or be related to any number of other factors. For example, Stan may be trying to figure out what he guesses I might want to hear. He could be hesitant to speak because it will open a flood of emotion, which he is defending against. He might be waiting for me to comment more on what he has said before he speaks. He might be trying very hard to figure out what is going on with me, including my assessment of him. I cannot know what keeps Stan quiet unless he eventually shares his feelings and thoughts with me. Without labeling what he is doing as resistance, I point out what I see him doing and invite him to comment on what this means to him. I am trying to open a dialogue regarding what he is thinking and feeling as he is in this session. I hope Stan will be able to talk more about his experience with me in his therapy.

As Stan's therapy progresses, I expect some resistance—hesitation, defenses, and barriers—at certain anxiety-provoking points. Growth and change, even when positive, can involve discomfort. Stan's resistance represents a familiar defensive strategy he has used to cope with anxiety in his daily life. He will decide whether this behavior is serving him well now. It is also good for him to learn that his defenses can interfere with his ability to change in a direction that could make his life fuller and more gratifying.

Stan has conflicting aspects within his personality. Although a large part of him would like to change, he fears the implications of changing. It is critical for him to be willing to identify his ambivalence regarding change and to talk about this in our sessions. Working from the perspective of motivational interviewing, I avoid labeling Stan as being "resistant" and look at my style of interacting with him to better understand my own part in creating resistant or noncompliant behavior on Stan's part. I want him to know that I am not judging him on his cautiousness and reservations. I adapt my approach and let Stan know that he will likely experience ambivalent feelings about change and that his motivation may ebb and flow during the course of therapy.

Guidelines for Dealing With Resistance in Clients

The various perspectives on resistance presented here provide a foundation for you to use when formulating your own perspective on the role of resistance in the counseling process. Doing so will assist you in respecting the difficulty your clients often experience. A summary of key points follows that may help you decide how to therapeutically work with the reluctance, defensive behavior, and resistance you may encounter as you work with clients.

- Realize that initially many clients are defensive about having to meet with you to deal with their problems. Many people have been given the message that asking for help is a sign of weakness, which may make them hesitant to be open.
- Adopt an open stance toward discussing with your clients how they are perceiving their work with you. Invite them to talk about any concerns they may have regarding the progress of therapy and their reactions to you.
- Avoid labeling and judging clients, and instead describe the behavior they are displaying. If you label certain behaviors your clients display as "resistance," they might feel judged and begin to think of resistance as something totally negative.
- Encourage clients to explore any form of resistance rather than demand that they give up their resistance.
- State your observations, hunches, and interpretations in a tentative way rather than making dogmatic pronouncements. Approach resistance respectfully and work with it therapeutically.
- Distinguish between the phenomenon of resistance, which is occurring in your client, and your reactions to the client's resistance. Monitor your reactions so that you don't escalate client resistance.
- Do your best to be accepting and nondefensive as you listen to your clients. If you understand and accept your client and do not react defensively, this will probably melt the intensity of the client's resistance. If you meet resistance with resistance, you are likely to entrench this pattern.
- Allow clients to express their feelings about prior negative experiences with counseling. Ask them what they would like to do differently with you.

- Provide clients with a brief explanation of how you work and strive to obtain genuine informed consent. Educate clients about ways they can use the relationship with you to help themselves.
- Let clients know that counseling often entails some setbacks. If they know from the beginning that personal learning is not always a smooth path, they are less likely to react with discouragement when they experience a plateau or a relapse.
- Strive to arrive together at a clear statement of the problem or the reason the client seeks counseling at this particular time. As soon as possible, design interventions in small, manageable steps that lead to a satisfactory solution. Assist clients in monitoring their progress and be receptive to any feedback they give you.
- Remain attentive to the types of resistance displayed by your clients. Talk openly with your supervisor about these patterns so that you can adjust some of your behaviors if they appear to exacerbate client resistance.

Concluding Comments

Resistance is not an enemy to be feared or a therapeutic evil to be eliminated; it can be an important aspect of the therapeutic process. Clients' resistance may have many sources; do not interpret it as evidence of your professional incompetence. If you are focused on defending yourself against the various forms of resistance you encounter with clients, you deprive your clients of the opportunity to explore the meaning of their resistance and thus limit what they can learn about themselves. Think of resistance as a normal process involving a lack of readiness on a client's part to get involved in counseling.

Realize that clients are often ambivalent when it comes to change, and consistently invite your clients to talk openly about their ambivalence. They often realize that there are both advantages and disadvantages to giving up some of their comfortable patterns. Clients may want to change certain behavioral patterns, but there is like to be anxiety associated with making changes. They may wonder if enduring this anxiety is worth the possible gains. Understand what this ambivalence means and explore it with clients rather than demanding that they be different.

To better understand the role resistance plays and how best to deal with it, be open to identifying resistive patterns within yourself. Appreciate your own ambivalence when it comes to change and realize that it is possible to want to change and at the same time to want to remain the same. Remember your difficulty in being open to your own growth, and use this as a model for understanding your clients. If you keep in mind how you deal with your own resistance, you will be less likely to personalize client resistance, which will better enable you to work therapeutically with resistance.

As a way to identify how you deal with resistance in yourself, take some time at this point to reflect on the following questions:

- When you consider yourself in the role of a counseling client, what might lead to resistance for you? What are some of the ways in which you are most likely to resist? What kind of resistive behaviors might you use?

- When you have experienced resistance, can you remember some of your bodily reactions? What kind of self-talk goes on within you when you experience resistance?
- What might help you to reduce your level of resistance or defensiveness? What would you want from your counselor when you are resistant?
- Take a few minutes to consolidate your thinking about resistance. What is your definition of resistance? As a counselor, what will help you to understand and deal with any resistance you might encounter from clients?
- Imagine the characteristics of a resistant and difficult client sitting in your office. How does this client affect you? What kind of resistive behavior do you think you would be most challenged by as a counselor? What kind of client is most likely to bring out your defensive reactions? Can you learn anything about yourself by paying attention to your reactions to your most difficult client?

CHAPTER SIX

Cognitive Focus in Counseling

Introduction

Cognitive behavioral approaches are quite diverse but all are based on the assumption that if we change our thinking we can also change our feelings and the way we act. The three most popular forms are rational emotive behavior therapy (REBT), founded by Albert Ellis; cognitive therapy (CT), developed by Aaron Beck; and cognitive behavior modification (CBM), developed by Donald Meichenbaum. All of these approaches place thinking at the core of emotional and behavioral disturbances and treatment. Their differences lie mainly in the style a therapist employs. In these approaches, the client must be active if change is to occur. Clients work collaboratively with the therapist, assuming the role of a learner in the therapy sessions and engaging in homework they practice in daily life.

Meichenbaum's (2007, 2008) cognitive behavioral modification approach combines some of the best elements of behavior therapy and cognitive therapy. This approach shares with REBT and Beck's cognitive therapy the assumption that distressing emotions are typically the result of maladaptive thoughts, implying that the best way to change behavior is to change thinking processes. Clients learn that psychological distress is a function of the interdependence of cognitions, emotions, behaviors, and resultant consequences. In therapy, clients learn to change their internal dialogue, which serves as a guide to new behavior. Meichenbaum's approach suggests that it may be more effective to *behave* our way into a new way of thinking than to *think* our way into a new way of behaving. A basic premise of cognitive behavior modification is that a prerequisite to behavior change involves the willingness of clients to notice how they think, feel, and behave and the impact they have on others.

All integrative approaches make room for the cognitive dimension—we are all thinking beings. I pay a great deal of attention to thinking as a vital component in counseling because the content of thought processes greatly influences both how we feel and how we act. An integrative approach requires dealing with self-talk, faulty thinking, core beliefs, automatic thoughts, and one's worldview.

I find many aspects of cognitive behavioral therapy (CBT) very valuable in my work, both during therapy sessions and in a variety of everyday life situations. Psychotherapy is essentially a psychoeducational process, which makes cognitive and behavioral methods most relevant. The psychoeducational focus of CBT is a clear strength that can be applied to many clinical problems and used effectively in many settings with diverse client populations.

Benefits and Limitations of a Cognitive Focus

Cognitive therapists are interested in what clients think, believe, and the way in which they perceive the world. Basic beliefs may be the product of considerable reflection and questioning, or clients may have acquired a number of beliefs without critically evaluating them. In either case, how clients feel and what they do in certain situations has a lot to do with their basic beliefs and thought patterns. Some beliefs may serve clients well, whereas others may lead to problems for clients.

Although significant others may have contributed to shaping clients' current lifestyles, clients are responsible for maintaining self-destructive ideas and attitudes that influence their daily transactions. Cognitive therapists see value in asking clients questions such as these:

- What are your assumptions and basic beliefs?
- Have you really examined the core ideas you live by to determine whether they are your own values or beliefs you have uncritically acquired from others?

Adlerian therapy, rational emotive behavior therapy, cognitive therapy, cognitive behavior modification, choice theory/reality therapy, narrative therapy, and solution-focused therapy share the basic assumption that clients' interpretations of situational events are crucial to understanding their clients. Instead of talking about events, therapists with a cognitive focus explore the personal meanings clients attach to these events.

Although clients benefit from a cognitive understanding of their problems, an overemphasis on the cognitive realm can shortchange the emotional dimension. For instance, it may be difficult for clients to identify and experience what they are feeling. Because of the anxiety of staying with painful emotions, clients might use some form of deflection and engage in intellectualizing. If clients too quickly try to figure out why they are feeling a certain way, they may avoid facing what they are feeling. For example, if a client doesn't get a job she wanted, she might engage in self-deception and rationalizations about why she didn't really want the job in the first place rather than experiencing her feelings and appropriately expressing them in the here and now.

Approaches that highlight cognition typically do not give much attention to exploring a client's past emotional issues. Working within a cognitive framework, therapists pay attention to clients' past without getting lost in the past and without assuming a fatalistic stance about earlier traumatic experiences. Past unresolved childhood experiences can be fruitfully explored in therapy if these earlier experiences are connected to a client's present level of functioning. From my perspective, painful early experiences need to be recognized, re-experienced, and worked through in therapy before clients can free themselves of their restrictive influences. Present beliefs about self and clients' current problems are often related to past hurt. Unless clients come to terms with these past traumas, the vestiges of these traumas tend to linger in the background and influence their current ways of being.

From my perspective, the cognitive behavioral approaches work best once clients have identified and dealt with their emotional issues. In practice, I don't see how it is effective to work *exclusively* in a cognitive way, or an emotive way, or a behavioral way. Because we are holistic beings, all of these domains need to be considered. In fairness, contemporary cognitive behavior therapy is based on the assumption that there is a high degree of interaction among the cognitive, affective, and behavioral domains. The grandfather of cognitive behavior therapy, Albert Ellis, consistently wrote and taught that rational emotive behavior therapy is highly interactive and that it is impossible to work on just a single dimension of personality. Aaron Beck, the father of cognitive therapy, emphasizes the integration of thinking, feeling, and behaving. Donald Meichenbaum, a leading figure in cognitive behavior modification, believes that our emotions and thinking are two sides of the same coin; the way we feel affects our way of thinking, just as how we think influences how we feel. With Meichenbaum's approach, clients learn about the role cognitions and emotions play in creating and maintaining stress through didactic presentations, curious questioning, and a process of guided self-discovery.

As you will see in Ruth's case, when dealing with certain core beliefs, she becomes emotionally touched and experiences various bodily sensations. In other words, when she thinks, she also feels and acts. When she acts, she feels and thinks. When she feels, she thinks and acts. Cognition, emotion, and behavior are not separate human functions; rather, they are interactive and integrated.

If you are interested in further reading on integrating cognitive therapy into a comprehensive approach, consult J. Beck (2005, 2011), Ellis (2001a, 2001b), Ellis and MacLaren (2005), Meichenbaum (1977, 2007, 2008), and O'Donohue and Fisher (2008). For a general treatment of cognitive perspectives, see Corey (2013d, chap. 10).

Becoming the Client: Experiencing Cognitive Behavioral Techniques

To be most creatively applied, cognitive and behavioral strategies must be tailored to the client's unique needs and situation. You can best appreciate the practical value of cognitive behavioral techniques by applying these interventions to yourself personally. Once again, assume that you are my client and consider how you might react to cognitive behavioral interventions. To increase cooperation, it is important that I respect your reactions to an intervention. These interventions are tools to be used in service of you, the client. Here are a few cognitive behavioral techniques from my integrative approach that I might employ with you as my client.

Paying Attention to Your Thinking

Do you engage in catastrophic thinking? Do you dwell on the most extreme negative scenarios in many situations? When you get stuck, I want you to imagine the worst possible outcome of the situation. Then ask, "What is the worst thing that could occur? If this happens, what would make this such a negative outcome?" You can learn to engage in more realistic thinking, especially if you consistently notice times when you tend to get caught up in catastrophic thinking.

As your therapist, I look for evidence to support or refute some of your core beliefs. Once we identify a number of your self-defeating beliefs, you can begin to monitor the frequency with which these beliefs intrude in situations in everyday life. During counseling sessions, I often ask you, "Where is the evidence for___?" Make it a practice to ask yourself this question, especially as you become more adept at spotting dysfunctional thoughts and paying attention to your cognitive patterns. For example, the statement "I must be approved of and accepted by all the significant people in my life" can be disputed with statements such as "Where is it written that I must have this approval?" "Why must I have their total approval to feel like a worthwhile individual?" An effective and functional belief might include this statement: "There is no evidence that I must be approved of by everyone, though I would like to be approved of by those whom I respect." You might also tell yourself, "I detest rejection, so if I keep to myself I won't be hurt." How would this belief affect the way you respond to others? I would ask you, "Even though rejection would hurt, could you prevent yourself from being derailed if you experience rejection? How might this fear of being rejected keep you from getting what you want in your relationships?" At this point, make a list of statements that might get in your way at times. What are a few examples of basic conclusions that you could challenge?

Doing Homework Assignments

The cognitive behavioral approaches place considerable emphasis on putting newly acquired insights into action. Homework is a valuable part of the process leading to change. Homework assignments enable you to practice new behaviors and assist you in the process of your reconditioning. The therapy hour is limited, and activities that you can practice in your daily life can augment therapy sessions. The best homework consists of activities you suggest, especially self-help assignments that grow out of the previous session. It is essential that I tailor homework assignments to your specific problems and that these activities be collaboratively developed by both of us. Again, let me stress that homework or any intervention is geared to what you want for yourself, not what I, as your therapist, think you should want—or what I want for you.

After you have identified some unsupported conclusions and faulty beliefs, between therapy sessions record and think about how your beliefs contribute to your personal problems. In this way you can work hard at critically examining your self-defeating cognitions. When you come to the next therapy session, bring up specific situations in which you did well or in which you experienced difficulty. As you consistently question the actual evidence for situations you encounter, you will become more effective in critically evaluating your self-talk. This allows you to determine whether your self-statements are based on accurate or erroneous information.

I will show you ways to carry on your own therapy, largely through homework activities, without my direct intervention. This provides you with tools you can use to continue learning once formal counseling ends. In my view, much of our counseling endeavor will deal with educating you, teaching you coping skills, and enabling you to see the connection between what you are learning in therapy sessions and everyday living. I particularly value the emphasis CBT puts on bibliotherapy and psychoeducational assignments such as listening to tapes, reading self-help books, keeping a record of what you are doing and thinking, and attending workshops. In this way you can further the process of change in yourself without becoming excessively dependent on me as your counselor. We will review psychoeducational assignments to assess the value of these assignments for you.

Drawing on Adlerian Concepts

Adlerian psychology pays particular attention to the cognitive aspects of personality and in many ways can be considered a cognitive approach to counseling. For Adlerians, feelings are aligned with thinking and are the fuel for behaving. Working within an Adlerian framework, my assumption is that first you think, then you feel, and then you act. Because emotions and cognitions serve a purpose and aim at a central goal in your life, much of our time during counseling is spent discovering and understanding your purpose and reorienting you in a useful way. You can expect to explore what Adlerians call "private logic," which includes concepts about yourself, others, and your life. The core of the therapy experience consists of discovering the purposes of your behavior or symptoms and the basic mistakes associated with your coping.

In therapy let's assume we discover that the structure of your private logic is captured by this syllogism:

- I am basically unlovable.
- The world is filled with people who are likely to reject unlovable persons.
- Therefore, I must keep to myself so I won't be discovered and rejected.

It is easy to see how depression or a sense of hopelessness might follow from this thinking. Learning how to correct such faulty assumptions will be central to your therapy. Through the therapeutic process, you will discover that you have resources and options to draw on in dealing with significant life issues and life tasks.

Working With Ruth From a Cognitive Perspective

See Session 6 (Cognitive Focus in Counseling) on the *DVD for Integrative Counseling: The Case of Ruth and Lecturettes.*

My integrative way of counseling Ruth involves exploring her *cognitive structures*, which include her belief systems, her thoughts, her attitudes, and her values.

More specifically, in family systems therapy attention is given to family rules; in behavior therapy attention is given to beliefs and assumptions that have an influence on her behavior. In rational emotive behavior therapy attention is on self-defeating beliefs and self-indoctrination; Adlerian therapy focuses on her basic mistakes and faulty thinking. In reality therapy the emphasis may be on Ruth's values and what she wants in her world; in feminist therapy we would conduct an assessment of the impact of gender-role messages (which is discussed in more detail in Chapter 12). Whatever terms are used, I tend to zero in on the underlying messages that Ruth seems to be hearing now in her life. I assume that her self-talk is relevant to her behavior.

From a cognitive behavioral perspective, I examine the ways in which Ruth's internal dialogue and her thinking processes are affecting her day-to-day behavior. I use an active and directive therapeutic style. Therapy is time-limited, present-centered, solution-focused, and structured. My task is to help Ruth recognize and change her self-defeating thoughts and maladaptive beliefs, so we concentrate on the content and process of her thinking by looking for ways to restructure some of her beliefs.

Rather than merely telling Ruth what faulty beliefs she has, I encourage her to gather data and weigh the evidence in support of certain beliefs. By using a Socratic discovery-oriented approach and the art of questioning, Ruth and I identify where her thinking, feeling, and behaving is problematic. The therapy process consists of assisting Ruth in detecting her problematic thinking, in learning ways of correcting her distortions, and in substituting more effective self-talk and beliefs. Here are a few of the questions I raise for Ruth to ponder and to answer: "What do you suppose it would be like if you were not to live up to the standards others have set for you?" "If you remain the way you are now, what do you imagine your life will be like in a few years?" "How might you feel different if you were able to ease up on yourself?"

A main cognitive technique I use with Ruth is disputing inaccurate beliefs. Much of her therapy involves her learning ways to argue with her internal dialogue. Here are some questions aimed at getting Ruth to examine the evidence for the validity of her beliefs: "Does having this belief help or hinder you in your life?" "Where is the evidence for your belief?" "Who told you that this belief is accurate?" Not only do I introduce debating methods during the therapy hour, but I also encourage Ruth to pay attention to her internal dialogue in daily life and to detect patterns of thinking that become problematic for her. She can then argue with her internal voices when she catches herself getting stuck in old patterns. I am especially inclined to employ cognitive interventions when it appears that Ruth is giving in to internal voices that reinforce a stance of powerlessness. Such techniques are called for in situations where she might make dire predictions about her future, when such conclusions are based on negative beliefs.

My interventions are aimed at getting Ruth to reflect on what she is saying and how this is influencing how she is feeling. My hope is that she will explore the facts involved in these situations, take another look at some of the conclusions she has arrived at, and develop an open stance in assessing new situations. My aim is to get her to think about her thinking and how it has a pervasive influence on her life today. In dealing with her cognitions from an Adlerian perspective, I might focus Ruth's attention on messages she incorporated as a child and on the decisions that she made. Eventually, she is likely to begin thinking about the reasons she made some early decisions. I challenge her to look at these decisions about life, about herself, and about others and to make necessary revisions that can lead her to form new assumptions about life. (The topic of early decisions and redecisions is elaborated on in Chapter 12.)

From rational emotive behavior therapy (REBT) I especially value the emphasis on learning to think rationally. I look for ways Ruth contributes to her negative feelings by the process of self-indoctrination with faulty beliefs. I guide her in testing the validity of the negative consequences she predicts. For example, she is extremely self-critical, she demands perfection, she believes that she must live up to what others expect of her at all times, and she drives herself by performance-oriented standards to the point of exhaustion. In our work together I teach Ruth ways to replace mistaken beliefs that have no validity with functional and realistic beliefs. Ruth must find for herself a new set of beliefs that allow her to enjoy life more fully. It is not my place to provide her with realistic and appropriate beliefs, but I work with her in creating constructive beliefs of her own. Although I do not think that merely examining her faulty logic is enough for personality change to occur, I do see this process of critically examining her thinking as an essential component of therapy.

Ruth has convinced herself that she must be the perfect daughter, the perfect wife, the perfect mother, and the perfect student. She has an underlying dysfunctional belief that she must be perfect in all that she attempts. If she is not perfect, in her mind, there are dire results. She is continually rating her performances, and she is bound to think poorly of herself because of her unrealistically high standards. Indeed, there is a judge sitting on her shoulder. I consistently remind her that rating herself as a person will take her on a path toward misery. Although she might continue to rate some of her actions, she can productively reflect on separating what she is doing from her personhood. I hope to teach her practical ways to talk back to her internal critic, to learn a new and functional self-dialogue, and to help her reevaluate her experiences as she changes her behavior.

Ruth hears this underlying message, which was given to her by her mother: "If you can't do a job well, don't do it at all." Because of this, she frequently experiences frustration and guilt. As I am talking with her about her perfectionism, she indicates that she wishes she could be kinder to herself and not feel and believe that she can never make a mistake. She says, "I'd like to ease up on myself." I suggest a role play in which she plays the part of herself that would like to ease up and I play the part of her that is the critical and driving self. Whenever she indicates that she wants to do less and not push herself so hard, I tell her that she cannot afford to get lax.

One of the desired outcomes of counseling is for Ruth to become less self-critical. My rationale for this cognitive role play with her is to facilitate an examination on her part of what she believes and where she got her beliefs. I hope Ruth will begin to question messages that she has uncritically accepted, then she can determine whether her beliefs are serving her at this point in her life.

Through a process of debating, disputing, and critically examining some of the messages that Ruth lives by, she will gain increased clarity of the many ways she is trying to measure up to external expectations. By arguing with me as I role-play a familiar side of her, she will be increasingly able to experience the depth to which her self-talk actually exhausts her. She says, "I am so tired of always having to measure up. I am just exhausted. But I don't know how to stop. I'm caught in a whirlwind and just don't know how to stop." She feels very tired of striving to live up to expectations. What is interesting therapeutically is that Ruth gets a clearer picture of what she is doing and how it is affecting her. Although she does not want to pursue the path she is going down, she is at a loss to know how to stop or even slow down. She becomes quite emotional as she talks about not knowing how to stop. She shares her exhaustion about always feeling that she has to measure up—and she adds that she just does not want to live this way anymore. Ruth is giving a clear message of wanting to make a basic change. Now we can use a host of interventions to help her change some of her core beliefs that lead to her exhaustion.

My expectation is that Ruth will realize that her feelings of anxiety are not caused by specific events she is experiencing at home and in her program at the university. For instance, if Ruth's children do very little for her but expect her to be "on call" whenever they want her, this very reality is not the factor that is causing her present psychological difficulties. The source of her problem is what she tells herself about the kind of inadequate mother she is. She operates from the basic belief that if her "mothering skills" are less than perfect, she is deficient as a person. In essence, she is making the mistake of globally rating herself as a person on the basis of some of her children's behaviors. My interventions are aimed at getting her to better understand the connection between some of her core beliefs and her ways of feeling and acting. I hope she can discover how her self-talk is influencing how she is feeling and what she is doing.

At some point in Ruth's therapy, it is likely that we will examine the validity of many of her interpretations about life situations and her conclusions about her basic worth. Beck's cognitive therapy emphasizes identifying and changing negative thoughts and maladaptive beliefs (also known as schemata). According to Beck's cognitive model of emotional disorders, to understand the nature of emotional problems it is essential to focus on the cognitive content of a client's reaction to an upsetting event or stream of thoughts. I draw on a range of cognitive, emotive, and behavioral techniques to demonstrate to Ruth that she produces her own emotional disturbances by the faulty beliefs she has acquired. In this and other sessions, we explore what cognitive therapists call "cognitive distortions" (see Beck & Weishaar, 2011), which include the following:

Arbitrary inferences: Ruth makes conclusions without supporting and relevant evidence. She often engages in "catastrophizing," or thinking about the worst possible scenario for a given situation.

Overgeneralization: Ruth holds extreme beliefs based on a single incident and applies them inappropriately to other dissimilar events or settings. For instance, because she and her husband are experiencing marital difficulties, she is convinced that she is a failure in all aspects of her marriage.

Personalization: Ruth has a tendency to relate external events to herself, even when there is no basis for making this connection. She relates an incident in which a professor did not call on her in class, even though her hand was raised. She was convinced that her professor did not value her thoughts and was bothered by her. She did not consider any other possible explanations for what happened.

Labeling and mislabeling: Ruth presents herself in light of her imperfections and mistakes. She allows a single problem situation to define her total being.

Dichotomous thinking: Ruth frequently engages in thinking and interpreting in all-or-nothing terms. Either she is a success as a mother or she is a total failure in mothering.

Over a number of sessions we work on specific beliefs. The aim is for Ruth to critically evaluate the evidence for her conclusions.

I view my role as promoting corrective experiences that will lead to changes in Ruth's thinking. I expect to assist her in discovering for herself how to distinguish between functional and dysfunctional beliefs. She can learn this by testing her conclusions. My assumption is that only through learning to apply rigorous self-challenging methods will she succeed in freeing herself from the self-defeating thinking that contributed to her problems. Although the cognitive dimension is emphasized, this cannot be accomplished without bringing in the behavioral dimension. Together we design behavioral homework assignments that put Ruth in situations where she is challenged to confront her self-defeating beliefs and her self-limiting behavior. I particularly like Donald Meichenbaum's view of what constitutes successful therapy: clients develop their own voices, take pride in what they have accomplished, and take ownership of the changes they are bringing about (personal communication, October 21, 2010). A measure of effective therapy involves clients becoming their own therapist and taking the therapist's voice with them.

For a more detailed description of working with Ruth from a cognitive behavioral perspective, see Albert Ellis's counseling with Ruth using REBT, Frank Dattilio's cognitive behavioral methods with Ruth, and my counseling with Ruth from a CBT approach in *Case Approach to Counseling and Psychotherapy* (Corey, 2013a, chap. 8).

Working With Stan From a Cognitive Perspective

See Session 8 (Cognitive Behavior Therapy) on the *DVD for Theory and Practice of Counseling and Psychotherapy: The Case of Stan and Lecturettes.*

In this session I work with Stan's faulty beliefs from a cognitive behavioral perspective. I challenge some of Stan's core beliefs through role reversal and cognitive restructuring techniques. Stan begins the session by sharing how he made a fool of himself by spilling a drink on his date. He is convinced that this act of clumsiness is proof of his social ineptness, and he is certain his date will never want to see him again. What troubles him is the degree to which he gives others the power to determine his self-worth. I find this awareness to be a hopeful sign because Stan has realized that he has constructed a world that empowers others instead of himself.

From a cognitive behavioral framework, I accept the assumption that it is not an event or a situation in life that actually causes problematic emotions. Rather, it is the evaluation of events and the beliefs people hold about these events that get them into trouble. Spilling a drink on his date may have been embarrassing, but it is not the only reason he is upset. I listen attentively to Stan's underlying assumptions as he participates in a role play with me to see if he has uncritically incorporated messages that are contributing to a negative and self-critical evaluation. I want him to understand that when he is less than perfect, his perception and self-evaluation contribute to his problems. Drawing from REBT, I have most likely explained to Stan the A-B-C model, as developed by Albert Ellis (2001b). This concept is based on the premise that A (the activating event) does not cause C (the emotional consequences); rather, it is mainly B (his belief about the activating event) that is the source of his problems. Much of my teaching will be about how he can change B (his belief system) and thereby make some significant emotional and behavioral changes.

A range of cognitive techniques can help Stan recognize connections between his cognitions and his behaviors. He can learn about his inner dialogue and the impact it has on his day-to-day behavior. I am interested in having Stan assess whether or not his thoughts are rational and functional. I look for the ways in which Stan contributes to his painful feelings by what he is telling himself, and much of our work centers on what he is telling himself about his interactions with others. Through cognitive restructuring work, Stan can learn new ways of thinking about his actions, new things to tell himself, and new assumptions about life. Our work together emphasizes Stan's role in self-discovery rather than direct teaching on my part. Lasting changes in his thinking and behavior will come about through his initiative, understanding, awareness, and effort.

Concluding Comments

People tend to maintain their core beliefs about themselves, their world, and their future, so the primary focus of cognitive therapy is on cognitive change. Clients are helped to examine their core beliefs and begin a process of restructuring those beliefs that are no longer functional. The restructuring process can occur by encouraging clients to gather and weigh the evidence in support of their beliefs. In cognitive therapy, clients are active, informed, and responsible for the direction of therapy and are partners in this enterprise. Efficiency is prized, and stress is placed on applying what is learned in therapy to coping with new problems in daily living.

Now that you have read this chapter, go back over some of the key themes I've identified from the cognitive approaches and apply them to yourself. Try to identify some of your basic convictions, core beliefs, and self-talk. Ask yourself where you acquired your basic beliefs and how they appear to be influencing the ways you feel and act today.

After reading this chapter on the cognitive focus in counseling, take time to reflect on the following questions as a way of clarifying your thoughts on the cognitive focus.

- What are some of the key concepts and techniques from the cognitive behavioral approaches that you most value in understanding yourself?
- How do you imagine it would be for you to be a client in cognitive behavioral therapy?
- What key concepts from cognitive therapy fit well with your personal philosophy of counseling?
- What are some cognitive techniques that you would most want to use with your clients?
- How likely are you to employ homework as a part of the therapy you provide? How could you collaborate with clients to create meaningful homework?
- What are some of the main benefits of a cognitive focus?
- What are some potential limitations of a cognitive focus?

CHAPTER SEVEN

Emotive Focus
in Counseling

Introduction

Paying attention to relational factors and to clients' emotions increases our understanding of our clients. I believe it is extremely important to facilitate an experiential process in clients rather than to immediately focus on modifying their cognitions or behaviors. When the therapist is able to affirm clients' experiences, they feel safe enough to generate new emotional meanings. An empathically attuned and respectful relationship provides the support necessary for clients to allow themselves to experience a range of feelings that they might otherwise block. This then opens the door for clients to modify their patterns of thinking and acting.

Benefits and Limitations
of an Emotive Focus

Just as cognition is essential to an integrative counseling style, so is the emotional dimension. Too often—especially with brief therapy aimed at discovering solutions to problems as efficiently and quickly as possible—what clients are feeling is relegated to a secondary position. Even in brief therapy, I want to be open to exploring emotions. Clients need to have an opportunity to talk before the therapist confronts their mode of thinking. Often the best route to getting clients to examine their cognitions is by encouraging them to identify, express, and talk about what they are feeling. Once clients experience an emotional catharsis, it is essential to work with the associated insights and cognitions underlying the emotional patterns.

Leslie Greenberg (2011) is a prominent figure in the development of emotion-focused therapy (EFT), and the key concepts discussed here are based on his integrative approach. EFT emphasizes the importance of awareness, acceptance, and understanding of emotion and the visceral experience of emotion in creating psychotherapeutic change. In EFT, clients are assisted in identifying, experiencing, accepting, exploring, transforming, and managing their emotions. A premise of EFT is that we can change only when we accept ourselves as we are. Furthermore, emotional change is fundamental to enduring cognitive and behavioral change. A number of strategies in EFT are aimed at the goals of strengthening the self, regulating affect, and creating new meaning.

EFT is considered as an integrative therapy because it synthesizes aspects of person-centered therapy, Gestalt therapy, and existential therapy. Other therapeutic approaches are increasingly focusing on emotions as well. For example, both psychoanalytic and cognitive behavioral approaches are giving more attention to the role of emotions and are rapidly assimilating many aspects of EFT. Greenberg makes the point that a strength of EFT is that it is an evidence-based approach, a concept increasingly being stressed in graduate programs.

Significant personal changes tend to come about when clients are taught how to transfer what they have learned in therapy sessions to everyday situations. Transferring this learning is not an automatic process. Therapists need to teach clients how to maintain these positive emotional and behavioral changes. This can be done by helping clients plan ways of coping effectively when they meet with frustration in the world and when they regress by seeming to forget the lessons they have learned. If therapy is aimed solely at emotional release, the likely result will simply be an emotional experience. With little attention to cognitive or behavioral follow up, clients are not likely to acquire a method for transferring their learning to a range of situations in daily life.

Becoming the Client: Experiencing Emotion-Focused Therapy

As I have asked you consistently to do, imagine yourself as the client now to grasp the power of emotion-focused therapy. I prefer to begin therapy by paying attention to what you are experiencing on an emotional level. I attend to how emotions are manifested in your body. I think the truth of many of your struggles can be found in what you are feeling and what your body is telling you. I ask, "What are you aware of at the moment and what do you want to do with that?" Noticing your emotional and bodily states can be significant routes to gaining awareness of what you are experiencing and doing. Without awareness, change is not possible.

Gestalt therapy experiments are designed to expand your awareness and to help you try out new modes of behavior. I create and use interventions, or experiments, to facilitate the exploration of material that emerges from our interactions in the session. Experiments enable you to become aware of aspects of experience that had previously been out of awareness. Within the safety of the therapeutic situation, you are given opportunities to "try on" a new behavior. The Gestalt way of creating experiments is a powerful and effective way to connect you to your emotions. Although Gestalt therapy offers rich pathways to your emotional experiencing, this approach taps whatever is in your awareness at the moment and, in that sense, it is truly integrative.

The interventions I make are geared to your thoughts, feelings, and actions and are routes to supporting your self-exploration. Such interventions have the purpose of facilitating your self-understanding, not promoting my personal agenda as your therapist or to meet my needs. I tend to avoid using planned techniques or exercises as catalysts to open up feelings. Experiments are more powerful when they grow out of the phenomenological context of therapy and when they are chosen for a specific therapy situation.

As a way to demonstrate an experiential, emotionally focused approach, let me present you with some "problems" that I encourage you to "adopt" as my client. You tell me that at this moment you feel a sense of sadness. I ask you to say more and to describe how you experience this sadness. You respond, "I'm feeling sad when I think of how hard I try to get approval from everyone. I'm so caught up in getting you to like me that I forget what it is I want for myself. I feel right now like I felt so much around my parents—always trying to do what they wanted so they would think well of me, yet never feeling that I was able to get what I wanted." You are saying a great deal, and I encourage you to keep talking. As you speak, I direct your attention to what you are experiencing in your body. You state that your heart is heavy and that it feels broken. I suggest that you stay with this bodily feeling as much as possible and put some words to what it is like for you to talk at this time. I might even ask you to give your heart a voice and give expression to your "heavy and broken heart." Where we go next depends on what emerges in your moment-to-moment awareness. Influenced by emotion-focused therapy and Gestalt therapy, I follow the leads you provide and support you in your efforts to stay focused on the images, feelings, thoughts, and sensations that come to the surface. I encourage you to stay with *what is* as fully as possible.

Operating within the framework of the Gestalt approach, I ask you to bring any concerns about what was or will be into the present and directly experience these concerns. Being in the present moment involves a transition between your past and your future. As a way to keep our work emotionally focused, I make use of experiments that are spontaneously created to fit your present situation. From the perspective of emotion-focused therapy, meaningful dialogue often results from staying with the changing flow of your present-centered awareness. By following whatever it is that you are experiencing and showing you how to follow your own energy, you will gradually increase your awareness.

To help you make contact with the present moment, I typically ask "what" and "how" questions but rarely ask "why" questions. To promote "now" awareness, I encourage a dialogue in the present tense by asking, "What is happening now? What is going on now?" "What are you experiencing as you share your struggle? What is your awareness at this moment?" "How are you experiencing your sadness?" "As you talk of your heavy heart, what is this like for you? If your heart could express itself, what would that be like for you?"

Now imagine yourself in this scenario. You say that you sometimes feel totally inadequate and that you have a hard time liking yourself. I ask you to tell me more about what it feels like to be this way. How did you come to these conclusions about your worth as a person?

I do not offer you immediate reassurance or tell you that you are an adequate person who is likeable. Although reassuring feedback may make you feel good for a short time, it is doubtful that this feeling would last very long. Your internal critic will not believe any positive feedback I might offer you—at least if I attempt to reassure you too soon. I am more interested in assisting you in exploring both your feelings and your thoughts. I also want to give you a chance to express what you often don't say. If you are able to talk fully about feeling inadequate and having difficulty liking yourself, you stand a better chance of arriving at your own solutions to the problems you face. I strive to create a therapeutic climate that will enable you to sort out your thoughts and feelings, which will lead to making better decisions and changes. Mere reassurance and advice do not facilitate self-examination, but a willingness to listen to you can encourage you to share what you are feeling in the moment, to engage in significant self-disclosure, and to explore your struggles.

Even though you may have stayed with some intense feelings and allowed yourself to experience the power of your feelings in your body, you might become uncomfortable and want to distance yourself from some feelings that arise as you talk with me. You may express fears about getting involved with me and display resistance toward any attempt at delving into deeply personal concerns. You tell me, "I'm afraid that if I get deep into my feelings I'll get stuck and won't be able to get out of it. I'm afraid if I let myself feel that, I'll get out of control. There is a part of me that wants to get into my emotions, yet another part of me wants to get into my head and keep control." Whether or not your fears are expressed, they tend to give rise to some ambivalence: the desire to reveal yourself is balanced by the reluctance to expose yourself. To work with your ambivalence, I suggest a role play in which we each take one of these two sides of yourself.

You will not be able to change an emotion unless you first allow yourself to experience the emotion. As Greenberg (2011) expresses this, "EFT works on the basic principle that people must first arrive at a place before they can leave it" (p. 80). If you avoid dealing with your feelings of worthlessness, insecurity, shame, and hopelessness, you cannot reduce these distressing feelings and change them. Greenberg states that "one of the most effective ways of managing emotions is to help clients to become aware of their emotions, to express them, and to decide what to do when emotions arise" (p. 72).

Gestalt therapy and psychodrama often employ an *empty-chair* or *two-chair technique*. This is another way to act out your present feelings in the therapy session. Having a dialogue with various aspects within yourself, or between yourself and another individual, is particularly useful when you are feeling ambivalent about a direction to pursue or when you are in some kind of conflict situation. I suggest that rather than talking about a situation, you make it present by actually bringing to life a conflict you are experiencing. You tell me that you often feel very young and awkward when you try to relate your accomplishments to your mother. I say to you: "So, sitting in the chair you are in now, become that young and awkward person and talk to this other (empty) chair—to your mother. What would you like your mother to know about your accomplishments? What are you saying to your mother in this scene?" Next I ask you to switch chairs and become your mother and reply the way you expect her to—or reply in the manner that you hope she would. By bringing emotionally laden material or a conflict into the present through this two-chair exercise, you and I get a better understanding of how you struggle with relationships or with feeling young and foolish. Emotion-focused methods adapted from psychodrama and Gestalt therapy tend to facilitate a deeper understanding and insight, as well as a greater emotional connection to your words.

An alternative way I might work with your feelings about your mother is to suggest that you participate in a *soliloquy*, another psychodrama technique. Imagine yourself in a place where you can think out loud (soliloquize) and say what you are thinking and feeling. This could be a useful follow-up intervention to the two-chair dialogue between you and your mother. This intervention facilitates clarification and an open expression of what you may be experiencing internally but not expressing verbally.

Future projection, another psychodrama technique, is designed to help you express and clarify concerns you have about your future. An anticipated event is brought into the present moment and acted out. In this case, you enact a version of the way you hope a situation will ideally unfold between you and your mother. Of course, you could enact a dreaded fear of tomorrow with the most horrible outcome. For instance, your mother might tell you that she does not expect you to ever accomplish anything of any merit. Once you clarify your hopes for a particular outcome, you are in a better position to take specific steps that will enable you to achieve the future you desire.

You may be wondering why it is essential to give primary attention to the role of emotions in our efforts to bring about change. Why is emotional release so important? My answer relates to the connection between physical health and emotional health. Abundant research reveals that many physical illnesses and psychosomatic symptoms are the result of bottling up emotions. If you repress your anger, you pay a price for this. If you are chronically under intense stress, your body may react with a host of illnesses. If you hold in your emotional pain, you expend a great deal of energy, and this takes a toll on your body. Clearly, there are links between repressing emotions and symptoms such as headaches, asthma, backaches, arthritis, and muscular tension. I am convinced that it takes a great deal of energy to deny emotional pain, and denied emotions often are expressed in the body. For example, if you are excessively blocked from your grief after a significant loss or death of someone you love, the result can be a chronic sense of pain. This unexpressed pain is likely to prevent you from being emotionally open to experiencing the fullness of other relationships. Experiential techniques borrowed from psychodrama such as empty-chair work, soliloquy, future projection, role reversal, and role playing can help to heal an emotional wound. Through an emotional release of pent-up feelings, the healing process is facilitated. Although catharsis is a natural part of many of the experiential or emotionally focused therapies (especially emotion-focused therapy, Gestalt therapy, existential therapy, person-centered therapy, and psychodrama), the emotional release not a goal in itself. Rather, it is an indicator of emotional expansion and integration.

The experiential therapies frequently involve some form of catharsis. Although there is value in catharsis, my experience with therapy groups has taught me time and again how essential it is to provide a context in which clients can come to an understanding of how their bottled-up emotions have affected both them and their relationships. It is important to find links between emotional release and new levels of cognitive and emotional awareness. Insight, or gaining an increased awareness of a problem situation, often follows the process of an emotional release. Insight is the cognitive shift that connects the awareness of the various emotional experiences with some meaningful narrative or growing understanding. Insights that you acquire in your therapy can add a degree of understanding to the catharsis and can allow you to begin the essential process of gaining control over ways of expressing and managing your feelings. Further, your insights may lead to the awareness that you no longer have to continue living as you did before. Integrating insights and developing and practicing more effective behaviors are essential components in the change process. Collaboratively designing homework toward the end of a therapy session is often an effective way to translate insight into action, which can lead to the changes you desire.

For a more detailed discussion of other techniques I might employ with you in an emotionally focused manner, refer to Chapters 9 and 11 of this book, Corey (2012, chap. 8), and Corey (2013d, chap. 8). A useful resource for the topic of this chapter is Greenberg (2011). See also Jon Frew's Gestalt approach with Ruth in (Corey, 2013a, chap. 6).

Working With Ruth in Identifying and Exploring Feelings

See Session 7 (Emotive Focus in Counseling) on the *DVD for Integrative Counseling: The Case of Ruth and Lecturettes.*

The person-centered approach stresses that one of the first stages in the therapy process involves identifying, clarifying, and learning how to express feelings. I encourage Ruth to talk about any feelings she is aware of, especially those that are a source of difficulty. These feelings may be vague and difficult to identify at first.

One of Ruth's main therapeutic goals is to come to terms with her inner truths, which involves her having a better sense of what she thinks and feels. To facilitate Ruth's experiential emotional process, I must establish a sense of safety in the therapy situation. If I can create a nonjudgmental and accepting environment, I hope that eventually Ruth will be able to unconditionally accept herself and all of her feelings. During the early stages of our sessions, I rely on listening with understanding. I encourage her to talk about what most concerns her and what recent events have led to her decision to come to therapy at this time.

If I can really hear Ruth's deeper messages, some of which may not be fully clear to her, I can respond to her in a way that lets her know that I have some appreciation for what it is like in her world. (Grasping the subjective or experiential world of clients is a key concept of many theoretical orientations including existential therapy, person-centered therapy, Gestalt therapy, and Adlerian therapy.) I need to do more than merely reflect what I hear her saying; I need to share with her my reactions as I listen to her, and perhaps how I am being affected by her in the session. The more I am able to communicate that I understand and accept the feelings she has, the less need she has to deny or deflect her feelings. As a result, her capacity for clearly identifying what she is feeling at any moment gradually increases.

There is a great deal of value in letting Ruth tell her story in the way she chooses. The way she walks into the office, her gestures, her style of speech, the details she chooses to go into, and what she decides to relate and what she withholds provide me with clues to her world. By being attentive and tracking what she is doing in the moment, I am getting a larger picture of her world. Certainly I am not getting the entire story, but it is possible to grasp significant samples of her story. At this time she is giving me the "short version" of her life story. I will inquire about her presentation as a way to understand the personal meanings of her thoughts and feelings pertaining to events in her life. My interventions are aimed at checking to make sure that I am understanding her accurately and conveying to her my understanding of her situation. Here I am influenced by concepts from the person-centered approach such as listening with understanding, presence, and focusing on the subjective aspects of Ruth's experiencing.

If I do too much structuring too soon or if I am too directive, I will interfere with Ruth's typical style of presenting herself. So, at this early stage of counseling, I agree with the person-centered therapists who stress attending and listening on the counselor's part and focus on the productive use of silence. Although I am not inclined to promote long silences early in counseling, there is value in not jumping in too soon when silences occur. Instead of coming to the rescue, it is better to explore the meanings of the silence.

To help Ruth express and explore her feelings, I draw heavily on Gestalt therapy experiments. I teach her to pay attention to what is emerging in her awareness. I am guided by the shifts in her awareness, and together we create experiments that grow out of her present-centered awareness. The emphasis is on our dialogue and the quality of contact we are able to make in the therapy session. Because she has yet to work through her feelings of not feeling valued for who she is, such concerns surface in her therapy. Ruth is aware that her value comes from the functions she performs for her family. She does not feel that she is valued apart from what she is able to do for others.

I invite Ruth to experience her feelings fully and bring whatever she is feeling into the present by reliving an event surrounding these feelings rather than by merely reporting outside events or long-standing themes in her life. For instance, if she says that she is sad when she thinks about how people in her family do not give her recognition in her own right, I ask that she stay with the sadness. If she can, I encourage her to share how she is experiencing her sadness. If she reports feeling tense, I ask her how she experiences this tension and where it is located in her body. I assist her in making contact with her feelings by asking her to "be that feeling." My rationale for doing this is based on my belief that *direct experiencing* is more therapeutic than talking about a feeling or event. Thus, if Ruth has a knot in her stomach, she can intensify her feeling of tension by "becoming the knot, giving it voice and personality." If I notice that she has moist eyes, I may direct her to "be her tears now." By putting words to her tears, she avoids abstractly intellectualizing about all the reasons she is sad or tense. Before she can change her feelings, she must allow herself to fully experience these feelings. The experiential therapies give me valuable tools for guiding her to the expression of feelings.

In this session I have made many different interventions, one of which is to ask Ruth to talk to me as if I am her husband. I ask her to stay with whatever she is experiencing, paying particular attention to her body and to the emotions welling up in her, doing her best to express these emerging feelings. Role-playing Ruth's husband gives me an opportunity to observe how she presents herself to her husband and to get some sense of how he might receive her verbal and nonverbal messages. Ruth's role play is likely to trigger feelings surrounding a specific situation with her husband, which brings her work to a deeper level than if she had merely reported a situation.

Working With Stan in Identifying and Exploring Feelings

See Session 4 (Existential Therapy) on the *DVD*
for Theory and Practice of Counseling and Psychotherapy:
The Case of Stan and Lecturettes.

In this session Stan explores his anxiety around death and the implications this has for finding meaning in his life. When Stan accepts the reality of his eventual death, he will experience his ultimate aloneness more dramatically. This awareness of mortality can jar him into realizing that his actions do count, that he does have choices concerning how he is living, and that he must accept the final responsibility for the quality of his life. Existential therapists believe there is a significant connection between the awareness of death and the meaning of life. Working with Stan's reactions to mortality provides many opportunities for him to express a range of feelings about his own death, including his fears of not living a meaningful existence. This emotional work is a catalyst for Stan to explore his spiritual values and what he wants his life to stand for. For Stan, this exploration of the meaning of life brings up a host of emotions that we will deal with in future sessions.

The catalyst for Stan's death anxiety was his father being hospitalized. This event caused Stan to think about the shortness of life and the purpose of his place in this world. As Stan talked about his relationship with his father and what would have happened if his father had died, he realized there was some unfinished business between them. Stan decides he wants to do more to change his relationship with his father.

Stan accepts my invitation to participate in a role-playing situation in which he talks to me as his father. When Stan says that he does not know where to begin, I suggest that he tell me (as his father) how difficult it is for him to know what to say to me. He begins with this, and continues by telling me of many of the ways that he feels he has not measured up to his father's expectations.

> Dad, no matter what I did, it never seemed right by you. I so much wanted your approval, but never knew how to go about getting it. I just wanted you to tell me that you loved me as I was and that you were proud of me.

Stan continued for a time talking in the past tense to me as his father. When I suggest that he shift to talking to me in the present moment, many intense feelings surfaced. Stan was able to give up some of his control and express the hurt within him.

After this symbolic role play, we processed what this was like for him and what he still wants from his father, which accessed even deeper feelings around trying so hard to win his father's love and acceptance. This work with Stan illustrates a key principle of emotion-focused therapy, which is that in order to change a feeling, it is necessary to feel the feeling. Simply talking about emotions and problems will not bring about emotional transformation.

As homework for Stan, I suggest that he write a letter to his father expressing some of the feelings that just came up for him. I stress to Stan that he is not to present this letter to his father—at least not now. Writing the letter may trigger memories, and he may experience further emotional release. I hope this will help him continue thinking about the current influence his father has on his life. By writing the letter, Stan is likely to gain clarity and a new perspective on how he wants to approach his father in real life. Even if the letter is burned or buried after writing, this can be a very therapeutic exercise because feelings are released that previously have not been expressed.

At our next session, I will ask Stan if he wrote the letter, and, if he did, what it was like for him to do so. What was he feeling and thinking as he was writing to his father? How was he affected when he read the letter later? Is there anything that he wants to share with me? The direction of our session will depend on his response, which will provide clues to where we need to go next. My hope is that Stan will learn that it is possible for him to act differently around his father, even if his father does not change.

Concluding Comments

I have emphasized the role of expressing feelings in the therapeutic process. I would like to present a few guidelines for doing experiential, emotionally focused work with your clients. It is important for you to be able to experience your own emotions and to express them in a healthy way. Your ability to be emotionally present for your clients hinges on how centered you are yourself and whether you have access to your own emotions. If you are frightened by your feelings, you won't be able to facilitate a process with clients that enables them to express and work through their feelings. If you are scared of your own anger or of anger directed toward you, it will be quite difficult for you to assist clients in dealing constructively with their anger. If you have denied your own pain over significant losses, you will not be able to be present for clients as they open painful subjects in their therapy. If you are extremely uncomfortable with conflict, it is unlikely that you will be instrumental in helping clients stay with a conflict long enough to bring resolution to a situation. If you are afraid to cry or lose control, how can you expect to deal with clients who keep their tears inside lest they get out of control? If your emotions make you uncomfortable, chances are that you will find some way to divert your clients' attention away from intense feelings. If a client is afraid of becoming engulfed in depression and you are frightened of depression, how can you therapeutically engage this individual?

If you are emotionally present for your clients, their stories are bound to affect you personally. Establish clear boundaries so you do not take onto yourself the pain your clients express. When the multiple stories of trauma that clients bring to therapy mirror a therapist's own personal struggles too closely, *empathy fatigue* may result (Stebnicki, 2008). Empathy fatigue shares some similarities with other fatigue syndromes such as compassion fatigue, secondary traumatic stress, vicarious traumatization, and burnout. The symptoms of empathy fatigue are common to professionals who treat survivors of stressful and traumatic events; those who treat people with mood, anxiety, and stress-related disorders; and those who work in vocational settings with people with mental and physical disabilities. Stebnicki emphasizes the importance of counselors preparing their mind, body, and spirit so they are more resilient in working with people at intense levels of interpersonal functioning.

To assist your clients, you need to be able to identify, express, and manage your own emotions. As clients relive painful memories attached to events, you will need to care about them without getting lost in their emotional pain. If you are easily triggered by the emotionally laden stories of your clients, you may not have what it takes to help them work through painful scenarios. As your clients affect you emotionally, be aware of the feelings this evokes in you. Recognize your own emotional reactions and be willing to explore them in your own supervision or therapy sessions. Over time, experienced counselors learn ways to use their emotional reactions to clients as helpful forms of information about the client, the process of therapy, and themselves.

I have placed a great deal of importance on assisting clients in the process of identifying, experiencing, and exploring their emotions. This does not imply that you should insist that your clients always deal with their emotions. Begin where your clients are, and determine what would be most useful for them at that particular time. If you push too hard for emotional expression, clients are likely to become uncomfortable and defensive. Keep in mind that the emotional work needs to be connected with what clients are thinking and doing. It may serve little therapeutic purpose to elicit feelings from clients if this is done mainly for dramatic effect.

After reading this chapter on the emotive focus in counseling, take time to reflect on the following questions as a way of clarifying your thoughts on the emotive focus.

- What are some of the main benefits and limitations of an emotive focus in counseling?
- What are some ways to integrate cognitive and behavioral work in assisting clients in processing an emotional experience?
- If you were a client in counseling, what value would you place on expressing and exploring your emotions?
- What are your reactions to this statement? "Often the best route to getting clients to examine their cognitions is by encouraging them to identify, express, and talk about what they are feeling."

CHAPTER EIGHT

Behavioral Focus
in Counseling

Introduction

No single theory undergirds the practice of contemporary behavior therapy, nor does this approach take a single form in practice. Behavior therapy includes both traditional behavior therapy and cognitive behavior therapy (CBT). The cognitive behavioral therapies currently represent the mainstream of contemporary behavior therapy, and most therapists practice CBT today. My integrated behavioral focus includes many behavior therapy methods, along with other action-oriented therapies, such as multimodal therapy, rational emotive behavior therapy, cognitive therapy, reality therapy, and solution-focused brief therapy. From an integrative perspective, I address some basic concepts that most of these theoretical orientations share and describe a range of behavioral techniques associated with these other action-oriented models.

The behavioral perspective stands in contrast to the relationship-oriented and experiential approaches described in previous chapters. Experiential approaches place considerable emphasis on clients' achieving insight into their problems as a prerequisite for change. Behavior therapists operate on the premise that changes in behavior can occur prior to understanding oneself and that behavioral changes may well lead to an increased level of self-understanding. I draw on a wide variety of behavioral techniques derived from social learning theory, such as reinforcement, modeling, cognitive restructuring, desensitization, in vivo exposure, relaxation training, coaching, behavioral rehearsal, mindfulness, and acceptance-based procedures. Indeed, behavioral interventions can be incorporated into many of the relationship-oriented therapies, and by doing so clients can consolidate their learning and continue to solve new problems more effectively.

The behavior-oriented perspective I describe in this chapter assists clients in exploring how past and present thoughts, feelings, and behaviors have worked for them and what they have cost. The action-oriented therapies provide methods that are measurable, plan-specific, and realistic. From an integrative perspective, behavioral methods can be usefully combined with the relationship-oriented approaches.

Benefits and Limitations of a Behavioral Focus

The behaviorally oriented models place emphasis on specifics and the need for a systematic application of therapeutic techniques. Clients often make global statements such as "I feel unloved; life has no meaning." Behavioral approaches aim toward greater specificity so that focused therapy can proceed. A behavior therapist might reply like this to such a global statement: "Who specifically is not loving you? What is going on in your life to bring about this meaninglessness? What are some specific things you might be doing that contribute to the state you are in? What specific behaviors, thoughts, or feelings would you most like to change?"

One of the major benefits of a behavioral focus is the wide variety of specific techniques available in counseling diverse client populations; these techniques have the advantage of empirical support for their effectiveness. The behavioral approach assumes that change can take place without insight into underlying dynamics. The behavioral emphasis is on *doing,* as opposed to merely talking about problems and gathering insights, and clients formulate plans of action for changing behavior. Behavior therapists believe that insight and increased self-understanding will flow from the behavioral changes clients make. Behavioral interventions can be employed to treat a wide array of problems: helping people stay with an exercise plan, managing stress, and treating depression, anxiety, and hypertension, to name a few. In my view, behavior therapy is at its best when it is used integratively. Clients who look for action plans and behavioral change are likely to cooperate with behavioral approaches because they include concrete methods for dealing with problems of living. In addition, a behavioral focus fits well with short-term counseling.

Behavioral practitioners state concepts and procedures explicitly, test them empirically, and revise them continually. Assessment and treatment occur simultaneously. The specific characteristics of behavior therapy include (1) conducting a behavioral assessment, (2) precisely spelling out collaborative treatment goals, (3) formulating a specific treatment procedure appropriate to a particular problem, and (4) objectively evaluating the outcomes of therapy. These characteristics can be incorporated into other therapeutic approaches, which makes behavior therapy an integrative perspective.

When using a behavioral perspective, it is crucial that you listen carefully to your clients and allow them to express and explore their feelings before implementing a treatment plan. The basic therapeutic conditions stressed by the person-centered therapist—active listening, accurate empathy, positive regard, genuineness, respect, and immediacy—can and should be integrated into a behavioral framework. If you are too eager to work toward resolving problems, you may pay little attention to exploring feelings. There are pitfalls in focusing too rigidly on clients' presenting problems and missing the deeper message. Thus, if you are teaching clients assertion skills that they can use in a job interview, remain open to addressing their thoughts (self-talk) associated with going to the interview as well as their emotional reactions (anxiety).

Understanding the Seven Modalities of Human Functioning

Assessment is a crucial step in using a behavioral approach to therapeutic change. Arnold Lazarus has provided a useful way to obtain information and target personal goals. The essence of Lazarus's BASIC I.D. model is that the complex personality of humans can be divided into seven major areas of functioning: B = behavior; A = affective responses; S = sensations; I = images; C = cognitions; I = interpersonal relationships; and D = drugs, biological functions, nutrition, and exercise (Lazarus, 1997a, 1997b, 2005, 2006, 2008). Although these modalities are interactive, they can be considered discrete functions. Clients are social beings who move, feel, sense, imagine, and think. A comprehensive assessment of these seven modalities of human functioning is an important part of the behavioral approach.

The BASIC I.D. is the cognitive map that provides systematic attention to each aspect of human functioning. Let's take a closer look at each of the modalities in the BASIC I.D.

1. *Behavior.* This modality refers primarily to overt behaviors, including acts, habits, and reactions that are observable and measurable. Some questions asked are: "What would you like to change?" "What would you like to start doing?" "What would you like to stop doing?"

2. *Affect.* This dimension refers to emotions, moods, and strong feelings. Questions asked include: "What emotions do you experience most often?" "What emotions are problematic for you?"

3. *Sensation.* This area refers to the five basic senses of touch, taste, smell, sight, and hearing. A typical question asked is: "Do you suffer from unpleasant sensations, such as pains, aches, dizziness, and so forth?"

4. *Imagery.* This area pertains to ways in which we picture ourselves, and it includes memories, dreams, and fantasies. A few questions asked are: "How do you see yourself now?" "How would you like to be able to see yourself in the future?"

5. *Cognition.* This modality refers to insights, ideas, opinions, self-talk, and judgments that constitute one's fundamental values, attitudes, and beliefs. Questions include: "What are the values and beliefs you most cherish?" "What are some negative things you say to yourself?" "What are the main 'shoulds,' 'oughts,' and 'musts' in your life?" "How do they impede effective living?"

6. *Interpersonal relationships.* This area refers to interactions with other people. Examples of questions include: "What do you expect from the significant people in your life?" "What do they expect from you?" "Are there any relationships with others that you hope to change?"

7. *Drugs/biology.* This modality includes more than drugs; it takes into consideration one's nutritional habits and exercise patterns. Typical questions are: "Do you have any concerns about your health?" "Do you take any prescribed drugs?" "What are your habits pertaining to diet, exercise, and physical fitness?"

Once this initial assessment is complete, more focused discussions can proceed in identified problem areas. This leads to identification of therapy goals, the first step in a treatment plan.

Becoming the Client: Experiencing Behavior-Oriented Therapy

In this section, I ask you to put yourself in the role of the client to experience the benefits of behavior-oriented therapy. The behavioral methods described in this section can be most useful in translating your insights into concrete action plans.

As my client, I will offer you a range of behavioral strategies, but I still want to attend to what you are thinking and feeling. We explore how your self-talk and thinking influences how you feel, and we explore how your thinking and feeling patterns influence what you are doing. By focusing on what you are doing, you can make an evaluation of the degree to which your present behavior is getting you what you want. In working on specific behaviors, we begin with an assessment to identify patterns. A place for us to start working is by doing a brief, but comprehensive, assessment using the BASIC I.D. model.

Once this initial assessment of the seven behavioral areas is completed, the next phase of work explores problem areas and allows me to understand you more fully. We are then ready to identify a set of therapy goals that both of us mutually agree are suitable for your therapy. Which of these behavioral goals will you set for yourself?

- Learning to ask clearly and directly for what you want
- Learning to be assertive without becoming aggressive
- Acquiring habits that lead to physical and psychological relaxation
- Developing specific habits for a healthy lifestyle (exercising regularly, controlling eating patterns, reducing stress)
- Monitoring your behavior or cognitions as a means to change
- Recognizing and challenging self-destructive thought patterns or critical self-statements that lead to problematic behaviors
- Learning communication and social skills
- Developing problem-solving strategies to cope with a variety of situations encountered in daily life

Once you have identified your goals, I help you break down these general goals into specific, concrete, measurable goals that can be pursued in a systematic fashion. For example, if you say you'd like to feel more adequate in social situations, I ask: "What are you doing or not doing that seems to be related to your feeling of inadequacy? What are the conditions under which you feel inadequate? Can you give me some concrete examples of situations in which you feel inadequate? In what specific ways would you like to change your behavior?"

Borrowing from reality therapy, I find Wubbolding's (2000, 2011) WDEP formulation to be especially useful in my work with you.

- W stands for exploring wants, needs, and perceptions. I do not tell you what you should change but encourage you to examine what you want.
- D stands for exploring the direction of your current behavior and your satisfaction with where you are going.
- E stands for evaluation, which consists of you making your own evaluation about what you are actually doing. It is up to you to decide how well your current behavior is working for you.
- P stands for designing a plan for change.

In applying reality therapy, we develop specific, realistic plans and then talk about how you might carry them out in everyday life. Knowing what you are willing to change is the first step. Through self-evaluation you determine what you have been doing that is not working. This lowers resistance and opens you up to other behaviors or directions. Knowing how to bring about this change is the next step. At each of these points in the WDEP model, specific questions get you to look at what you are doing and figure out better ways to arrange your life.

After you and I work through the steps in the WDEP model and identify therapeutic goals, we decide on the various avenues by which these goals can be accomplished. You may have trouble reaching your goals because your plans are not sufficiently thought out, which makes them difficult to implement. By developing and assessing behavioral strategies together, we can move in the direction of making your vision a reality.

An aspect I particularly like about behavior therapy and related action therapies is the wide range of behavioral techniques available to assist you in moving in the direction you desire. Here is a sample of the behavioral strategies we might apply to meet your personal goals:

- You indicate that you experience a good deal of anxiety. You find yourself rushing and doing many things at once. I teach you a few basic relaxation procedures that you agree to practice once a day.
- To address your habit of trying to do too many things at once, I teach you the principles of mindfulness, which require that you stay in the here and now, focusing on *what is* rather than *what if*. With this focus you can observe your moment-to-moment experiencing and concentrate on one thing at a time. Mindfulness is a nonjudgmental way of being and a form of acceptance.
- You say that you want to get better at asking for what you want, without sounding apologetic. I use strategies such as coaching, modeling, and social skills training to teach you how to approach others more effectively.
- You want to improve your time management skills. You find that you procrastinate a great deal and then rush to complete projects. Together we brainstorm possibilities for effectively dealing with procrastination. We come up with a number of specific points for better managing your time as a student: focus on demanding subjects first, set goals in number of pages of a reading assignment, create a reward system, avoid guilting yourself about what you don't do, give yourself credit for what you do, stop the interruptions, allow for short breaks.
- You would like to reduce your anxiety when you feel you are being tested, which prevents you from going on job interviews. I begin with a specific analysis

of the nature of your anxiety by asking how you experience this anxiety in specific situations, including what you actually *do* in these situations: "When did it begin? What are some situations when you most experience this anxiety? What do you do at these times? What are your feelings and thoughts in these situations? How do your present fears interfere with obtaining what you want? What are the consequences of your behaviors in threatening situations?" After this assessment, we define specific behavioral goals, and I introduce strategies to help you reduce your anxiety to a manageable level. For example, you state one of your goals as: "I will arrange for one job interview during this week and report back at our next session." I get a commitment from you to work toward this goal, as well as any others you agree to at later times, and together we evaluate your progress toward meeting these goals throughout the duration of therapy.

• You are expected to actively work outside of your counseling sessions. At each of your sessions we collaboratively design homework activities that enable you to take into your daily life what you are learning in the office. Homework is carefully designed and is aimed at getting you to carry out positive actions and induce emotional and attitudinal change. This practice extends the value of the brief time we have during a session and fosters an active stance on your part in working on your goals. Toward the end of therapy, I encourage you to review your progress, make plans, and identify strategies for dealing with continuing or potential problems.

Going back to the multimodal BASIC I.D. assessment grid, you can now see how it is possible to have a behavioral orientation in a broad sense. Behavior includes emotions, sensations, imagery, cognition, interpersonal relationships, and health. Because you are an integrated being functioning in all of these modalities, a behavioral focus in counseling must attend to more than simply what you are doing. Your thoughts, feelings, and physiological reactions influence your behaving. As we work on specific behaviors that we have targeted for exploration, I also need to be mindful of thoughts and feelings you are experiencing pertaining to the behavioral dimension.

Throughout our work together, I encourage you to see the value in actively trying new behavior rather than leaving action to chance. One way of fostering an active stance is to formulate a clear contract that includes writing out a plan of action. In this way you are continually being confronted with what you want and what you are willing to do.

Developing a Behavioral Contract

Contracts are a useful frame of reference for evaluating the outcomes of counseling, but developing an effective contract is not as easy as it may seem. I borrow some specific aspects of formulating and carrying out a plan from a prominent reality therapist, Robert Wubbolding (2000, 2011). Here are some specific suggestions for creating an effective plan.

• Plans are based on the client's personal goals. Begin by having the client specify desired changes. Goals should be measurable, attainable, positive, and significant to the client.

- Goals must be translated into target behaviors. Ask what specific behaviors the client wants to increase or decrease. Design plans around the answer to this question.
- Once behavioral changes the client wants to acquire are evaluated, an action program to bring about change is devised.
- Encourage the client to come up with clear plans for what he or she will do today, tomorrow, and the next day to bring about change and to anticipate what might get in the way of these plans.
- It is a good idea to begin the plan as soon as possible. Ask the client, "What are you willing to do today to begin to change your life?" "What are you going to do now to attain your stated goals?"
- Good plans are simple and easy to understand. Plans should be flexible and open to modification as the client gains a deeper understanding of the specific behaviors she or he wants to change.
- The plan should be within the limits of the client's motivation and capacities. Like goals, plans should be realistic, attainable, and reflective of what the client needs and wants.
- Good plans are specific. Develop specificity by addressing questions such as "What?" "Where?" "With whom?" "When?" and "How often?"
- Plans are best stated in positive terms by pointing out what will be done rather than what won't be done.
- It is a good idea to develop plans the client can carry out alone. Plans that are contingent on what others will do or not do can be restrictive and difficult to evaluate.
- In choosing action-oriented steps, it is essential that the client considers his or her internal and external resources and limitations.
- Effective plans are repetitive and, ideally, are performed daily.
- Effective planning involves process-centered activities, such as applying for a job, writing a letter to a friend, taking a yoga class, devoting two hours a week to volunteer work, or taking a vacation.
- It may be necessary to revise the plan from time to time. Ask the client, "Is your plan helpful?" If the plan does not work, it can be reevaluated and alternatives considered.
- When a plan is not working, it is often the result of having a mismatch between the client's goals and the plan, or failure to break each step down into manageable parts.

Creating and carrying out behavioral plans enables clients to gain effective control over their lives. This is clearly the teaching aspect of counseling, which is best directed toward providing clients with new information and assisting them in the discovery of more effective ways of getting what they want and need.

For further discussion of behavior therapy and other action-oriented approaches, see Corey (2013d, chap. 9), Corsini and Wedding (2011, chap. 7), Lazarus (1997a), Neukrug (2011, chap. 8), Prochaska and Norcross (2010, chap. 9), Sharf (2012, chap. 8), and Wubbolding (2011).

Working With Ruth Using a Behavioral Focus

See Session 8 (Behavioral Focus in Counseling) on the *DVD for Integrative Counseling: The Case of Ruth and Lecturettes.*

My initial focus is on doing a thorough assessment of Ruth's current behavior. I use the BASIC I.D. model to obtain useful information and target personal goals. As I am doing this assessment, I ask Ruth to monitor what she is doing so that we can create baseline data to evaluate any changes. We then continue our work by collaboratively developing concrete goals. I use a wide range of cognitive and behavioral techniques to help Ruth achieve her goals, including stress-reduction techniques, social skills training, behavior rehearsals, modeling, coaching, systematic desensitization, in vivo exposure, flooding, mindfulness and acceptance methods, and relaxation techniques. I emphasize learning new coping behaviors that Ruth can use in everyday situations. She practices these activities both during her therapy sessions and during the week outside of the office.

Ruth indicates that she has difficulty focusing her attention and that she continually thinks about all the things she "should" be doing. To assist her in learning how to direct her attention to whatever she is doing each moment, I introduce mindfulness practice, which can help her to become alive to the moment. Mindfulness is the act of being intentional in experiencing in a nonjudgmental way what is happening in the present. Mindfulness is like meditation in that both practices aim to achieve a clear mind and a calm body. Although being in the moment sounds simple, most people find it quite challenging to be fully present and alive to present experiencing. I teach Ruth specific mindfulness skills in the therapy sessions. Then, for homework, I ask her to monitor her experience of mindfulness practice each day in her journal. We then discuss her progress in using mindfulness skills as a way to center herself and reduce stress in her life. I also suggest that she read Jon Kabat-Zinn's (1990) book, *Full Catastrophe Living*, and use his mindfulness meditation practice tapes daily at home. Ruth and I discuss Kabat-Zinn's notion that each moment of our waking life is a moment that can bring us greater stillness and awareness. We also discuss Kabat-Zinn's statement: "Mindfulness practice provides an opportunity to walk along the path of your own life with your eyes open, awake instead of half unconscious, responding consciously in the world instead of reacting automatically, mindlessly" (p. 442).

Mindfulness is the intentional process of observing, describing, and participating in the moment in a nonjudgmental way. In mindfulness practice Ruth will train herself to focus on her present experience, while at the same time achieving a distance from it. She will learn to focus on one thing at a time, or to develop an attitude of "one mindfully." My hope is that Ruth will acquire an attitude of mindfulness in every aspect of her daily life including standing, walking, and eating. I encourage Ruth to practice formal mindfulness meditation for 45 minutes daily, using Kabat-Zinn's mindfulness meditation tapes. In our sessions each week, I ask how her practice is going and whether she is progressing on applying these mindfulness principles to her everyday living. For more on the use of mindfulness in counseling, See Germer, Siegel, and Fulton (2005) and Greason (2011).

How do Ruth and I determine the degree to which she is progressing? What criteria do we use to make this determination? A fundamental part of behavior therapy consists of the work clients do outside of the therapy hour. Ruth carries out homework assignments, and then we evaluate the results during our therapy sessions. This gives us both an index of her progress. Furthermore, behavioral interventions have measurable results. The techniques we used are continually verified to determine how well they are working. Actual changes in Ruth's behavior provide critical information for making this evaluation. Her own evaluation of how much progress she sees and how satisfied she is by the outcomes is a major factor in assessing therapeutic results.

In a particular counseling session, Ruth tells me that she feels encouraged to go forward and make some of the changes that are important to her. She brings up the subject of her weight. As we talk about what her weight means to her, Ruth mentions that she does not exercise and that she does not have much energy. I need to be careful not to make a decision for her regarding developing an exercise program and managing her weight. Instead, it is critical to ascertain what she wants in these areas. Although I am utilizing behavioral strategies with her, I also employ techniques from feminist therapy such as gender-role analysis and gender-role intervention. This involves asking her to recall parental messages she received related to weight and appearance. The technique of gender-role intervention places Ruth's concern about her weight in the context of society's role expectations for women. My aim is to provide her with insight into the ways social issues and unrealistic standards of the "perfect body" are affecting her psychologically. This leads to a discussion of unrealistic strivings and a critical appraisal of how she measures her worth.

After discussing which messages Ruth wants to change, we implement a plan for creating these changes. She states that she wants to develop a regular exercise program. If her program is to work well for her, she must identify what type of exercise is appropriate for her. Once she is clear that she wants to commit herself to regular exercise, we are ready to formulate an action plan that will help her get what she wants. Together we determine that walking will be a vital part of her exercise program. We work out the details, including how often she will walk and for how long. I encourage her to use her friend as a source of support in helping her stick with her plans. Furthermore, I strongly recommend that she find ways to monitor her progress and keep herself accountable in following her plans for appropriate eating and exercising habits.

Working from an integrative perspective, it is imperative that I also attend to Ruth's thoughts and feelings about her weight and her body image in general. Her self-talk is not helpful to her in this area. She castigates herself about not looking right and about being weak because she is overweight. Her negative self-talk leads to feelings of defeat, depression, and anger with herself. When her clothes don't fit, she tells herself she is totally unattractive and feels upset and discouraged. It will not be enough to simply chart out the steps in a behavioral program for weight control through exercise and dieting. We will also need to address her thoughts and emotions at the same time as we are working behaviorally. Placing her concerns about her body in the context of societal standards that dictate what constitutes the ideal physical appearance may aid in Ruth's understanding. Because her concerns involve her thoughts, feelings, and actions, it is necessary to work on all these levels to some extent, even though we may focus on one particular dimension at certain times in counseling.

For a detailed description of a multimodal-behavior therapist's perspective on Ruth, written by Arnold Lazarus, see *Case Approach to Counseling and Psychotherapy* (Corey, 2013a, chap. 8). See also Sherry Cormier's work with Ruth from a behavioral perspective in the same chapter.

Working With Stan Using a Behavioral Focus

See Session 7 (Behavioral Focus in Counseling) on the *DVD for Theory and Practice of Counseling and Psychotherapy: The Case of Stan and Lecturettes.*

This session illustrates behavioral methods of teaching Stan assertiveness training and setting up realistic homework. Stan can spend a great deal of time gathering insights about why he is the way he is. He can learn to express feelings that he kept hidden for many years. He can think about the things he tells himself and even begin to acquire a more realistic set of beliefs. Although acquiring insight, changing core beliefs, and expressing feelings are of value, focusing exclusively on these levels is not enough to bring about substantive personality change. Addressing what Stan is *doing* is a way of bringing these feelings and thoughts together by applying them to real-life situations in various action programs. I greatly value the contributions of Adlerian therapy, behavior therapy, reality therapy, rational emotive behavior therapy, cognitive therapy, narrative therapy, and solution-focused brief therapy, all of which give central emphasis to the role of action in the real world as a prerequisite for change.

Behavior therapy offers many techniques aimed at bringing about behavioral change. In Stan's case I am especially inclined to work with him in developing a self-management program. For example, he complains of often feeling tense and anxious. By learning and practicing daily relaxation procedures, Stan is gaining more control over his physical and psychological tension. Through mindfulness practice, Stan is experiencing more success in getting himself centered before he goes to his classes, meets women, or talks to friends. He is making significant changes by monitoring his behavior in everyday situations. Through this self-monitoring, he is gaining increased awareness of what he tells himself, what he does, and how he feels. He has been keeping up with writing in a journal, which is itself therapeutic and is enabling him to behave in novel ways. In his journal he has been recording events that lead up to his feeling depressed (or anxious or hurt). In addition, he is writing about what he actually did in these situations and what he might have done differently. By paying attention to what he is *doing* in daily life, Stan is beginning to gain more control of his behavior.

Stan would like to participate more actively in class discussions, but his negative self-talk gets in the way. He does not like being invisible in class, and he would like his professors to get to know him better. He is committed to getting the most from his education, and he realizes that his reluctance to ask for help from his professors stems from not wanting to bother them. We talk about ways Stan might behave more assertively to get what he wants. For several sessions Stan practices initiating conversations with his professor during her office time. After several behavioral rehearsals, Stan feels more confident in asking a professor for some time. Together we carefully design a homework assignment that will enable Stan to carry his behavioral rehearsals into the school setting. Homework is an excellent way for Stan to become an active agent in his therapy. He must *do* something in daily situations if change is to occur. The degree to which he will change is directly proportional to his willingness to experiment by trying out new ways of behaving.

Stan agrees to meet with his professor before our next therapy session. At the beginning of the following session I ask Stan how things went with the meeting with the professor. He is apologetic and informs me that he failed to carry out his assignment. Together we explore what stopped him from doing what he said he wanted to do. If his self-talk and his thoughts are stopping him, it can be helpful for Stan to learn about the mindfulness principle of recognizing that a thought is just a thought.

Resolutions and plans are empty unless there is a decision to carry them out. It is crucial that Stan commits to a definite plan that he can realistically accomplish. I draw upon the WDEP model in reality therapy in teaching Stan what constitutes an effective plan. Each week we discuss Stan's progress toward meeting his goals and review how well he is completing his assignments. If he does not do an assignment or if he does not like the way he carried out an assignment, we can use this as an opportunity to talk about what this means to him. Rather than judging his behavior in performing assignments, the emphasis is on what can be learned and how he can learn new skills that will lead to success. We spend a good deal of time refining and practicing skills so Stan can approach situations differently. Much of our work together is based on using the sessions for behavioral practice and fine-tuning a plan of action to be implemented between our sessions.

The ultimate responsibility for making plans and implementing them rests with Stan. My task is to consistently encourage Stan to learn specific information and skills to cope with a range of challenges he may encounter in day-to-day living. Soon Stan will become his own counselor, applying his new skills for effective living not only to present problems but also to future difficulties.

Concluding Comments

An emphasis on evidence-based therapies as a part of the assessment and treatment process is a hallmark of behavior therapy. Behavior therapists are committed to examining the effectiveness of their procedures in terms of their generalizability, meaningfulness, and durability of change. It is up to practitioners to demonstrate that therapy is working. If progress is not being made, therapists look carefully at the original assessment and treatment plan and make modifications as necessary.

A significant feature of behavior therapy is the collaboration between therapist and client. The client is encouraged to become an active participant and to provide feedback to the therapist regarding the usefulness of specific interventions. Therapists modify their treatment procedures based on this feedback. Clients have a major stake in formulating therapy goals and are expected to experiment for the purpose of enlarging their repertoire of adaptive behaviors. Clients need to be willing to practice behavioral changes and to continue to implement new behaviors outside of the therapy office. The impact of therapy is not realized until the client transfers the new behaviors from the office to everyday life.

I recommend that you review the key themes of the behavioral approaches described in this chapter and apply them to yourself. Apply the WDEP model (of reality therapy) to identify a behavior you are willing to change. This might be a behavior you'd like to reduce or a behavior that you'd like to acquire. Once you have selected your target behavior, apply the guidelines for developing an action plan to yourself.

After reading this chapter on the behavioral focus in counseling, take time to reflect on the following questions as a way of clarifying your thoughts on the behavioral focus.

- What is one of your behaviors that is not working for you at this time?
- What is the importance of developing a specific and realistic action plan as a requisite for change?
- What are the characteristics of an effective plan? What are some guidelines you would use to help your clients design a plan for change?
- What importance would you place on the therapeutic relationship when working from a behavioral perspective?
- How do you imagine it would be for you to be a client in behavior-oriented therapy?
- What concepts and techniques from the behavioral approaches fit into your personal approach to counseling?

CHAPTER NINE

An Integrative Perspective

Introduction

Psychotherapy integration is best characterized as looking beyond and across the confines of single-school approaches to see what can be learned from other perspectives. In an integrative approach, diverse theories and techniques are combined to contribute to an effective framework for clinical practice (Stricker, 2010). Integrative counseling is a creative synthesis of contributions from diverse theoretical orientations that fit your unique personality and style. Norcross and Wampold (2011a, 2011b) maintain that effective clinical practice requires a flexible and integrative perspective. Using an identical therapy relationship style and treatment method for all clients is inappropriate and can be unethical.

Two of the most common pathways to achieving this integration are technical integration and theoretical integration. *Technical integration* tends to focus on differences, uses techniques drawn from many approaches, and is based on a systematic selection of techniques. This path calls for using techniques from different schools without necessarily subscribing to the theoretical positions that spawned them. Arnold Lazarus (1997a; 2008), founder of multimodal therapy, espouses technical (or systematic) eclecticism, which is more commonly referred to as technical integration. Multimodal therapists borrow from many other therapy systems, using techniques that have been demonstrated to be effective in dealing with specific problems. Clinical effectiveness is determined by the degree of a therapist's flexibility, versatility, and technical eclecticism (Lazarus, 2008).

In contrast, *theoretical integration* is a conceptual or theoretical creation that goes beyond blending techniques. This path creates a conceptual framework that synthesizes the best of two or more theoretical approaches to produce an outcome richer than that of a single theory (Norcross, 2005). Theoretical integration is the most complex, sophisticated, and difficult of all types of integration because it requires bringing together concepts from disparate approaches (Stricker, 2010). *Emotion-focused therapy* (EFT), which is informed by the role of emotion in psychotherapeutic change, is a form of theoretical integration.

Lazarus (2008) raises concerns about theoretical integration because he believes blending aspects of different theories is likely to obfuscate therapeutic practice. He contends that by remaining theoretically consistent, but technically eclectic, practitioners can spell out precisely what interventions they will employ with various clients, as well as the means by which they select these procedures.

A third path to psychotherapy integration is *assimilative integration*, described by Stricker (2010). This route is grounded in a single psychotherapeutic orientation but draws techniques from other therapeutic models, which are integrated in as seamless a fashion as possible. Although a single theoretical perspective informs the therapist's understanding of the needs of the client, a diverse range of techniques can be employed in constructing an individualized treatment plan. Stricker's assimilative integration is based on a relational psychodynamic theory, and technical interventions are drawn from cognitive, behavioral, experiential, and systems approaches.

I see many advantages to incorporating a diverse range of techniques from many different theories, but I also think it is possible to incorporate key principles and concepts from various theoretical orientations. Some concepts from the experiential approaches blend quite well with cognitive behavioral approaches. For example, the experiential approaches emphasize here-and-now awareness, the therapeutic relationship, and an exploration of feelings—all concepts easily incorporated into action-oriented therapies. Clients can be asked to decide what they want to do with present awareness, including making behavioral plans for change. All the action-oriented therapies depend on a solid therapeutic alliance between client and therapist. Techniques will not take root if there is not a good working relationship, and clients are more likely to cooperate with a therapist's cognitive and behavioral interventions if they believe the therapist is genuinely interested in them.

Searching for Common Factors Across Therapy Schools

Another route to psychotherapy integration is the *common factors approach,* which starts by identifying specific effective ingredients of any group of psychotherapies. This approach to integration searches for common aspects across different theoretical systems. Despite many differences among the theories, a recognizable core of counseling practice is composed of nonspecific variables common to all therapies. Some examples of these common factors include a therapeutic alliance, expectations of the therapist and client for a positive therapeutic experience, and a systematic way of using techniques to address problems (Stricker, 2010). These common factors are thought to be at least as important in accounting for therapeutic outcomes as the unique factors that differentiate one theory from another (Norcross, 2005).

According to Lambert (2011), of all the common factors investigated in psychotherapy, none has received more attention and confirmation that a facilitative therapeutic relationship. The importance of the therapeutic alliance is a well-established critical component of effective therapy. Interpersonal, social, and affective factors common across therapeutic orientations are more critical than techniques employed when it comes to facilitating therapeutic gains. Wampold's (2001, 2010) review of psychotherapy research support's Lambert's findings that no specific form of treatment has been proved to be clearly superior to another. Rather, the common factors that are part of all theoretical orientations—such as the therapist's ability to form an alliance with the client—are critical to therapeutic outcomes. The various therapy models and techniques work equally well because they share the key factor accounting for change—the client (Bohart & Tallman, 2010).

Creating an integrative approach to practice is not a simple task. You cannot simply pick pieces from theories in an unsystematic manner or based on personal whim. The kind of integration I am suggesting is based on common factors across therapeutic schools. However, blending theoretical constructs is more demanding than utilizing diverse techniques from different schools. If you attempt to blend theoretical constructs from different orientations in your own integrative model, you need to make sure that these concepts are compatible and that these frameworks lend themselves to a workable merger. Some blending simply does not make much conceptual sense. For instance, psychodynamic theory, which focuses on unconscious factors as the source of present-day problems, does not blend nicely with theories that reject the unconscious, such as rational emotive behavior therapy and reality therapy. Likewise, psychodynamic theories are geared around central concepts such as exploration of past traumatic events, exploration of dreams, working through the transference relationship, and awareness and management of countertransference. Some therapy models do not provide a framework for exploring these theoretical constructs.

For various perspectives on psychotherapy integration, I recommend Stricker (2010) *Psychotherapy Integration*, and Stricker and Gold (2006), *A Casebook of Psychotherapy Integration*. These books will give you a sense of the direction being taken by the psychotherapy integration movement. In addition to these sources, the following textbooks dealing with counseling theory have a chapter on integration of therapies: Corey (2013d, chaps. 15 & 16); Prochaska and Norcross (2010, chaps. 15 & 16); and Sharf (2012, chaps. 16 & 17).

The Foundation of My Integrative Approach

In this section I present some elements of my integrative approach to counseling. Existential theory comes closest to my worldview and serves as the foundation for constructing my theoretical orientation, but I also draw heavily from two other related theories—Gestalt therapy and psychodrama. After briefly describing some of the key concepts and themes from the existential, Gestalt, and psychodrama orientations, I discuss how I incorporate basic concepts and techniques from a number of the action-oriented therapies as well.

Existential Therapy as a Philosophical Base

My own philosophical orientation is strongly influenced by the existential approach, which conceives of counseling as a life-changing process. Counseling
is a journey in which the therapist is a guide who facilitates client exploration.
A number of key themes from the existential approach seem to me to capture
the essence of this therapeutic venture. According to the existentialist view, we
are capable of self-awareness, which is the distinctive capacity that allows us
to reflect and to decide. With this awareness we become free beings who are
responsible for choosing the way we live, and thus we create our own destiny.
I like the emphasis on freedom and responsibility, for this notion challenges
us to redesign our lives. I encourage people to look at the choices they *do* have,
however limited they may be, and to accept responsibility for choosing for
themselves. However, making choices gives rise to existential anxiety, which
is another basic human characteristic. This anxiety is heightened when we reflect on the reality of death. Facing the inevitable prospect of eventual death
gives the present moment significance as we become aware that we do not have
forever to accomplish our goals. The reality of death is a catalyst that can challenge us to create a life that has meaning and purpose. We strive toward a
meaningful life by recognizing our freedom and by making a commitment to
choose in the face of uncertainty.

Both existential therapy and person-centered therapy place central prominence on the person-to-person relationship. Client growth occurs through this
genuine encounter, and a key factor influencing the outcome of therapy is the
quality of the therapeutic relationship. I am convinced that emphasizing the
human quality of the therapeutic relationship lessens the chances of making
counseling a mechanical process.

The conceptual propositions of existential therapy can be creatively integrated with many other therapeutic orientations (Schneider, 2008; Schneider &
Krug, 2010). In thinking about therapy from an existential perspective, I am
not overly concerned with which techniques I might employ or with creating
an agenda for my client. It is not the techniques I use that make a therapeutic
difference; rather, it is the quality of the relationship with my client that heals.
My main interests are in being as fully present as I am able to be for the client,
establishing a trusting relationship, creating safety, and moving into the client's subjective world. If my client is able to sense my presence and my desire
to make a real connection, then a solid foundation is being created for the hard
work that follows.

Because the existential approach is concerned with the goals of therapy,
basic conditions of human existence, and therapy as a shared journey, I do not
feel bound by a specific set of techniques. Interventions are used in the service
of broadening the ways in which clients live in their world. Techniques are tools
to help clients become aware of their choices and their potential for action. Although I incorporate techniques from various therapeutic models, these interventions are made within the context of striving to understand the subjective
world of the client. An existential view provides me with the framework for
understanding universal human concerns, including facing and dealing with

the problems of personal freedom, self-alienation and estrangement from others, the fear of death and nonbeing, living with courage, exploring the meaning of life, and making critical life choices.

For further discussions of existential therapy, see Deurzen (2002, 2010), Corey (2013d, chap. 6), Corsini and Wedding (2011, chap. 9), Elkins (2009), Frew and Spiegler (2008, chap. 5), Neukrug (2011, chap. 5), Prochaska and Norcross (2010, chap. 4), and Sharf (2012, chap. 5).

Gestalt Therapy: A Holistic Perspective

Gestalt therapy is truly an integrative orientation in that it focuses on whatever is in the client's awareness. From the Gestalt perspective, feelings, thoughts, body sensations, and actions are all used as guides to understand what is central for the client in each moment. The centrality of whatever is in the client's awareness is an ideal way to understand the world of the client. I attempt to approach clients with an open mind and focus on what occurs phenomenologically with my client. By paying attention to the verbal and nonverbal cues provided, I have a starting point for exploring the client's world.

Functioning within a Gestalt framework, I view my main goal as striving to increase the client's awareness of "what is." Change occurs through a heightened awareness of what the client is experiencing in the present moment. Awareness, choice, and responsibility are cornerstones of practice. This approach is phenomenological because it focuses on the client's perceptions of reality and is existential because it is grounded in the notion that people are always in the process of becoming, remaking, and rediscovering themselves.

The Gestalt approach is characterized by many key concepts that can be fruitfully blended into other orientations. Gestalt therapy (and psychodrama) techniques encourage clients to bring painful memories and feelings pertaining to both past and present events to center stage. Through the skillful and sensitive use of Gestalt therapy interventions, it is possible to assist clients in heightening their present-centered awareness of what they are thinking and feeling as well as what they are doing. The client is provided with a wide range of tools, in the form of Gestalt experiments, for making decisions about changing the course of living. Although the therapist suggests the experiments, this is a collaborative process with full participation by the client. Therapists create experiments within a context of the I/Thou dialogue in a here-and-now framework. Gestalt experiments take many forms: setting up a dialogue between a client and a significant person in his or her life; assuming the identity of a key figure through role playing; or reliving a painful event.

Gestalt therapy utilizes the experiment to move clients from talk to action and experience. This is a perspective on growth and enhancement, not merely a system of techniques to treat disorders. With the emphasis given to the relationship between client and therapist, there is a creative spirit of suggesting, inventing, and carrying out experiments aimed at increasing awareness.

For specific examples of Gestalt experiments when working with the emotive dimension, review Chapter 7 of this book. For further discussion of Gestalt therapy, see Corey (2013d, chap. 8), Corsini and Wedding (2011, chap. 10), Frew and Spiegler (2008, chap. 7), Neukrug (2011, chap. 6), Prochaska and Norcross (2010, chap. 6), Sharf (2012, chap. 7), and Woldt and Toman (2005).

Psychodrama: An Integrative Approach

Psychodrama is primarily an action approach to group counseling in which clients explore their problems through role playing, enacting situations using various dramatic devices to gain insight, discover their own creativity, and develop behavioral skills. The scenes are played as if they were occurring in the here and now, even though they might have their origins in a past event or in an anticipated situation. Although psychodrama is primarily used in group therapy, many psychodrama techniques can be useful in individual counseling. Using psychodrama, the client acts out or dramatizes past, present, or anticipated life situations and roles. This is done in an attempt to gain deeper understanding, explore feelings and achieve emotional release, and develop new ways of coping with problems. Significant events are enacted to help the client get in contact with unrecognized and unexpressed feelings, to provide a channel for the full expression of these feelings and attitudes, and to broaden the role repertoire.

Integrated with other systems—such as psychodynamic, experiential, and cognitive behavioral approaches—psychodrama offers a more experiential process, adding imagery, action, and direct interpersonal encounters. In turn, psychodrama can utilize methods derived from the other experiential approaches and the cognitive behavioral approaches to ground clients in a meaningful process.

I value psychodrama's active techniques and role playing because these methods lead clients to directly experience their conflicts to a much greater degree than is the case when they *talk about* themselves in a storytelling manner. This direct experiencing tends to bring emotions to the surface. While the emotional aspects of an enactment are of therapeutic value, a degree of cognitive integration is required to maximize the impact of experiencing emotions. Participants in a psychodrama can be encouraged to reflect on how their beliefs and decisions may be contributing to the emotional turmoil they experienced in the psychodrama.

Psychodrama uses a number of specific techniques designed to intensify feelings, clarify implicit beliefs, increase self-awareness, and practice new behaviors. One of the most powerful tools of psychodrama is role reversal, which involves the client taking on the part of another person. Through role reversal, people are able to get outside of their own frame of reference and enact a side of themselves they would rarely show to others. In addition, by reversing roles with a significant person, the client is able to formulate significant emotional and cognitive insights into his or her part in a relationship. This technique also creates empathy for the position of the other person.

The concepts and methods of psychodrama offer imagery, action, and direct interpersonal encounters to a range of therapeutic approaches. Psychodramatic techniques can be adapted to fit well within the framework of other theoretical models, including psychoanalytic therapy, cognitive behavior therapies, Gestalt therapy, existential therapy, Adlerian therapy, play therapy, family therapy, and group therapy. According to Blatner (2006), psychodrama's value lies in the fact that its methodology can be integrated with other therapeutic approaches rather than acting in seeming competition.

The underlying philosophy of psychodrama is consistent with many of the premises of existential therapy, person-centered therapy, and Gestalt therapy, all of which emphasize understanding and respecting the client's experience and the importance of the therapeutic relationship as a healing factor. Although practitioners who employ psychodramatic methods assume an active and directive role, these techniques are most effective when the counselor adopts a person-centered spirit. Practitioners who are authentic, who are able to make connection and to be psychologically present, who demonstrate empathy, and who exhibit a high level of respect and positive regard for their clients are most effective in implementing a range of psychodrama techniques.

For a more detailed discussion of psychodrama applied to group counseling, see Blatner (1996, 2006), Corey (2012, chap. 8), Horvatin and Schreiber (2006), and Moreno, Blomkvist, and Rutzel (2000).

Drawing on the Action-Oriented Therapies

As important as it is to work with the emotional realm, I think it is essential to incorporate concepts and techniques from the action-oriented approaches to bring about both cognitive and behavioral changes. Here are some of the ways I utilize the action-oriented therapies in my integrative model.

Adlerian Therapy

The basic goal of the Adlerian approach is to help clients identify and change their mistaken beliefs about self, others, and life and thus participate more fully in a social world. The therapeutic process helps clients make some basic changes in their style of living, which leads to changes in the way they feel and behave. I especially like the Adlerian perspective on therapy as a cooperative venture. Therapy is geared toward assisting clients in being able to translate their insights into action in the real world.

Adlerian therapy rests on a central belief that our happiness is largely related to social connectedness. Because we are embedded in a society, we cannot be understood in isolation from that social context. We are primarily motivated by a desire to belong. As social beings, we have a need to be of use to others and to establish meaningful relationships in a community. As socially embedded individuals, our lives and contributions flourish when we experience a sense of belongingness to the community.

The Adlerian model lends itself to versatility in meeting the needs of a diverse range of clients (Carlson, Watts, & Maniacci, 2006). Adlerians are not bound to follow a specific set of procedures, which gives them a great deal of freedom in working with clients in ways that are uniquely suited to their own therapeutic style. Adlerian therapists are resourceful in drawing on a variety of cognitive, behavioral, and experiential techniques that they think will work best for a particular client. Some of these techniques are encouragement, confrontation, summarizing, interpretation of experiences within the family and early recollections, suggestion, and homework assignments.

One of Adler's most important contributions is his influence on other therapy systems. Many of his basic ideas have found their way into other psychological schools, such as family systems approaches, Gestalt therapy, reality therapy, rational emotive behavior therapy, cognitive therapy, person-centered therapy, solution-focused brief therapy, and existentialism. These approaches all are based on a similar concept of the person as purposive and self-determining and as striving for growth and meaning in life.

Adlerian theory addresses the client's past, present, and future. The notion of teleology, or striving for meaning and purpose, is central, and the spiritual concerns of clients can be addressed. The concept of social interest—that we need to contribute to making the world a better place—can be a part of any theoretical system. Going beyond the self and getting involved in making a difference in the lives of others is integrative in its very nature. All of these concepts can be adapted to any theoretical model.

Contemporary Adlerian theory is an integration of cognitive, psychodynamic, and systems perspectives, and in many respects resembles the social constructionist theories. Contemporary social constructionist theories share common ground with the Adlerian approach. Some of these common characteristics include an emphasis on establishing a respectful client–therapist relationship, an emphasis on clients' strengths and resources, and an optimistic and future orientation (Carlson, Watts, & Maniacci, 2006).

For further discussion of Adlerian therapy, see Carlson, Watts, and Maniacci (2006), Corey (2013d, chap. 5), Corsini and Wedding (2011, chap. 3), Neukrug (2011, chap. 4), Prochaska and Norcross (2010, chap. 3), and Sharf (2012, chap. 4).

Behavior Therapy

A basic assumption of the behavioral perspective is that most problematic cognitions, emotions, and behaviors have been learned and that new learning can modify them. Although this modification process is often called "therapy," it is more properly an educational experience in which individuals are involved in a teaching/learning process. There are many parallels between counseling and education. Counseling is educational in that people develop a new perspective on ways of learning, and they also try out more effective ways of working with their cognitions, emotions, and behaviors. Techniques from the action-oriented approaches such as role playing, behavioral rehearsal, coaching, guided practice, modeling, feedback, mindfulness skills, and homework assignments can be used to attain humanistic goals that characterize the experiential therapies. Furthermore, behavioral strategies can be integrated with many other models, regardless of theoretical orientation.

Contemporary behavior therapy stresses clients' active role in making decisions about their treatment, and behavior therapists and clients alter goals throughout the therapeutic process as needed. The therapist works collaboratively with clients in formulating specific measurable goals that are clear, concrete, understood, and agreed on by the client and the counselor. In this action-oriented therapy, counselor and client determine specific steps the client can take to achieve her or his goals. Behavioral treatment interventions are individually tailored to specific problems experienced by clients. Evidence-based strategies that have research support for use with a particular kind of problem are used to promote generalization and maintenance of behavior change. Many of these research-based behavioral interventions can be fruitfully integrated into other therapeutic approaches.

For further discussion of behavior therapy, see Corey (2013d, chap. 9), Corsini and Wedding (2011, chap. 7), Craske (2010), Frew and Spiegler (2008, chap. 8), Neukrug (2011, chap. 6), Prochaska and Norcross (2010, chap. 9), and Sharf (2012, chap. 8).

Multimodal Therapy

Multimodal therapy is a branch of behavior therapy. As you learned in Chapter 8, it is a comprehensive, systematic, holistic approach to behavior therapy developed by Arnold Lazarus (1997a, 2005, 2006, 2008). Basing his practice on social learning theory, Lazarus endorses drawing techniques from just about all of the therapy models. In his integrative model new techniques are constantly being introduced and existing techniques are refined, but never used in a shotgun manner.

I incorporate many multimodal concepts and strategies in my personal integrative style of counseling. Not only is multimodal therapy useful from a treatment perspective, but it provides an excellent context for doing a comprehensive assessment that can inform treatment. Multimodal methods allow me to challenge self-defeating beliefs, offer constructive feedback, and provide positive reinforcement. I am able to coach, train, and model for my clients. Using this approach, I can function actively and directively by providing information and instruction. I am constantly adjusting my techniques to achieve the client's goals in therapy. I ask the question, "What is best for this particular person?" I make a careful attempt to determine precisely what relationship and what treatment strategies will work best with each client and under which particular circumstances. Because individuals are troubled by a variety of specific problems, it is appropriate that both a multitude of treatment strategies and different therapeutic styles are used to bring about change.

For further discussion of multimodal therapy, see Corey (2013a, chap, 7; 2013d, chap. 9), Lazarus (1997a, 2005, 2006), and Sharf (2012, chap. 17).

Cognitive Behavior Therapy

Most of the contemporary therapies can be considered "cognitive" in a general sense because they have the aim of changing clients' subjective views of themselves and the world. However, the cognitive behavioral approaches differ from both psychodynamic and experiential therapies in that the major focus of cognitive behavior therapy (CBT) is on both undermining faulty assumptions and beliefs and teaching clients the coping skills needed to deal with their problems.

In many respects rational emotive behavior therapy (REBT) can be considered as a comprehensive and integrative therapeutic practice. Numerous cognitive, emotive, and behavioral techniques can be employed in changing one's emotions and behaviors by changing the structure of one's cognitions. Like

REBT, Beck's cognitive therapy is an integrative approach, drawing on many different modalities of psychotherapy. Cognitive therapy serves as a bridge between psychoanalytic therapy and behavior therapy. Cognitive behavioral approaches provide a structured, focused, present-centered, time-limited, and active approach.

A feature I particularly value in all the cognitive behavioral therapies (and in feminist therapy as well) is the demystification of the therapy process. Clients are active, informed, and responsible for the direction of therapy. Being based on an educational model, these therapies all emphasize a working alliance between therapist and client. These approaches encourage self-help, provide for continuous feedback from the client on how well treatment strategies are working, and provide a structure and direction to the therapy process that allows for evaluation of outcomes. Cognitive behavior therapists are concerned with teaching clients how to be their own therapist. Typically, a therapist will educate clients about the nature and course of their problem, about the process of cognitive therapy, and how thoughts influence their emotions and behaviors. The educative process includes providing clients with information both about their presenting problems and about *relapse prevention,* which consists of procedures for dealing with the inevitable setbacks clients are likely to experience as they apply what they are learning to daily life.

For further discussion of cognitive behavior therapy, see Beck (2011), Corey (2013d, chap. 10), Corsini and Wedding (2011, chap. 8), Frew and Spiegler (2008, chap. 9), Ledley, Marx, and Heimberg (2010), Neukrug (2011, chap. 10), Prochaska and Norcross (2011, chap. 10), and Sharf (2012, chap. 10).

Reality Therapy/Choice Theory

Choice theory underlies the practice of reality therapy and is grounded on phenomenological and existential premises. From the perspective of choice theory, we choose our goals and are responsible for the kind of world we create for ourselves. We are responsible for what we choose to do, no matter what has happened in the past. Reality therapy is grounded on existential principles; it also shares many concepts with the cognitive behavioral therapies.

One concept of reality therapy I find particularly useful is total behavior, which teaches that all behavior is made up of four inseparable but distinct components: *acting, thinking, feeling,* and the *physiology* that must accompany all of our actions, thoughts, and feelings. The main emphasis is given to acting and thinking, for these aspects of total behavior are easier to change than are the feeling and physiology components. The key to changing a total behavior lies in choosing to change what we are doing and thinking because these are the behaviors that we can control.

I value the basic notion of the need to assume personal responsibility for our feelings that is stressed by reality therapy. This philosophy takes us out of a passive role and challenges us to accept our part in creating our feelings by what we are doing and how we are thinking. For example, depression is not something that simply happens to us but is an active choice we make. Glasser (1998, 2001) speaks of "depressing" or "angering" rather than "being depressed" or "being angry." This process of "depressing" keeps anger in check, and it also allows us to ask for help. By using action words ending in "ing," the therapist emphasizes that feelings are behaviors. Clearly, the emphasis of this theory is on how we act and think, and in this sense it shares many of the themes of cognitive behavioral approaches.

The core of reality therapy is learning how to make better and more effective choices and gaining more effective control of our lives. Although the past may have contributed to a current problem, the past is not the focus of therapy. Regardless of what occurred in the past, to function effectively people need to live and plan in the present. Reality therapy practitioners focus on what clients are able and willing to do right now to change their behavior. Therapists consistently ask clients to evaluate the effectiveness of what they are choosing to do to determine if better choices are possible. Skillful questioning and various behavioral techniques are employed to help clients make this self-evaluation. The counselor assists clients in making plans to change those behaviors that clients determine are not working for them.

For further discussion of reality therapy and choice theory, see Glasser (1998, 2001), Corey (2013d, chap. 11), Frew and Spiegler (2008, chap. 10), Neukrug (2011, chap. 11), Sharf (2012, chap. 11), and Wubbolding (2000, 2011).

Solution-Focused Brief Therapy

Solution-focused brief therapy (SFBT) is based on the optimistic assumption that people are healthy, competent, resourceful, and possess the ability to construct solutions and alternative stories that can enhance their lives. The philosophy of this approach rests on the assumption that people can become mired in unresolved past conflicts and blocked when they focus on past or present problems rather than on present and future solutions. SFBT therapists emphasizes strengths and resiliencies by focusing on exceptions to their clients' problems and on creating solutions rather than talking about these problems. Some common techniques include the use of miracle questions, exception questions, scaling questions, homework, and summary feedback. Some therapists ask the client to externalize the problem and focus on strengths or unused resources. Others challenge clients to discover solutions that might work.

Solution-focused practitioners adopt a *"not knowing"* position to encourage clients to become the experts about their own lives. In this approach, the therapist-as-expert is replaced by the *client-as-expert*, especially when it comes to what the client wants in life. The role of the counselor is to help clients recognize the resources they already possess, such as resilience, courage, and ingenuity.

Practitioners with a solution-focused orientation tend to engage clients in conversations about what is going well, future possibilities, and what will likely lead to a sense of accomplishment. Therapists often ask clients: "Tell me about times when your life was going the way you wanted it to." These conversations illustrate stories of life worth living. On the basis of these conversations, the power of problems is lessened and new directions and solutions are made possible. A key concept is, "Once you know what works, do more of it." If something is not working, clients are encouraged to do something different. With this approach, clients are involved in the therapeutic process from beginning to end, which increases the chances that therapy will be successful.

For a further discussion of solution-focused brief therapy, see Corey (2013d, chap. 13), deShazer (1985, 1988, 1991), deShazer and Dolan (2007), Murphy (2008), Neukrug (2011, chap. 13), Prochaska and Norcross (2010, chap. 14), and Sharf (2012, chap. 12).

Motivational Interviewing

Motivational Interviewing (MI) is a humanistic, client-centered, directive coun-seling approach that was developed by William R. Miller and Stephen Rollnick in the early 1980s. Over the past 25 years, clinical and research applications of motivational interviewing have grown at a remarkable pace. The strategies and skills in MI involve using open-ended questions, employing reflective listen-ing, affirming and supporting the client, summarizing and linking at the end of sessions, and eliciting and reinforcing *change talk*. Therapists guide clients to make a commitment to change and help them clarify where they want to go (Arkowitz & Miller, 2008; Levensky, Kersh, Cavasos, & Brooks, 2008).

MI is rooted in the philosophy of the person-centered approach, but with a "twist." The twist is that, unlike the unstructured person-centered approach, MI is deliberately directive and has the specific goals of reducing ambivalence about change and increasing intrinsic motivation (Arkowitz & Miller, 2008). The therapeutic relationship is crucial in achieving successful outcomes. In both person-centered therapy and MI, the counselor provides the conditions for growth and change by communicating attitudes of accurate empathy and unconditional positive regard.

Like solution-focused therapy, MI emphasizes the *relational context* of ther-apy, which is known as the "MI spirit." This MI spirit involves the counselor es-tablishing a collaborative partnership with the client, drawing on the ideas and resources of the client, and preserving the autonomy of the client (recognizing that all choices ultimately rest with the client rather than with the counselor). It is crucial for therapists to understand and act in accordance with the spirit of MI rather than simply implementing techniques and strategies. MI empha-sizes the internal frame of reference of clients, their present concerns, and dis-crepancies between values and behavior. MI activates clients' own motivations for change and their desire to adhere to treatment goals. The counselor assists clients in becoming their own advocates for change and the primary agents of change in their lives.

Motivational interviewing stresses client self-responsibility and promotes an invitational style for working cooperatively with clients to generate alterna-tive solutions to behavioral problems. MI therapists avoid arguing with clients and understand that resistance is the client's best effort to cope with difficul-ties. Therapists roll with resistance, express empathy, and listen reflectively. By viewing resistance as something that emerges from the interaction between cli-ents and counselors, the functions resistance often serves are illuminated and practitioners can adapt their approach to it. MI therapists do not view clients as opponents to be defeated but as allies who play a major role in their present and future success.

Miller and Rollnick (2002) developed these five basic principles of motivational interviewing:

1. MI practitioners strive to experience the world from the client's perspective without judgment or criticism. MI emphasizes reflective listening, which is a way for practitioners to better understand the subjective world of the client.

2. MI is designed to evoke and explore ambivalence. Counselors pay particular attention to the clients' arguments for changing compared to their arguments for not changing. Change is not easy and there are good reasons to remain as one is as well as to make life changes. Therapists elicit and reinforce *change-talk* by employing specific strategies to strengthen discussion about change. MI practitioners encourage clients to determine whether change will occur, and if so, what kinds of changes will occur and when.

3. MI therapists strive to enhance client agency about change and are interested in their clients' ideas about change. MI practitioners believe in clients' abilities, strengths, resources, competencies, and inherent ability to make decisions. They are mainly interested in exploring what is working well for clients rather than dwelling on their problems.

4. Although clients may see advantages to making life changes, they also may have many concerns and fears about changing. During the early phase of MI therapy it is common for clients to express ambivalence about changing, and individuals may have insufficient motivation to do what is necessary to bring about change. The therapist listens carefully and attempts to understand both sides of this ambivalence from a client's perspective.

5. When clients show signs of readiness to change through decreased resistance to change and increased talk about change, a critical phase of MI begins. In this stage, clients may express a desire and ability to change, show an interest in questions about change, experiment with possible change actions between therapy sessions, and envision a future picture of their life once the desired changes have been made. Therapists shift their focus toward strengthening clients' commitments to change and helping them implement a change plan. Levensky, Kersch, Cavasos, and Brooks (2008) stress that it is critical for therapists to make an accurate assessment of a client's readiness for change. Once clients gives evidence of being motivated to change, the role of the therapist is to assist clients in developing their own plan of action. A clinician might ask, "So, what do you see as your next step?" When clients formulate their own plans, with the help of the therapist, they increase their self-efficacy.

For a comprehensive discussion of motivational interviewing, see Miller and Rollnick (2002).

Feminist and Systemic Therapies

Feminist therapy is generally relatively short-term therapy aimed at both individual and social change. At the individual level, therapists work to help women and men recognize, claim, and embrace their personal power. As a consciously political enterprise, feminist therapists work toward social transformation. The major goal is to replace the current patriarchal system with feminist consciousness and thus create a society that values equality in relationships, that stresses interdependence rather than dependence, and that encourages women to define themselves rather than being defined by societal demands.

Feminist therapists are committed to actively breaking down the hierarchy of power in the therapeutic relationship through the use of various interventions. Some of these strategies are unique to feminist therapy, such as gender-role analysis and intervention, power analysis and intervention, assuming a stance of advocate in challenging conventional attitudes toward appropriate roles for women, and encouraging clients to take social action. Therapists with a feminist orientation understand how important it is to become aware of typical gender-role messages clients have been socialized with, and they are skilled in helping clients identify and challenge these messages. Feminist therapy principles and techniques can be applied to a range of therapeutic modalities such as individual therapy, couples counseling, family therapy, group counseling, and community intervention.

Few individual counseling theories place a primary focus on the role of systemic factors in influencing the individual. Both feminist and systemic therapies are based on the assumption that individuals are best understood within the context of their relationships. An individual's problems cannot be understood by focusing solely on the individual's internal dynamics. Rather, the individual's dysfunctional behavior grows out of the interactional units of the family, the community, and social systems. Thus, solutions to an individual's problems need to be designed from a contextual perspective.

Brown (2010) contends that feminist therapy is an integrative approach because practitioners typically draw upon a diverse range of interventions from other theoretical orientations. Techniques are drawn from psychodynamic, CBT, mindfulness-based approaches, and humanistic therapies. Interventions from other models include role playing, bibliotherapy, psychoeducation, assertiveness training, behavior rehearsal, cognitive restructuring, psychodrama techniques, identifying and challenging untested beliefs, and journal writing. Interventions are tailored to enhance clients' strengths and to assist them in gaining personal power. Therapists collaborate with clients on the goals of therapy and create a strong working alliance. The primary goals of empowerment, egalitarianism, and an analysis of power, gender, and social location are always kept in mind. According to Brown, the intent is to shift power and privilege to the voices and experiences of those who come to counseling, and away from those who deliver it.

Incorporating concepts from the client's external world is of paramount importance in my integrative approach. Concepts from feminist, systemic, and multicultural approaches add an essential dimension to understanding how individuals can best change by addressing both their internal and external worlds. In my approach I deal with the systemic (family, community, cultural) variables that contribute to an individual's core problems and draw on these factors as resources to foster the change process.

For further discussion of feminist therapy and systemic therapy, see Brown (2010), Corey (2013d, chaps. 12 & 14), and Sharf (2012, chaps. 13 & 14).

Working With Ruth in Cognitive, Emotive, and Behavioral Ways

See Session 9 (An Integrative Perspective) on the *DVD*
for Integrative Counseling: The Case of Ruth and Lecturettes.

As a basis for selecting techniques to employ with Ruth, I look at her as a think-ing, feeling, and behaving person. I work with these three dimensions in an in-teractive fashion rather than in a linear fashion. Thus, I do not work with Ruth's cognitions, then move ahead to her feelings, and finally proceed to behaviors and specific action programs. All of these dimensions are interrelated. When I am working with her on a cognitive level (such as dealing with decisions she has made or one of her values), I am also concerned about the feelings gener-ated in her at the moment and about exploring them with her. Cognitive and emotive dimensions have an interactive influence on actions. Therefore, we ex-plore how her thoughts and feelings are influencing what she is doing and also what she can do differently. Ruth can try out new behaviors in the session and practice new skills that she can apply to problems she encounters in daily life. As a basis for this integrative style, I draw on the experiential therapies, which stress expressing and experiencing feelings; on the cognitive therapies, which pay attention to the client's thinking processes, affecting behavior and beliefs; and on the action-oriented therapies, which stress the importance of creating a plan for behavioral change.

In one counseling session I employ a role-playing technique in which I as-sume the persona of Ruth while she takes on the role of her husband, John. My purpose in doing this reverse role play is to teach her how she can assertively approach her husband and let him know of her desire that they go on a retreat for married couples. We rehearse a number of ways that she could deal with John in the session. Ruth is aware that when she does not get what she wants she has a tendency to shut down. I try to get her to talk out loud, at least in the therapy sessions, when she has a tendency to fade away. Before the session ends, I asked her if she feels ready to deal with her husband in real life. She indicates that she does want to ask John to go on the couples' retreat, and I ask her to design some homework that would enable her to apply the role-playing situations we did in the office to her situation at home.

My integrative approach takes into account that Ruth is part of a system. To be able to more completely understand her, it is necessary to explore how she fits into her family of origin and the quality of her relationships with her present family. She has identified strained relationships with her mother and father and also with her children and husband. My hope is that we will have at least one session with all of the members of her family of origin. The focus will be on Ruth gaining greater clarity on how her interpersonal style is largely the result of her interactions with her family of origin. I accept that it is not pos-sible to understand Ruth apart from the context of the system of which she is a part. I agree with family therapists who would claim that to understand her present development it is necessary to go back three generations to see the impact of her family of origin. Most likely she is unaware of how her family of origin is influencing how she thinks, feels, and acts. Lacking this awareness, she makes assumptions in her present relationships, especially with her husband and her children.

If I work individually with Ruth, the emphasis can still be on the many ways her current struggles are related to her family system. Rather than trying to change the members of her family, we will largely work on discovering what she most wants to change about herself in relation to how she interacts with them.

For a more complete discussion of counseling Ruth from a family systems perspective, multicultural approaches, and integrative perspectives, see *Case Approach to Counseling and Psychotherapy* (Corey, 2013a, chaps. 12, 13, & 14).

Working With Stan in Cognitive, Emotive, and Behavioral Ways

See Session 13 (Integrative Approach) on the *DVD*
for Theory and Practice of Counseling and Psychotherapy:
The Case of Stan and Lecturettes.

In this session. which is part of the termination process, Stan and I review what he has learned in his therapy and how he can continue using his new insights and new behaviors in daily living. The focus is integrative because our task is to talk about changes on all levels of human experience. Even at this stage in Stan's therapy, I continue to provide him with information about the therapy process. I explain to Stan how his beliefs, behaviors, and feelings are interrelated. We both talk about how change in one of these dimensions has affected functioning in other modes. During this time I want Stan to take credit for any of the changes he has made. I reinforce the idea that it took courage and determination on his part to make life-changing decisions and to carry them out. It is important that Stan be reminded of the time we have left and that he be given the opportunity in the remaining sessions to bring in any new concerns he wants to explore, to address any unfinished business, and to identify resources for continuing his work after ending therapy.

As we move toward termination, we talk about where Stan can go from here. We develop an action plan and talk about how he can best maintain his new learning. We explore many ways that he can involve himself in reaching out to people. In essence, he can continue to challenge himself by doing things that are difficult for him yet at the same time broaden his range of choices. Now he can take the risk and be his own therapist, dealing with feelings as they arise in new situations.

Evaluating the process and outcomes of therapy are key parts of termination. I ask Stan to reflect on what he has learned ("What stands out the most for you? What did you learn that you consider the most useful to you?") and to consider how he can consolidate his learning ("What can you do now to keep practicing new behaviors?"). We also explore potential difficulties he expects to face when he no longer comes to weekly counseling sessions ("What will you do if you experience any setbacks?"). I introduce some *relapse prevention strategies* to help Stan cope constructively with future problems. These cognitive behavioral techniques improve the retention, accessibility, and implementation of adaptive coping responses once treatment has ended and are designed to help clients maintain the longevity of self-managed treatment gains (Newring, Loverich, Harris, & Wheeler, 2008). By addressing potential problems and stumbling blocks that he might have to deal with, Stan is less likely to get discouraged if he experiences any setbacks. If any relapses do occur, we talk about viewing such events as part of continual learning rather than as evidence of failure. I let Stan know that termination of formal therapy does not mean that he cannot return for future sessions if he thinks that would be useful for him. A follow-up session to assess his progress after termination may be scheduled at this time as well.

Study a Primary Theory—But Be Open to Integration

For those of you who are beginning your counseling career, my general suggestion is to select the primary theory closest to your basic beliefs. Learn that theory as thoroughly as you can, and at the same time be open to examining other theories in depth. If you begin by working within the parameters of a favored theory, you will have an anchor point from which to construct your own counseling perspective. But do not think that simply because you adhere to one theory you can use the same techniques with all of your clients. Even if you adhere to a single theory, you will need to be flexible in the manner in which you apply the techniques that flow from this theory as you work with different clients.

As you think about your client and the therapy sessions to come, ask yourself this question: "*What* treatment, by *whom*, is the most effective *for this* individual with *that* specific problem, and under *what* set of circumstances?" (Paul, 1967, p. 111). Regardless of what model you may be working with, you must decide *what* techniques, procedures, or intervention methods to utilize, *when* to use them, and with *which* clients. You will most likely encounter a diverse range of client populations. For counseling to be effective, it is necessary to utilize techniques and procedures in a manner that is consistent with clients' values, worldview, life experiences, and cultural background. Although it is unwise and possibly unethical to stereotype clients because of their cultural heritage, it is useful to assess how the cultural context has a bearing on their problems. Some techniques may be contraindicated because of clients' socialization. Thus, clients' responsiveness (or lack of it) to certain techniques is a critical barometer in judging the effectiveness of these methods.

Effective counseling involves proficiency in a combination of cognitive, affective, and behavioral techniques. Such a combination is necessary to help clients think about their beliefs and assumptions, to experience on a feeling level their conflicts and struggles, and to translate their insights into action programs by behaving in new ways in day-to-day living.

A pivotal assessment question is, "What does this particular person most need in order to more effectively cope with his or her problems?" The techniques that you will use can best be determined by your assessment of the client, which is why it is important to integrate assessment with treatment. Once you know what your client's target problems and goals are, the next step is to design specific techniques that can be effective with that client. Wampold (2010) offers sound advice in stating that if clients do not respond to a particular approach, then the therapist must adjust the therapy accordingly. He adds that therapists need to be competent in providing multiple treatment approaches to accommodate variability in clients' characteristics, attitudes, values, and preferences. "The process of becoming an effective therapist is a lifelong pursuit involving deliberate practice. The goal is not to select the 'right' theory but to use a particular theory—or more likely theories—effectively" (Wampold, 2010, p. 113). Wampold encourages students and practitioners to keep an open mind because diverse theoretical approaches all have something of value to offer.

Benefits and Limitations of Integration

I believe it is needlessly restrictive to apply only a few techniques from a single theory to most clients. I like to incorporate a wide range of procedures in my therapeutic style. However, unless you have an accurate, in-depth knowledge of theories, you cannot formulate a true synthesis. Simply put, you cannot integrate what you do not know (Norcross, 2005; Norcross & Beutler, 2011). Constructing your integrative orientation to counseling practice is a long-term venture that is refined with experience. Synthesizing various techniques or approaches in a systematic way is not accomplished merely by completing a course in counseling theory. The challenge is for you to think and practice integratively—but critically.

There are some limitations to encouraging the development of an integrative model, as opposed to sticking primarily with one theory. At its worst, eclecticism can be an excuse for sloppy practice—a practice that lacks a systematic rationale for what you actually do in your work. If you merely pick and choose according to whims, it is likely that your work will reflect your lack of knowledge. It is important to avoid the trap of emerging with a hodgepodge of unamalgamated theories thrown hastily together. According to Norcross (2005), a haphazard eclecticism is mainly an outgrowth of pet techniques and inadequate training and an arbitrary blend of methods. Psychotherapy integration rests on the assumption that different clients require different methods, yet this blending of concepts and methods needs to be done systematically. Norcross (2005) expresses a hope for psychotherapy integration that "will engender an open system of informed pluralism, deepening rapprochement, and evidence-based practice, one that leads to improved effectiveness of psychosocial treatments" (p. 19).

Concluding Comments

Throughout this book I have presented the advantages of constructing a systematic, consistent, personal, and disciplined approach to integrating various elements in your counseling practice. Whatever the basis of your integrative approach to counseling, you need to have a basic knowledge of various theoretical systems and counseling techniques to work effectively with a wide range of clients in various clinical settings. Sticking strictly to one theory may not provide you with the therapeutic flexibility that is required to deal creatively with the complexities associated with clinical practice.

One reason for the trend toward integrative counseling is the recognition that no single theory is comprehensive enough to account for the complexities of human behavior, especially when the range of client types and their specific problems are taken into consideration. Consider the contributions of the various counseling models and work toward creating your own integrative perspective. If you are open to an integrative perspective, you may find that several theories play a crucial role in your personal approach. By accepting that each theory has strengths and weaknesses and is, by definition, "different" from the others, you have some basis to begin developing a counseling perspective that fits you.

After reading this chapter on an integrative perspective, take time to reflect on the following questions as a way of clarifying your thoughts on using an integrative approach in counseling practice.

- What do you understand by the concept of an integrative approach to counseling?
- What are the differences between technical eclecticism and theoretical integration?
- What are some potential advantages of incorporating a diverse range of techniques from various theories?
- In what way is the client–therapist relationship a common denominator among the various theoretical models?
- What are the main benefits and limitations of an integrative approach?
- Is an integrative therapy approach a good fit for you?
- What have you learned thus far that will help you in designing your own integrative approach to counseling practice? What do you need to learn about approaches and methods in developing an integrative approach?

CHAPTER TEN

Working With Transference and Countertransference

Introduction

Transference occurs in many different kinds of relationships, but especially in intensive forms of therapy. Clients bring unresolved feelings with significant others into the therapeutic relationship and project them onto their counselors. Regardless of whether your theory explicitly makes room for concepts such as transference and countertransference, it is my belief that these factors operate in most counseling relationships.

Contrasting Views of Transference

Transference is common in the therapeutic process, and it is essential that you understand what transference means and that you know how to deal with it ethically and effectively. In developing your own integrative approach, you will need to conceptualize a way to understand both transference on a client's part and your reactions to the client's transference with you—or your countertransference.

In psychodynamic approaches, transference and countertransference are viewed as central to the therapy process. An unconscious process, *transference* typically has its origins in the client's early childhood, and it constitutes a repetition of past conflicts. Because of this unfinished business, the client perceives the counselor in a distorted way. When these reactions and feelings of the client are transferred to the counselor, the intensity of the feelings have more to do with unresolved issues in the client's life than to the present counseling situation. For example, the client may transfer unresolved feelings toward a stern and unloving father to the therapist, who, in the client's eyes, becomes stern and unloving. Or the client may develop a positive transference and seek the love, acceptance, and approval of an all-powerful therapist. A central part of psychoanalytic therapy involves the therapist becoming a psychological substitute for significant others.

Transference allows clients to understand and resolve unfinished business from these past relationships through the present relationship with the therapist.

In essence, working through a similar emotional conflict in the therapeutic relationship counteracts the effects of a client's early negative experiences. Reflect on these questions: Do you remember times in your personal counseling when you experienced transference toward your counselor? What was this like for you? What did your counselor do that was helpful to you? If you have not been in personal counseling, think about transference reactions you have experienced toward authority figures such as teachers, employers, and supervisors. What were some of the reactions you had toward them? What might have been useful to you in understanding and dealing with these reactions so that you could perceive these individuals more realistically?

The psychoanalytic model offers the oldest perspective for grasping the implications of both transference and countertransference, and these concepts are a basic part of my integrative approach. Altman (2008) contrasts the classical psychoanalytic model with the contemporary relational model of psychoanalytic therapy. In classical psychoanalysis the analyst remains outside the relationship and strives for a detached and objective stance from which to make observations and interpretations of the client's psychodynamics. In contrast, the immediacy of the therapeutic relationship is much more central in the contemporary relational approach to psychoanalytic therapy. The modern analytic model recognizes that the participation of the therapist in the therapeutic process cannot be eliminated.

All interventions that therapists make involve elements of their subjective experiences as well as their objective observations. Furthermore, clients influence the experience of therapists as well as vice versa. In the contemporary relational model, basic concepts such as transference and countertransference pertain to a more general mode of here-and-now interactions within the therapeutic situation. Transference may be the result of the client's interpretation of the therapist's behavior and is not necessarily a distortion carried over from the client's past. Likewise, countertransference may be influenced by the therapist's unresolved conflicts from other past or present relationships rather than being tied to any feature of the relationship with the client. The therapist's unconscious emotional responses to the client may result in a distorted perception of the client's behavior. In the broad sense, *countertransference* can be thought of as any projections that can potentially get in the way of the therapist helping the client, whereas *transference* can be described as any feelings clients project onto their counselor, whether the source of these feelings is in past or present relationships.

Psychoanalytic practitioners consider the transference situation to be valuable because its manifestations provide clients with the opportunity to reexperience a variety of feelings that would otherwise be inaccessible. Transference also provides many clues to here-and-now interactions between therapist and client. Transference can be understood and worked with in other therapy systems as well. I mention this so that you do not get the picture that the only way of understanding and exploring transference in the therapeutic relationship is via the psychoanalytic route.

Reality therapy, rational emotive behavior therapy, and behavior therapy do not have a framework for addressing transference and countertransference.

Reality therapy, as taught by William Glasser (1998, 2001), rejects the concept of transference. Since the inception of reality therapy, Glasser has consistently maintained that reality therapists should make no effort to be anyone but themselves. He contends that transference is a way for people to avoid taking personal responsibility in the present.

Rational emotive behavior therapists tend to take a dim view of working with transference phenomena. According to Ellis (1999), transference is not encouraged, and when it does occur, the therapist is likely to confront it. The therapist wants to show that a transference relationship is based on the irrational belief that the client must be liked and loved by the therapist (or parent figure). Ellis believes that devoting any length of time to reliving earlier traumatic situations or exploring transference feelings is "indulgence therapy," which might result in clients feeling better, but will rarely aid them in getting better.

Although cognitive behavior therapists may not use the terms "transference" and "countertransference," I think many of them recognize that these phenomena do occur in the therapeutic relationship and they address these issues. Cognitive behavioral practitioners place considerable emphasis on the working alliance and a collaborative partnership. When there are ruptures in this working alliance, especially when they are due to what is going on in the here-and-now therapeutic interaction, CBT practitioners would be inclined to discuss any factors that might be impeding the therapeutic relationship.

The Connection Between Transference and Countertransference

Your clients will bring past reactions to significant others and place them on you in the present. A client may view you with a mixture of positive and negative feelings, and at different times the same client may express love, affection, resentment, rage, dependence, and ambivalence. Transference can be a path that enables clients to gain insight into how they operate in a wide range of relationships. Clients may experience transference with many people, not just with you as their counselor.

The psychoanalytic perspective holds that it is essential for you as a therapist not only to know your clients, but also to know yourself. One way of attaining this self-knowledge is to monitor and reflect upon your behavior in the context of the here-and-now interactions with your clients. Be attentive to your own reactions toward clients and how you work with them therapeutically. The transference reactions your clients have toward you will very likely evoke reactions in you as a counselor. These reactions can become problematic if they result in countertransference. It is important to be alert to the possibility of countertransference so that "your problem" does not become your client's problem. However, if you can recognize and monitor your countertransference, this phenomenon does not have to be a destructive aspect in the therapeutic relationship. In fact, as Levenson (2010) points out, from the viewpoint of time-limited psychodynamic therapy, *interactive countertransference* can be viewed as a more universal reaction to the client's dynamics. Levenson maintains that the therapist's internal and external reactions often provide important sources of information for understanding the client's lifelong dysfunctional patterns and his or her dynamics. From this vantage point, the therapist's countertransference can be used to further therapeutic gains rather than being an impediment to the progress of therapy.

Working With Transference Therapeutically

Put yourself in the role of a counselor as you read this section. What kind of client behaviors will be particularly challenging for you? Reflect on a client's transference toward you and how you are likely to deal with these reactions. When you encounter clients whom you perceive as being problematic, do not put the exclusive focus on them. Rather than zeroing in on problematic behaviors manifested by your clients, reflect on your reactions to your clients. See what these reactions tell you, both about yourself and about your client. Here are some examples of transference situations you are likely to encounter with clients whom you counsel. Ask yourself what your response might be to a client's feelings toward you, and what feelings are likely to be evoked in you.

❧ Clients Who Make You Into Something You Are Not   Some clients will want you to be a parent substitute for them. They may see you as a savior who will take care of them and solve all their problems. They see you as an all-knowing person who will provide them with answers. Other clients may immediately distrust you because you remind them of a former spouse, a critical parent, or some other important figure in their life. Some clients will not let themselves get emotionally close to you because they feel that as children they were abandoned by people they cared for. Clients who feel their parents did not care for them and who felt abandoned may be very careful about letting you into their lives.

❧ Clients Who See You as Perfect   A client may use superlative adjectives to describe you. Consider a client who sees you as always understanding and supportive. He is sure that you have the ideal family and cannot imagine that you might have any personal difficulties. He credits you with the changes he is making in his counseling with you. How would you deal with this client and all the adulation that he is directing toward you?

❧ Clients Who Become Excessively Dependent on You   Some clients may not make decisions without first finding out what you think. They want to call you at any time of the day or night. They may want to run over the allotted time for their session. Dependent clients may view you as all knowing and all wise. They are convinced that you have the right answers for them and at the same time never think of finding their own answers. They are likely to want you to affirm them and convince them that they are special in your eyes.

You can inadvertently foster client dependence in subtle way. Even though you may intellectually understand the value of promoting autonomy, there may be payoffs for encouraging dependence. For example, if your clients depend on you and tell you how important your input is to them, this can reinforce your need for feeling important and for being needed. Do you have any needs that could be met by allowing certain clients to develop dependence on you? How can you monitor this situation?

🌸 Clients Who Are Not Able to Accept Boundaries

Some clients have problems understanding or accepting appropriate boundaries. Much of their behavior within the counseling relationship may be aimed at testing you so that they know how far they can go with you. Some of your clients may transgress therapeutic boundaries and want to enter into a friendship or develop some kind of social relationship with you. Wanting more than a client–therapist relationship can be a manifestation of transference. As children, these clients knew no boundaries, and now they are likely to be lost and to feel anxious because they are not certain where they stand with you. In working with such clients, it is essential not to fall into the trap of allowing them to treat you as they did a parent. One way you can do this is by being clear about your own boundaries. Know your role and function in the therapeutic relationship, and avoid relaxing appropriate boundaries so as to be liked by your clients.

🌸 Clients Who Displace Anger Onto You

Some clients will strike out at you with displaced anger. These clients are likely to tell you that because you are supposed to be helping them you have no right to express your own feelings. Recognize that you are probably getting more of this client's anger than you deserve. Avoid getting into a debate. If you take what you are getting too personally, you are bound to begin to react defensively, and possibly with countertransference.

🌸 Clients Who Fall in Love With You

Some clients will make you the object of their affection. They may see you as the ideal person and want very much to become a person just like you. They are convinced that they could find a resolution to their problems if only they found a person like you who would love and accept them. How might you respond to being the object of adulation? This may be an appropriate time for self-disclosure on your part. For example, if you feel uncomfortable with accolades being showered on you by clients, you can share with them that it is difficult to hear some of what they are telling you. For example, you might say: "I do appreciate your liking and valuing me, yet at times I become uncomfortable with it. At times I sense that you perceive me as being without faults. By elevating me as high up as you do, it is likely that at some point I will fall far short of your expectations. That can be a very difficult moment for both of us."

These few illustrations of transference behaviors demonstrate how essential it is for you to gain awareness of your own needs and motivations. Dealing with which of these transference behaviors would require the most skill? If you became entangled in a client's transference reactions, how open would you be to seeking supervision or personal therapy? If you are unaware of your own dynamics, you might tie into your clients' projections and get lost in their distortions. You are likely to avoid focusing on key therapeutic issues and instead focus on defending yourself. If you understand your own reactions to clients, you'll have a better frame of reference for understanding their reactions to you.

As you reflect on ways that you may be emotionally triggered in working with certain clients, think about how you are affected by those clients you perceive as being especially difficult. How do you respond to the different forms of transference? What kind of transference tends to elicit intense emotional reactions on your part? Do you take intense reactions of a client in a personal way? Do you blame yourself for not being skillful enough? Do you become combative with clients who project a range of feelings toward you?

When clients appear to work very hard at getting you to push them away, it can be therapeutically useful to explore what they are getting from this self-defeating behavior or how what they are doing serves them. You might say to such a client: "You know, I would very much like to work with you. Sometimes I get the sense that you are trying hard to get me not to like you. Are you aware of trying to get me to push you away?" Handled properly in the therapeutic relationship, clients can experience and express feelings toward you that more properly belong to others who have been significant in their lives. When these feelings are productively explored, clients become aware of how they are keeping old patterns functional in their present relationships.

It is a mistake to think that all feelings your clients have toward you are signs of transference. Clients may become realistically angry with you because of something you have done or not done. Their anger does not have to be an exaggerated response triggered by past situations. If you are consistently late for sessions, for example, clients may become upset with you over not giving them the time and respect they deserve. Their reactions may well be justified and should not be "explained away" as a mere expression of transference.

Likewise, clients' affection toward you does not always indicate transference. Perhaps some clients genuinely like your traits and enjoy being with you. You can err both by being too willing to accept unconditionally whatever clients tell you and by interpreting everything they tell you as a sign of transference. In short, it is difficult to identify certain reactions as being rooted either in transference or in reality.

Addressing Countertransference Issues

The other side of transference is *countertransference*—unrealistic reactions you might have toward your clients that may interfere with your objectivity. It is important for you to consider countertransference as a potential source of difficulty that may develop between you and a person with whom you are working. You do not have to be problem-free, but it is crucial that you be aware of how your own problems can affect the quality of your working relationships with clients.

Simply having feelings toward a client does not automatically mean that you are having countertransference reactions. You may feel deep empathy and compassion for some of your clients as a function of their life situations. Countertransference occurs when your needs become too much a part of the relationship or when your clients trigger old wounds of yours. Just as your clients will have some unrealistic reactions to you and will project onto you some of their unfinished business, so will you have some unrealistic reactions to them. Your own vulnerabilities will be opened up as you are drawn into some of the transference reactions of those you help. Norcross and Guy (2007) suggest that practitioners would do well to "leave their clients at the office." Learning to manage our reactions to clients who exhibit problematic behavior is an essential aspect of self-care.

Although your countertransference has the potential for getting in the way of working effectively with certain clients, this does not mean that all countertransference is problematic or necessarily harmful. Countertransference can have both positive and negative effects on the counseling process. Countertransference becomes problematic when it is not recognized, understood, monitored, and managed. Recognizing countertransference is the most important first step in learning how to manage it. If your own needs or unresolved personal conflicts become entangled in your professional relationships and blur your sense of objectivity, you have lost control and your countertransference reactions will probably interfere with the client's capacity to change. Hayes, Gelso, and Hummel (2011) consider countertransference to be inevitable because all therapists have unresolved conflicts, personal vulnerabilities, and unconscious "soft spots" that are activated through their professional work. Monitor your feelings during therapy sessions, and use your responses as a source for increased self-awareness. Doing so will help you to better understand your clients and so you can help them come to a deeper understanding of themselves.

Your countertransference reactions can teach you a great deal about yourself. Be alert to the subtle signs of countertransference, and do not be too quick to pin the blame for your reactions on your clients. For example, you may find that certain clients evoke a parental response in you. Their behavior can bring out your own critical responses to them. Knowing this about yourself will enable you to work through some of your own projections or places where you get stuck.

If you use your own feelings as a way of understanding yourself, your client, and the relationship between the two of you, these feelings can be a positive and healing force. Even though you may be insightful and self-aware, the demands of the counseling profession are great. The emotionally intense relationships that develop with your clients can be expected to bring your unresolved conflicts to the surface. Because countertransference may be a form of identification with your client, you can get lost in the client's world. When you become entangled in your client's dynamics, you limit your ability to be a therapeutic agent. If you become aware of certain symptoms—such as a strong aversion to certain types of clients or a strong attraction to other types of clients—seek consultation, participate in supervision, or enter your own therapy for a time to work out these personal issues that stand in the way of your clinical effectiveness. Making use of personal therapy and clinical supervision can be most helpful to you in better understanding how your internal reactions influence the therapy process and how you can use your countertransference reactions to further the progress of therapy (Hayes et al., 2011).

You will not be able to eliminate countertransference altogether, but you can learn to recognize it and deal nondefensively with whatever your clients evoke in you. Your own supervision is a central factor in learning how to deal effectively with both transference and countertransference reactions. Your blind spots can easily hamper your ability to deal with "difficult clients" or with your own old wounds. Focus on yourself in your supervision sessions rather than talking exclusively about a client's problem. Spend some time exploring your thoughts, feelings, and reactions toward certain clients. A good way to expand your awareness of potential countertransference is by talking with colleagues and supervisors about your feelings toward clients. This is essential if you feel stuck and don't quite know what to do in some of your sessions.

Self-knowledge is your most basic tool in dealing effectively with transference and countertransference. It is good to remember that being instrumental in the changes your clients are making will certainly influence you. If you are reluctant to acknowledge your own personal problems, it will be difficult for you to challenge clients to work through their transference issues.

Self-Disclosure in the Therapeutic Relationship

The traditional or classical model of psychoanalytic therapy discourages therapists from engaging in self-disclosure in the therapeutic relationship. Therapists functioning from a classical psychoanalytic model typically assume an anonymous stance, sometimes called the "blank-screen" approach, engaging in very little self-disclosure and maintaining a sense of neutrality. By doing so, therapists are attempting to foster a transference relationship in which their clients will make projections onto them. If the therapist reveals little and rarely shares personal reactions, it is assumed that whatever the client feels toward the therapist is largely the result of projections associated with other significant figures from the past. These projections, which have their origins in unfinished and repressed situations, are considered the very essence of the psychoanalytic endeavor. As we have seen, contemporary relational psychoanalytic therapy assumes that the therapeutic relationship is of central importance in terms of facilitating client change. The contemporary relational version allows for appropriate self-disclosure on the part of the therapist, especially his or her reactions to what is happening within the here and now of the therapeutic situation.

Many therapeutic models do not call for therapist detachment and remaining anonymous. In fact, person-centered therapy, existential therapy, and Gestalt therapy call on counselors to engage in appropriate self-disclosure as a way of creating an authentic relationship. Indeed, therapy is seen as an I/Thou encounter in which both counselor and client are deeply affected. Many cognitive behavior therapists, reality therapists, feminist therapists, and family therapists make use of self-disclosure as a basic procedure and relationship tool. A certain degree of self-disclosure to your clients is one way to diminish their projections of unrealistic reactions toward you. If you are not a mysterious figure and your clients know something about you, they are less likely to make up scenarios about you in fantasy.

From the person-centered approach I appreciate the emphasis given to immediacy and to an open discussion of how both parties are experiencing the therapeutic relationship. Perhaps the most important type of self-disclosure is the kind of here-and-now immediacy that focuses on what is transpiring between you and your client. This could be especially useful in cases in which clients are involved in a transference relationship with you. If you are having a difficult time listening to a client, for example, it could be useful to share this information. You might say: "I've noticed at times that it's very difficult for me to stay connected to what you're telling me. I'm with you when you talk about yourself and your own feelings, but I tend to get lost as you go into great detail about all the things your daughter is doing or not doing." In this statement the client is not being labeled or judged, but you are giving your reactions about what you hear when your client tells stories about others. Letting clients know how you are perceiving and experiencing them is an important form of immediacy. Selectively discussing some of your reactions toward them may be useful, especially if you encourage clients to discuss the feedback you give them.

Although I caution against indiscriminately revealing your personal problems to your clients, sharing yourself can be a powerful intervention in making contact with your clients. Judging the appropriate amount of self-disclosure can be a problem for even seasoned counselors. In determining the appropriateness of self-disclosure, consider *what* to reveal, *when* to reveal, and *how much* to reveal. Either disclosing too little or disclosing too much can be problematic. If you try too hard to be genuine and self-revealing, you may burden your client with inappropriate personal details. It is critical that what you reveal is appropriate and timely, and that it is done for a client's benefit. If your feelings are very much in the foreground and inhibit you from fully attending to a client, it may be helpful for you and your client if you share how you are being affected. To determine if your self-disclosures are in the service of a client, ask yourself these questions:

- What motivated me to disclose?
- To what extent do my disclosures help clients talk more honestly and specifically about themselves?
- Does what I share about myself with clients help them put their problems into a new perspective or help them consider new alternatives for action?
- To what extent is my self-disclosing helping clients translate their insights into new behavior?

I want to emphasize that self-disclosure does not mean telling clients detailed stories about your personal past or present problems. Too much sharing of yourself can easily distract both you and your clients from productive self-exploration. Sometimes merely letting clients know that you have similar personal issues or similar feelings about a life situation, without going into elaborate detail, is very healing for them. Your disclosure can help them accept some of their reactions as normal and can result in a sense of being understood by you. Admittedly, you are vulnerable when you share your own experiences, feelings, and reactions. Yet can you expect your clients to be willing to be vulnerable in front of you if you remain unknown?

Becoming the Client: The Value of Personal Therapy

In this section I encourage you to consider the value of experiencing your own personal therapy. By becoming a client you will learn about yourself personally and also acquire a great deal of knowledge and skill that you can apply as a professional. I believe it is very important that you have the experience of being a client at some time, if for no other reason than to learn to appreciate the courage and persistence it takes to be on the receiving end of the therapy process. In your personal therapy you may experience transference and thus know firsthand how it is to view your therapist as a parent figure. Making use of personal therapy could be an extremely valuable resource, both as a way to resolve some of your personal issues and as way to increase your self-awareness and ability to work with others. Your own therapy provides you with an avenue to explore and process your countertransference reactions to clients.

Personal counseling is useful in helping you recognize how you may overidentify with certain clients, how you might meet some of your needs at the expense of your clients, and how control issues may be played out between you and a client. I am convinced that to the extent that you have not dealt with your past problems or unresolved interpersonal conflicts, these issues will influence your reactions to your clients. If you have not explored your own pain over certain events in your life, you may be carried away on a client's emotional tidal wave. A commitment to working on your own current and past problems is a crucial part of self-care. It is essential to remember that your degree of self-care is directly related to your effectiveness as a therapist.

There will always be residual feelings attached to certain events you've experienced in your life, and you will have your own sources of vulnerability. However, you can become aware of the signs of these reactions and can deal with these feelings in your own therapy and supervision sessions. Over time, you can begin to use your countertransference reactions to become more sensitively attuned to your client's experiences.

You should be aware of what your conflicts are and how they are likely to affect you as a counselor. It is critical for you to recognize and express yourself when you are triggered. For example, if you have great difficulty in dealing with anger, chances are that you will do something to dilute these emotions when they occur in your clients. If you are extremely uncomfortable with conflict and find yourself withdrawing in the face of conflict, it is a good bet that you are likely to find ways to skirt around conflict, even when your clients bring up conflicts they are having outside of the session. If you have not allowed yourself to grieve over some significant loss, you may find it challenging to remain present with clients when they are dealing with feelings surrounding loss and grief. How can you be present for your clients and encourage them to express feelings that you are so intent on denying in yourself?

Through being a client yourself, you have an experiential frame of reference from which to view yourself as you are. It gives you a basis for compassion for your clients, for you can draw on your own memories of reaching impasses in therapy, of both wanting to go further and at the same time wanting to stay where you were. Being willing to participate in a process of self-exploration can reduce the chances of assuming an attitude of arrogance. Even if your program does not require any form of personal counseling, I hope you will find ways to avail yourself of therapeutic experiences. Through various therapeutic modes, such as individual and group counseling, you can come to a better understanding of how you operate in your interpersonal world. Indeed, experiencing counseling as a client is very different from merely reading about counseling theories and techniques. By reflecting on your own experience as a client, you can identify aspects of the counseling process that are foundational. You will learn what attitudes and behaviors of therapists actually facilitate working through resistance with clients. This personal and experiential dimension can only enhance your knowledge and skill base in the process of becoming a counselor.

For more information on the topic of personal therapy for mental health practitioners, I highly recommend *The Psychotherapist's Own Psychotherapy: Patient and Clinician Perspectives* (Geller, Norcross, & Orlinsky, 2005). For an excellent discussion of therapist self-care, I recommend *Leaving It at the Office: A Guide to Psychotherapist Self-Care* (Norcross & Guy, 2007).

Working With Transference and Countertransference With Ruth

See Session 10 (Working With Transference and Countertransference) on the *DVD for Integrative Counseling: The Case of Ruth and Lecturettes.*

Ruth displays reactions toward me that can be described as transference. Consider these statements that Ruth made to me in a session: "No matter how hard I try, I'm not able to please you. I'm not doing something right. I feel you are critical of me. You are judging me, and I'm not enough, just like with my Dad. I feel that I can't please you or meet your expectations. You must be disappointed that I'm taking so long to get better." Because Ruth brought up these reactions, I think there is therapeutic merit in encouraging her to express herself in some detail. At some point in the session I might ask her to explore connections she is making between her father and me, especially if it is apparent that transference is occurring.

What about my part in this relationship? If I deal with Ruth's transference reactions toward me appropriately, this can be an avenue of increased self-understanding on her part. However, it is essential that I monitor my potential countertransference. The assumptions she makes about me might well strike a sensitive chord for me, as indeed it did in this session. If I am caught up in my own countertransference, I might respond defensively and become irritated. I am aware that I tend to get impatient and defensive when clients tell me how I am and then treat me on the basis of their perceptions—without including me in this checking-out process. If Ruth continues to make conclusions about who I am and what I think of her without including me in this process, I am likely to feel misunderstood or unappreciated by her. Then I might become caught up in justifying my position or protecting myself. If I am expending a great deal of energy defending myself, I will not be able to deal with her reactions in a therapeutic manner.

However, in the session under discussion, I recognize my own vulnerability and I let her know how I am affected by hearing what she is saying and how it affects me when I feel judged by her. If I can suspend my tendency to convince Ruth that I am different from the person she is perceiving me to be, we can work through this transference. If she were to say to me "I can't imagine that you'd want to invest the energy and time in really listening to my pain or really understanding me," I could respond with "I'd like to hear more about how you came to this conclusion about me." I invite more exploration of the transference rather than negating it.

I also engage in self-disclosure and let Ruth know that some of her feelings of "not being enough" touched me personally. Operating on the assumption that I can actually use my personal reactions in a therapeutic manner by appropriately disclosing to Ruth, I tell her: "There are times when I also feel that I am not enough. When I am told how I am, and when I feel judged, this taps into old issues for me. When I am extending myself and feel that I am not appreciated, it is easy for me to tell myself that I am being judged as inadequate." Disclosing this opened up a dialogue that she could use to reflect on her experience in therapy. Later in the session, I tell Ruth that I do not always say the right thing, nor am I always as sensitive as I might be. I admit that perhaps some of my shortcomings make it difficult for me to acknowledge the work that she has done in these sessions. My self-disclosure had an impact on Ruth, for she becomes silent and then gets teary. I ask her to talk about the tears. She indicates that she is surprised that I am not blaming her and that I am willing to consider my part in how she is perceiving and reacting to me. One of Ruth's fears is that I would tell her that what she is telling me is just about her father. Furthermore, that we both had in common the struggle with feeling enough personally was affirming for her to hear.

It is critically important that I am increasingly able to recognize countertransference patterns in myself and that I take steps to monitor my reactions. I certainly need to be cognizant of the ways my reactions could blur my vision and hamper my effectiveness with Ruth. Through supervision, and perhaps personal therapy, I can learn to identify and accept some immediate reactions that are stirred up inside me when I feel judged or negatively evaluated. It may not be important or appropriate for me to share this with my client, but knowing myself is critical in maintaining a sense of objectivity.

Working With Transference With Stan

See Session 2 (Psychoanalytic Therapy) on the *DVD* *for Theory and Practice of Counseling and Psychotherapy:* *The Case of Stan and Lecturettes.*

In this session, Stan lets me know that he likes working with me and looks forward to his therapy sessions. He is also aware that he wants my approval and wonders if he is meeting my expectations. He is concerned that he is not a "good client" at times, and he worries about what I think of him. Stan shares that if he says too much about himself it might come back to haunt him later. He claims that in the past he has been burned by being too honest and by saying too much about himself, especially with people in his family. He perceives his father as being stern and critical. He never has been able to have the relationship with his dad that he wants. In some ways, Stan views me in similar ways as he does his father. I, too, might be critical, harsh, and judgmental. Stan is bringing his past history into his relationship with me as his therapist. He admits that he feels and behaves in my presence in many ways as he does with his father. His transference reactions to me can be most beneficial in gaining a further understanding of his dynamics, including early wounding with significant others. It allows us to understand his vulnerability with respect to being judged and his struggle to measure up to expectations. Exploring his feelings toward me, and what he is attributing to me, can lead to insights regarding unresolved conflicts with his father. I frequently suggest to Stan that he talk about his perceptions of me and share his experience of being in therapy. In many ways, Stan's father is very much alive within him, and he is making others into his father. I ask Stan to free-associate to the word "father," which he does but in a censored way. Still, this technique gives us further information about the central role of his father in his life and provides clues that we explore in more depth.

Practicing within a psychoanalytic model, I view Stan's transference as providing valuable clues in the here-and-now interactions between us. The transference situation allows Stan an opportunity to reexperience a variety of feelings that would otherwise be inaccessible, and it also allows him to understand and deal with unfinished business from his past relationships. By productively exploring his transference reactions, Stan can gain insight into how he is keeping old patterns functioning in his present relationships. Given how therapeutically valuable it is to explore all the manifestations of transference, this becomes a key part of the work that Stan and I do together.

Concluding Comments

I encourage you to reflect on how you might be affected by the intensity of your professional work. If you can remain open to identifying and exploring areas of your countertransference, this will surely influence your ability to function effectively with others. As this chapter has demonstrated, being able to deal therapeutically with clients' reactions to you is a major challenge in the client–therapist relationship. It is imperative for you to recognize and deal with internal conflicts and past pain that are triggered by your work as a counselor.

The emotionally intense relationships we develop with clients can be expected to tap into our own vulnerability. Our clients' stories and pain are bound to affect us, and we need to find some way to deal with what is opened up for us. We don't have to numb ourselves to the pain experienced by our clients, and, indeed, we can be touched by their stories and express compassion and empathy. However, we have to realize that it is their pain and not carry it *for* them lest we become overwhelmed by their life stories and render ourselves ineffective in working with them.

After reading this chapter on working with transference and countertrans-ference, take time to reflect on the following questions as a way of clarifying your thoughts on how these concepts may be used therapeutically in counseling practice.

- What is your understanding of the concept of transference?
- What value do you place on working with transference in the therapeutic relationship?
- What is your understanding of countertransference?
- If you became aware of countertransference reactions to a client, what course of action would you be inclined to take?
- What value do you see in therapist self-disclosure?
- What are your thoughts about requiring (or recommending) psychotherapy for those studying to become counselors?
- What value do you place on receiving your own personal therapy?
- How is therapist self-care related to a therapist's ability to provide effective services to clients?

CHAPTER ELEVEN

Understanding How the Past Influences the Present and the Future

Introduction

Some approaches, such as reality therapy, behavior therapy, rational emotive behavior therapy, cognitive therapy, and solution-focused brief therapy, do not examine the historical determinants of behavior. Their premise is that present conditions, rather than traumas or faulty learning during early childhood years, influence clients' problems, and that cognitive and behavioral techniques can change the relevant current factors that influence clients' behaviors. However, I believe that the past offers a context for understanding and dealing with a client's present cognitive, emotional, and behavioral difficulties.

Understanding How the Past, Present, and Future Are Intertwined

Bringing the Past Into the Present

The psychoanalytic model holds that the shadow of the past can haunt the present, and I continue to see the vital connection between the past and the present in the work I do. Typical problems that people bring to counseling include an inability to freely give and accept love; difficulty recognizing and dealing with feelings such as anger, resentment, rage, hatred, and aggression; an inability to direct one's own life; difficulty separating from one's parents and becoming a unique person; a need for and a fear of intimacy; and difficulty accepting one's own sexual identity. From the psychoanalytic perspective, these problems of adult living have their origin in early development. Early learning is not irreversible, but to change its effects we must become aware of how certain early experiences have contributed to our present personality functioning. I have incorporated these basic psychoanalytic concepts in my personal integrative approach to counseling.

A common misconception about psychoanalytic therapy is that it resembles an archaeologist digging out relics from the past, dwelling on the past to the exclusion of present concerns. Kernberg (1997) indicates that there is an increasing interest by contemporary psychoanalytic therapists in focusing on the unconscious meanings in the here and now before attempting to reconstruct the past. Among the contemporary psychoanalytic therapists are those who subscribe to object-relations theory and view the internal and external world of relationships as central to therapy. The object-relations model of therapy is largely based on the early relations of a child and mother and how this early relationship shapes the child's inner world and later adult relationships. As the therapist moves back and forth in time, the aim is to understand how early patterns are repeated in the present. Modern psychodynamic practitioners are interested in their clients' past, but they intertwine that understanding with the present. From a relational analytic perspective, there is a shift from focusing on the there and then to the here and now, which allows therapeutic work to proceed in a more enlivened and accelerated way (Levenson, 2010).

Insight can be a vehicle that enables clients to relinquish old behaviors from the past that intrude into the present. It is useful for clients to understand and use historical data in their therapy, but they also need to be aware of the pitfalls of getting lost in their past by recounting endless and irrelevant details of their early experiences. A preoccupation with the past can be uselessly time consuming and can inhibit progress, as well as being a form of resistance. Discussion centering on childhood events is less useful than dealing with the past in relation to here-and-now interactions between client and therapist.

Envisioning the Future

Our vision of our future can have an impact on our present functioning, just as our past can. Beitman, Soth, and Good (2006) claim that we are influenced to think, feel, and act through our images of our future: "Psychotherapy integration is achieved when therapists and clients collaborate to reshape problematic expectations of the future images that are based on the debris of the past" (pp. 43–44). A number of therapeutic approaches emphasize future strivings. Along with valuing the Gestalt and psychodrama approaches for dealing with the future, I find a number of useful concepts in narrative therapy, solution-focused therapy, Adlerian therapy, reality therapy, and existential therapy—all of which have concepts dealing with future aspirations.

Solution-oriented therapy eschews the past and emphasizes the present and, especially, the future. It is so focused on what is possible that it has little interest in or understanding of the client's problem. DeShazer (1991) has suggested that therapists do not need to know a problem to solve it and that there is no necessary relationship between problems and their solutions. By focusing on the future and using techniques such as the miracle question (deShazer & Dolan, 2007), solution-focused therapists encourage clients to move toward their vision of a better life.

Narrative therapy is both present-centered and future oriented. The therapist believes that clients have abilities, talents, positive intentions, and life experiences that can be the catalysts for new possibilities for future action. The counselor needs to demonstrate faith that these strengths and competencies can be identified, even when the client is having difficulty seeing them. A narrative therapist is likely to ask a client to speculate about what kind of future could be expected from the strong, competent person that is emerging. As the client becomes free of problem-saturated stories of the past, he or she can envision and plan for a less problematic future.

Both solution-focused and narrative therapists rely on questioning as the centerpiece of therapy. Open-ended questions about the client's attitudes, thoughts, feeling, behaviors, and perceptions are one of the main interventions in these therapies. Especially useful are future-oriented questions that challenge clients to think about how they are likely to solve potential problems they encounter in the future. In narrative therapy, *unique possibility questions* enable clients to consider future possibilities and to reflect upon what they have achieved in the present. Based on their successes, they can consider what their next steps might be. Here are some examples:

- Given your present discoveries and understandings, what do you think your next steps might be?
- Having observed people responding in a supportive manner to your self-caring, what plans do you have for yourself to not let go of your ability to nurture yourself?
- Now that you are prepared to question and reexamine the direction your life is taking, what does this behavior suggest to you about the personal qualities and abilities you are exhibiting right now?

I very much agree with the Adlerian premise that clients can be understood best by looking at where they are going and what they are striving to accomplish. Adlerians are interested in the future, but they do not minimize the importance of past influences. They assume that our decisions are based on our experiences, on the present situation, and on the direction in which we are moving. I appreciate the perspective of the Adlerians, who look for continuity, or a pattern, in life. Adlerians look for this continuity in the client's lifestyle, which reveals ways the past is still operating in the present.

Becoming the Client: Examining Your Past, Present, and Future

We have looked at how the past, present, and future are inseparable. Now would be a good time for you to consider how your own past is affecting your present and ways that your past experiences could influence your future. In this section I ask you to "become a client," and I encourage you to reflect on the personal applications of dealing with your past, present, and future. Your past experiences have implications for who you are now. What you are striving to become also has implications for the person you are today. Your past is still alive in the person you are today, and it can influence your future direction. As your therapist, I ask you to reflect on the following questions:

- What themes stemming from your childhood are still a part of your personality today?
- What unresolved conflicts from your childhood get in the way of your enjoyment? To what extent do your present behavior or current problems indicate areas of unfinished business?
- What events occurred during your childhood or adolescence that you might bring into your personal counseling sessions?
- Is there a significant person in your life that you would like to bring into this session? Are you willing to engage in a role-play session with me acting as that person?
- What value do you see in reexperiencing some difficult situation you have been through earlier and talking about how you are feeling in the moment in therapy?

Think of one particular relationship in your life right now that you'd like to improve. Imagine that you are having a dialogue with that person one year from now. What would you most want to say to him or her? What would you most hope to hear from this person?

Exploring your vision of your future would certainly be a factor in my work with you. How valuable do you think that imagining yourself in the future might be for you personally? The miracle question, a technique often used in solution-focused brief therapy, is one way I help you clarify your future goals and strivings. In our therapy session, I ask, "If a miracle happened and the problem you have was solved overnight, how would you know it was solved, and what would be different?" I then encourage you to enact "what would be different" in spite of the perceived problems. By formulating this future perspective, you are focusing on what you want in your life and how you can go about getting it.

Working With Ruth's Past, Present, and Future

See Session 11 (Understanding How the Past Influences the Present and the Future) on the *DVD for Integrative Counseling: The Case of Ruth and Lecturettes.*

🐾 **Dealing With the Past in an Integrative Style**   Utilizing my integrative approach to counseling Ruth, I am interested in understanding and exploring (within the restrictions of our time frame) her early history and assisting her in gaining insight into how her past connects to some of the problems she is experiencing today. When the past seems to have a significant bearing on Ruth's present attitudes or behavior, we bring it into the present as much as possible through the use of Gestalt techniques. I heavily construct my integrative practice around Gestalt therapy concepts as a way to illuminate the connections between the past and the present.

When Ruth speaks about a past event, I ask her to bring whatever feelings surface into the present by reliving them through a variety of role-playing techniques. This is more potent than merely talking about past events. For example, I suggest to her that she become the hurt child and talk directly to her father in fantasy. I say: "Bring your father into this room now, and let yourself go back to the time when you were a child. Tell him now, as though he were here and you were that child, what you most want to say." By paying attention to what is occurring moment by moment with Ruth, I get additional clues as to how best to intervene. She may now say all the things she wanted to say to her father as a child but, because of her fear, kept deep inside herself. She might tell her father what she most wanted from him then and what she still wants with him now. The theoretical rationale for most of these techniques is rooted in the assumption that the emotions that were overwhelming to her as a child were dealt with by some form of distortion or denial. By reliving an experience as though it were happening now, emotions that were repressed can come to the surface.

In the supportive, accepting, and safe therapeutic environment, Ruth can allow herself to experience feelings that she has cut off from awareness, and she can now express these feelings that are keeping her stuck. By challenging her assumptions of how her father is, she is able to establish a new basis for relating to him. Through this process, she relives the hurt, yet she also can experience understanding and resolution of a painful situation. By symbolically dealing in the here and now with people in her life with whom she feels unfinished, she can bring closure to some painful events.

Let's look at a few critical situations between Ruth and her father, along with how I intervened. One critical incident took place when she was 6 years old. She reported: "My father caught me 'playing doctor' with an 8-year-old boy. He lectured me and refused to speak to me for weeks. I felt extremely guilty and ashamed." Ruth is likely to have guilt regarding sexuality stemming from this incident.

To help her explore this past incident and how it still has a current impact, I use Gestalt methods. I ask Ruth to be herself (at the age of 6) and talk to me now (as her father). I say to her: "Imagine I'm your father, and I'm not going to say anything. I'll just listen to you. I just caught you with this neighbor boy. Tell me what is going on with you right now." As she talks, I simply listen on the assumption that what is important now is to allow her to express feelings that she has kept to herself for so long. She tells me how embarrassed, ashamed, and sorry she is for letting that happen. She is sure that I (as her father) view her as bad and dirty, that I am greatly disappointed in her, and that I won't love her anymore. It is clear that she is still affected by her past and her rigid upbringing. She is convinced that she did something very wrong in the eyes of her father and her church.

Because Ruth brings up the matter of her church, it seems an appropriate transition to move to an exploration of how her religious upbringing has a current influence on her. I suggest a second role play in which she becomes the "voice of her church," the past, and her father. I ask her to talk to me from that stance. For my own part in the role play, I assume the more accepting part and the voice that she would like to hear. She is able to get into her part with great conviction because she is saying aloud what she heard for so many years grow-ing up and what she has told herself silently. She has incorporated the critical and judgmental voice of her father and the church without really examining the validity of the messages she is receiving from either of these sources. In role-playing the "accepting side," I want to get across that "Even though I have my faults and am imperfect, I am certainly not a bad person." As Ruth's assertive side, a central message I'm striving to get across is that Dad's approval costs me my integrity: "I have been striving all my life, Dad, to get your approval. But to be what you want I have to be scared and always feel guilty. I don't want to do that anymore. To get your approval costs too much."

This gives Ruth an idea of what she would like to be able to say and really believe. She says: "I sure wish I could talk to my father that way!" We devote several sessions to discussing how her father played a central role in the moral and religious values that she believed she had to accept to stay in his "good graces." Eventually, Ruth gets the insight that she does not want to live by the religious dogma her father preached, nor does she want to accept for herself the messages he continues to give her about the "right path for living."

The two role plays we do here demonstrate working with both feelings and beliefs that have been an integral part of Ruth's being for so long. The enact-ment of these role plays brings the past into the here and now and allows her to give expression to beliefs and feelings that have roots in her early childhood. My intervention is designed to enable her to clarify how she wants to think, feel, and believe today.

Along with Gestalt methods, I draw on concepts and techniques from psy-chodrama to help Ruth understand her past. In psychodrama, she would enact conflicts as if they were occurring in the present moment, rather than narrating past events. For instance, I could ask her: "Show me what happened when you were a young child and your father caught you with the neighborhood boy." Psychodrama offers encouragement to her to speak in the present tense and to use action words. Placing the client in the present, regardless of when the scenes actually happened, reduces verbal reporting and assists clients in di-rectly experiencing an event. When she engages in showing me what she is thinking or feeling, she moves toward concrete experiencing and cuts through defenses. She will also move away from abstract and impersonal discussions about a topic by plunging into personal enactment of a concern.

A basic tenet of psychodrama, much the same as Gestalt therapy, is that reliving and reexperiencing a scene from the past will give Ruth both the op-portunity to examine how that event affected her at the time it occurred and a chance to deal differently with the event now. By replaying a past event in the present, Ruth gains a deeper understanding of the past event and can as-sign new meaning to it. Through this process, she can work through unfinished business and develop a new and different ending to an earlier situation.

❧ Dealing With the Present in an Integrative Style   I am counseling Ruth from a present-centered perspective. Most of our discussions deal with her thoughts and beliefs, her emotional states, and what she is doing currently. Even though I am open to exploring some of her past experiences, my focus is

on examining ways that her past still has a present influence. Ruth and I can direct attention to her immediate feelings as well as to her thoughts and actions. It seems essential to me that we work with all three dimensions—what she is thinking, how her thoughts and behaviors affect her feeling states, and what she is actually doing. By directing her attention to what is going on with her during our sessions, Ruth becomes aware of how she interacts in her world apart from therapy.

🌿 Dealing With the Future in an Integrative Style

The technique of making a past situation a present one can be applied to future events as well. The rationale for doing this is the same as working with the past. If the future comes alive through enactment, there is less chance of dealing with abstractions. I frequently utilize both Gestalt and psychodrama techniques to assist clients in experiencing their hopes, fears, and expectations for the future. If Ruth is afraid of a future confrontation with her father, I ask her to live her expectations in the here and now by speaking directly to her father in a role-play situation. By expressing her fears and hopes in the safety of the therapy context, she is likely to gain clarity about what she would like to say to her father in real life. Thus, she may say in a role play to her symbolic father: "I want to tell you how much I'd like to be close to you, but I'm afraid that if I do so, it won't matter to you. I'm afraid of saying the wrong things and pushing you even further away. Sometimes I think I have disappointed you because I haven't become the person you expected."

Psychodrama is also highly useful for exploring some anticipated event in the future. In psychodrama, the past, present, and future are all significant tenses, yet the action is played out in the present moment. Psychodrama can enable Ruth to bring the future into the now: "Show me how you'd like to be able to talk with your father one year from now. Let me be your father and try on some of the things you'd like to be able to say to him."

A technique in psychodrama known as "future projection" can be appropriate in counseling Ruth, especially when she brings up wanting improvements in her significant relationships (with her husband, her children, and her parents). When I ask her to participate in living out a scenario in the future, my goal is to help her express and clarify concerns she has about the future. Her future concerns are not merely discussed, but an anticipated event is brought into the present moment and acted out. These concerns may include her wishes and hopes, fears of tomorrow, and goals that provide some direction to her life. In implementing this technique, I have her imagine a future time and place with selected people, bring this event into the present, and get a new perspective on a problem. Ruth may act out either a version of the way she hopes a given situation will ideally unfold or her version of the worst possible outcome.

Once Ruth clarifies her hopes for a particular outcome, she is in a better position to take specific steps that will enable her to achieve the future she desires. For example, she can be asked to carry on the kind of dialogue with her father that she would ideally like one year hence. A role-reversal technique can be powerful if used in a timely manner. I might suggest to her: "Let yourself become your father. You know the words you'd most like to hear from him. As your father, speak to me (as Ruth) and tell me what you wish he would say and how you would hope he would act." Through reversing roles with her father, Ruth is able to formulate significant emotional and cognitive insights into the situation involving her father. She can also project herself forward and tell him how she has acted differently toward him during the previous year. If she gets a clearer sense of the kind of relationship that she would like with him and if she accepts her own responsibility for the quality of this relationship, she can begin to modify some of the ways in which she approaches her father.

For a review of both Gestalt therapy and psychodrama, see *Theory and Practice of Group Counseling* (Corey, 2012). See also *Theory and Practice of Counseling and Psychotherapy* (Corey, 2013d) for more elaborate discussions of Gestalt therapy and existential therapy. For a more complete discussion of ways to work with Ruth's past, see *Case Approach to Counseling and Psychotherapy* (Corey, 2013a, chap. 2).

Working With Stan's Past, Present, and Future

See Session 3 (Adlerian Therapy) on the *DVD for Theory and Practice of Counseling and Psychotherapy: The Case of Stan and Lecturettes*.

In this session I work with a series of Stan's early recollections. This technique shows how a client's early memories are often connected to present-day themes.

Dealing With Stan's Past   I am very interested in exploring Stan's early history and assisting him in understanding how his past is connected to what he is doing today. I believe we can illuminate themes that run through our life if we are able to come to terms with significant experiences from our childhood. My emphasis is on having Stan begin to question the conclusions he came to about himself, others, and life. Here are a few of Stan's mistaken conclusions and self-defeating perceptions that grew out of his earlier experiences:

- If I get close to people, they will take advantage of me.
- Because my own parents didn't want me and didn't love me, I'll never be loved by anybody.
- If only I were a better person, maybe people would accept me.
- Being a man means being strong at all times.

An Adlerian perspective provides tools for doing some productive cognitive work both in and outside the therapy sessions. In this way, Stan can critically evaluate some of his basic mistakes and eventually begin to replace these mistaken conclusions with constructive notions.

One way of getting a better sense of significant events from Stan's past is to ask him to report early recollections, which I use as part of the assessment process. Early recollections are *specific* incidents that Stan can recall, along with the feelings and thoughts that accompanied these childhood incidents. These recollections are quite useful in better understanding Stan. He reports several early recollections, but one stands out most vividly. This is the time that he saw children throwing a kitten off the roof. He felt extremely sad, yet felt helpless to do anything. Stan had reported several early recollections, then we went back to this particular memory and talked about the feelings it evoked in him now as he shared it. Stan talked at some length about how he felt helpless in many situations when he was a child and how this helpless stance is part of his life today. He often reports feeling a sense of powerlessness, especially when trying to address injustices. Stan began to see that not having power as a child does not have to be a pattern in his adult life. This insight served as a point of departure for further therapeutic work.

❧ Dealing With Stan's Present In counseling Stan, I keep the focus on his present life. I am interested in his past history mainly as a way to get a richer appreciation for his present struggles. By paying attention to what is going on in the here and now during the counseling session, I get clues about what is unfinished from Stan's past. Thus, I am consistently attempting to bring Stan into the here and now, whether he is talking about something from his past or an anticipated future situation. My assumption is that power is in the present.

To assist Stan in exploring present concerns, I draw heavily from Gestalt therapy, which emphasizes moment-to-moment experiencing. Most Gestalt techniques are designed to put clients into closer contact with their ongoing experiencing and increase their awareness of what they are presently feeling. One of the most important contributions of Gestalt therapy is the emphasis on learning to appreciate and fully experience the present. The past is gone, and the future has not yet arrived, whereas the present moment is lively.

Just as there are advantages to focusing on the here and now, there can be disadvantages to this exclusive focus. Polster (1987) observes that too tight a focus, with a highly concentrated emphasis on the here and now, will foreclose on much that matters, such as continuity of commitment, the implications of one's acts, dependability, and responsiveness to others. Polster stresses the importance of having clients flesh out their stories, which may include working with the past, the present, and the future. In keeping with this framework, my work with Stan involves an integration of his past, present, and future. This involves listening to stories from his childhood and constructing a future story of his life.

❧ Dealing With Stan's Future Being influenced by the Adlerian philosophy, I operate on the assumption that Stan lives by goals and purposes, is moved by anticipation of the future, and strives to create meaning. My assumption is that working with Stan's past, present, and future are dynamically interrelated: his decisions are based on what he has experienced in the past, on his present situation, and on the goals that he is moving toward. As Stan and I look for a continuity in his life, the emphasis is on the goal-directed nature of all his behavior. From an Adlerian perspective, I am especially interested in where Stan is heading. What does Stan want for himself? If he decides that his present behavior is not getting him what he wants, he is in a good position to think ahead about the changes he would like to make and what he can do now to actualize his aspirations. The present-oriented behavioral emphasis of the action therapies is a good reference point for getting Stan to speculate on what he would like to say about his life five years hence. Once Stan has a clearer picture of the kind of future he wants, he is in a good position to formulate a systematic plan that will help him achieve his goals.

Concluding Comments

It is one thing to read about the concepts and techniques I've described in my integrative approach, but it is quite another matter to apply them to yourself. The more you are able to identify personal themes of significance associated with your past, present, and future, the greater your chance of coming to appreciate some of these concepts. If you see value in counseling clients from the perspective I've described, you are likely to find ways of using techniques aimed at bringing both past and future concerns into the present with your clients. To engage clients in experiential role-playing scenarios in the here and now, you need to feel comfortable making these interventions. Although the emphasis of this chapter has been mainly on identifying and expressing feelings, there is plenty of room for exploring cognitive and behavioral patterns associated with the past, present, and future.

After reading this chapter on understanding how the past influences the present and the future, take time to reflect on the following questions about how your own past has influenced your present and future goals.

- What are some of your past experiences that continue to influence who you are today?
- If you could revise one of the chapters of your life, how would you rewrite it?
- To what extent do you see your past as giving you an appreciation of the struggles of the clients with whom you will work?
- Consider three aspects of your current existence that you would most like to change. If you were successful in changing them, how do you imagine that your life would be different?
- What kind of life would you like to have five years from now? Are there any steps you can take now to move closer to your goals?
- How much time do you devote to thinking about future goals and aspirations? To what degree do you think that your vision of your future has an influence on how you think, feel, and act today?
- As a counselor, how do you think your own experience with your past could influence the way you work with a client?
- As a counselor, what emphasis would you place on your client's past, present, and future? Which would gain your primary focus?

CHAPTER TWELVE

Working Toward Decisions and Behavior Change

Introduction

Existential therapy is the foundation of my integrative approach to counseling, and I operate on its assumption that we each can be the architects of our own lives. If you don't like the design of your present existence, you can take steps to revise the blueprints. If you were one of my clients, I would invite you to look at your life as a plan and to evaluate the blueprints that influence who you are today.

In Chapter 11 we explored at how the past, present, and future are interrelated. These issues are closely related to the topics we now consider—early decisions and behavior change. As critical as it is for clients to understand where they've come from and to appreciate some of the motivations for their present behavior, this is only part of the story. Understanding the context of early decisions may be useful to clients in getting a better picture of their development, but self-understanding needs to lead to action if clients are to make significant behavioral change. Insight without action will not help clients make existential decisions. This chapter addresses ways of helping clients to understand their earlier decisions and to increase their capacity to make new decisions.

Understanding Redecision Therapy

Redecision therapy rests on basic concepts of injunctions, early decisions, and new decisions. Redecision therapy, developed by Mary and Robert Goulding (1979), is a form of transactional analysis (TA) that offers a useful framework for understanding how learning during childhood extends into adulthood. A key concept that forms the foundation of this therapeutic approach is the Gouldings' belief that as adults we make decisions based on past premises that at one time were appropriate to our survival but that may no longer serve us well. This approach stresses the capacity to change early decisions and is oriented toward increasing awareness, with the goal of enabling clients to alter the course of their lives. In redecision therapy, clients learn how the rules they received and incorporated as children now influence their actions.

Injunctions and Early Decisions

An injunction is a parental message that tells children what they have to do and be to get recognition and acceptance. Although some of these injunctions may be given in a verbal and direct manner by parents to children, more often than not these messages are inferred: "Don't be separate from me," "Don't be the sex you are," "Don't want," "Don't need," "Don't think," "Don't be important," "Don't feel," and "Don't be a child" (Goulding & Goulding, 1979).

When you were a child, you decided either to accept these parental messages or to fight against them. Here are a few examples of these injunctions and possible early decisions based on them. You may have heard the message "Don't talk" and decided that you have no voice. You may have accepted the injunction "Don't feel" and made an early decision that your feelings are of no value. A common message is "Don't make mistakes." If you heard and accepted this message as a child, you may fear taking risks so as not to look foolish. You might equate making mistakes with being a failure. A possible early decision you may have made is, "Because I made a dumb choice, I won't decide on anything important again!" Another common injunction is "Don't be close." Related to this injunction are the messages "Don't trust" and "Don't love." Based on these messages, you may have made a decision such as this: "I let myself trust another person by getting close, and it failed. In the future I will keep myself distant, and that way I won't risk rejection." These early decisions became a basic part of your personality. By making decisions in response to real or imagined injunctions, you have contributed to keeping some of these decisions alive. If you hope to change the impact of early messages, you must become aware of what these "oughts" and "shoulds" are and of how you allow them to operate in your life. Many of these decisions may have been appropriate in certain situations in childhood, but they are inappropriate when carried into an individual's adult years. A major part of the therapy process consists of becoming aware of messages clients may still listen to and the impact of these early decisions in present-day living.

Understanding the Influence of Your Family

Operating within the mind-set of family therapy, I would inquire about the kind of rules you experienced in your family. Family rules may be spoken or unspoken, but they are powerful influencers of how you think, feel, and act currently. These rules, which are often couched in terms of "shoulds" or "should nots," become strong messages that govern interactions within a family.

It is impossible to grow up without rules such as these: "Never be angry with your father." "Always keep a smile on your face." "Don't bring attention to yourself." "Never let people see your weaknesses; show neither love nor anger." "Don't talk back to your parents; always try to please them." "Don't talk to outsiders about your family." "Children are to be seen but not heard." "Have fun only when all the work is finished." "Don't be different from other family members." As a child, you may have decided to accept a rule and live by it for reasons of both physical and psychological survival. However, such a pattern may be self-defeating when carried into your adult interactions.

Applying Redecision Therapy to Behavior Changes

You do not have to be a victim of decisions you made in early life. You cooperated in making the early decisions that direct your life, so you can now make new decisions that are appropriate and that will allow you to experience life differently. Making an intellectual decision to be different is rarely enough to counteract years of past conditioning. It often helps to employ experiential techniques to go back to the early childhood scenes in which these decisions were made. Many of the Gestalt techniques described in Chapters 7, 9, and 11 can help you become emotionally and cognitively aware of the impact of earlier decisions and can facilitate the process of redecision.

Awareness is an important first step in the process of changing clients' ways of thinking, feeling, and behaving. In the early stages of counseling, many of the techniques are aimed at increasing clients' awareness of their problems and their options for making substantive changes in their lives. As therapy progresses, clients explore the "shoulds" and "shouldn'ts," the "dos" and "don'ts," by which they live. Once clients have identified and become aware of these "internalized voices," they are in a better position to critically examine these messages to determine whether they are willing to continue living by them.

Whatever injunctions clients have received, and whatever the resulting life decisions were, redecision therapy maintains that clients can change by making a new decision in the present. Clients are challenged from the outset to make new decisions for themselves. They are frequently required to imagine returning to the childhood scenes in which they made self-limiting decisions. Counselors facilitate this process with interventions such as these: "As you are speaking, how old do you feel?" "Is what you are saying reminding you of any times when you were a child?" "What pictures come to your mind right now?" "Could you exaggerate the frown on your face?" "What scene comes to mind as you experience your frowning?" "What are you feeling as you describe this scene?"

Once clients are able to identify an early scene (such as the one Ruth recalled in Chapter 11), it is helpful to allow them to reexperience the scene. Clients might reexperience the scene in fantasy through the use of a Gestalt experiment where some past scenario is brought into the present moment, which can bring about a corrective emotional experience. As part of replaying this earlier experience, it is important for clients to be able to examine the decisions they once made in response to such messages to determine if an early decision is still useful.

In redecision work, clients enter the past and create fantasy scenes that help them to safely give up old and currently inappropriate early decisions. Armed with an understanding in the present that enables clients to relive the scene in a new way, they see that a particular decision was the best they could do at a difficult time but that now they can modify that decision. It is possible to give a new ending to the scenes in which original decisions were made—a new ending that often results in a *new beginning* in which clients think, feel, and act in revitalized ways.

For a more detailed treatment of the topics of injunctions, decisions, and redecisions, see *Changing Lives Through Redecision Therapy* (Goulding & Goulding, 1979), and *Theory and Practice of Group Counseling* (Corey, 2012, chap. 12).

Becoming the Client: Experiencing the Redecision Process

As a way to personalize the notions of injunctions, early decisions, and redecisions, I am asking you to "become the client" as I apply some aspects of the blend of redecision therapy and Gestalt therapy in my integrative approach. I especially value the integration of concepts from redecision therapy, which emphasizes the cognitive dimensions, with the techniques of Gestalt therapy, which tends to accent the affective dimensions. These basic principles of redecision therapy are quite useful in the overall context of understanding how you make certain decisions about yourself and your place in the world. I base my work with you on the existential notion that what has been decided can be redecided. If you choose, messages and past decisions can be modified in the present.

During the working and action-oriented phase of counseling, there is considerable focus on examining past decisions and looking forward to making new decisions. At this phase of your counseling, I ask you to review what you have learned about your early decisions as a result of participating in therapy (an approach characteristic of existential therapy, redecision therapy, cognitive therapy, rational emotive behavior therapy, and reality therapy). To stimulate this review, I typically pose these kinds of questions:

- Do you see your early decisions as still being appropriate for you now?
- Do you want to revise any of your early decisions?
- What new decisions do you want to make?

A variety of cognitive behavioral techniques can assist you in understanding early decisions in the form of core beliefs and self-talk (see Chapter 6). Cognitive restructuring can be incorporated into most forms of therapy. Once decisions and core beliefs have been identified and explored, you are then in a position to critically evaluate these beliefs and decisions and modify them. Through techniques such as cognitive disputing, debating, Socratic questioning, reframing, and cognitive restructuring, you can actively incorporate a sound set of beliefs and create a more effective way of life.

The action-oriented phase of counseling is a time for you to translate your insights into action by solving problems and making decisions. During this time, you and I consider possible alternatives and their consequences, evaluate how these alternatives will meet your goals, and decide on a specific course of action. The best alternatives and new possibilities for action are ones you generate.

A major part of the counseling process consists of making new decisions based on the expanded information you have acquired about yourself. By immersing yourself in behavioral homework, you can learn to become your own counselor, and you can reinforce this redecisional process. Utilizing an Adlerian technique, I encourage you to *act as if* you are the person you want to be, which can serve to challenge your self-limiting assumptions. I ask you to *catch yourself* repeating old patterns that have led to ineffective behavior. It is essential that you set tasks for yourself and do something specific about dealing with your problems. By taking action, your new insights and new decisions lead to concrete actions. Small steps can lead the way to significant changes.

Working Toward Redecisions With Ruth

See Session 12 (Working Toward Decisions and Behavior Change) on the *DVD for Integrative Counseling: The Case of Ruth and Lecturettes.*

Identifying Family Rules and Messages   Ruth and I spend some time identifying and exploring family rules and messages. She comes up with as many family rules as she can recall in growing up as a child. She recollects parental messages such as these: "Don't think for yourself." "Follow the church obediently, and conform to God's will." "Never question the Bible." "Live a moral life." "Don't get close to people, especially in sexual ways." "Sexuality is bad and wrong, unless you are married." "Always be proper and appropriate." We spend time identifying and dealing with gender-role messages Ruth still struggles with such as these: "Your main concern should be your family." "Don't put your career needs before what is expected of you as a woman." "Defer to what men want." "Always be ready to nurture those who need care and attention."

Exploring Early Decisions   In working with Ruth's early decisions, I borrow concepts from both the psychoanalytic and family therapy models. The psychoanalytic approach emphasizes reconstructing the past and working through early conflicts that have been repressed to resolve these unconscious conflicts. In some approaches to family therapy, Ruth would work to understand family behavior patterns three generations back to unravel patterns and emotional baggage she may have acquired from her family background.

In working with Ruth on her early decisions, I employ a directive and action-oriented approach. Functioning as a teacher, attention is given to what she can learn that will lead to changes in the way she is thinking, feeling, and behaving. Once we have identified some of the major messages she has internalized, I ask her to begin thinking about the decisions she made about herself, others, and the world. I also ask her to reflect on the direction in which her early decisions are taking her. Ruth sees with increasing clarity that she has lived much of her life in ways that were designed to get her father's approval. She feels that unless she gets her father's acceptance and approval she will not feel good about herself. She reasons that if her own father could not love her then nobody ever could. Drawing from Adlerian and cognitive behavioral concepts, I proceed by getting her to look at themes in her life and by guiding her in critically evaluating several faulty assumptions she continues to make.

At this stage of her therapy, Ruth is increasingly challenging her thinking and her value system. She is raising questions about the meaning of her life. She is looking at beliefs and values she has accepted to determine if she still wants to base her life on them. Does she want to spend the rest of her life in a futile attempt to "win over" her father, or some other man? What will it take for her to finally gain her father's acceptance and love?—if this is possible. What might she think of the person she must become to gain his acceptance? Pursuing these questions gets her to *think* and *decide* for herself on her standards for living.

Because Ruth has let me know that she wants to reconsider her value system, I have an investment in assisting her in this process. Our counseling requires her to carefully consider what part of her value system she wants to retain and what she wants to modify. I do not expect her to reject all that she was taught. The experiential and relationship-oriented approaches emphasize the importance of Ruth critically examining her values so that these value can become her own. Authenticity consists of living by values she chooses rather than living by unexamined values given to her by others.

🌿 Ruth's Existential Quest

The goal of our therapeutic endeavor is for Ruth to become increasingly capable of making self-directed choices and influencing the quality of her future through her choices. She is challenged to re-create herself through her projects. Much of our work together involves my inviting her to raise core questions about her existence, such as "Who am I?" "Who have I been?" and "Where am I going?"

A basic existential premise that I accept in my relationship with Ruth is that she is not the victim of circumstances. To a large extent, she is what she has chosen and is choosing to be today. For much of her life, Ruth has lived a restricted existence. She has tended to see few options for dealing with life situations, and she often reports feeling trapped or helpless. One of my central tasks is to invite her to examine the ways she is living a restricted existence.

I encourage Ruth to reflect on the direction of her life, to recognize her range of alternatives, and to make decisions without any firm guarantees about the future. Once she becomes aware of factors in her past and of stifling modes of her present existence, she can begin to accept responsibility for changing her future. As she recognizes some of the ways in which she has passively surrendered control, she can start on a path of consciously shaping her own life and designing the future she wants.

🌿 Feminist Perspective

The feminist therapy model provides me with a valuable lens to understand some of Ruth's core struggles. The intervention of gender-role analysis is especially useful. Gender-role analysis can be employed to increase her insight about how societal gender-role expectations have adversely affected her and to help her understand how women and men are socialized differently. Through this process, Ruth will learn to identify gender-role messages (verbal, nonverbal, and modeled) she has experienced in her lifetime. Through her therapy Ruth will be in a position to examine the socialization messages she received from society as a whole, from her family of origin, and from her religion. As a result, she will learn that many of her conflicts about her life and identity are due to the fact that she wants to step outside her traditionally defined female gender role. She is now able to identify the positive and negative consequences of following those gender-role messages. Ruth is learning how she has internalized certain gender-role messages in conscious and unconscious ways. My hope is that she will be able to acquire a full range of behaviors that are freely chosen rather than those prescribed by gender-role stereotypes.

For a more detailed description of working with Ruth from a feminist therapy model, see the piece by Kathy M. Evans, Susan R. Seem, and Elizabeth A. Kincade in *Case Approach to Counseling and Psychotherapy* (Corey, 2013a, chap. 10).

Encouraging Ruth to Act   As much as possible, I structure situations in the therapy session that will facilitate new decisions on Ruth's part. Her redecisions have to be made on both the emotional and cognitive levels, but it is also important that she commit herself to some course of action aimed at changing herself and bringing about environmental change. Here I like the reality therapy emphasis on getting Ruth to decide on a plan of action and then making a commitment to carry it out.

Therapy is a place of safety where clients can experiment with new ways of being to see what behavioral changes they really want to make. Ruth has learned that insight without action is incomplete. She must apply the lessons learned in therapy to real-life situations. I consistently encourage her to carry out homework assignments that challenge her fears and inhibitions in a variety of practical situations.

Because Ruth sincerely wants to be different, we use session time for role playing and behavioral rehearsal. Then I ask her to try out her new learning in different life situations, especially with her family. For me, translating what is learned in the sessions into daily life is the essence of what therapy is about. One assignment Ruth carried out was to approach an instructor in the fitness class at her college and request a place in the class as an added student, even though the class was closed. Regardless of the outcome, she is learning that she has a right to ask for what she wants. Her old style would be to assume that since the class was closed there would be absolutely no way that she could ever add it. This assignment helped her understand that she does not have to give up so soon.

Ruth is starting to think more about getting on with her life without formal therapy. She has learned that she can make new decisions and that she can follow her own lead. Because there are many tasks to accomplish as part of the termination process, more than one additional session will be needed. I ask Ruth to think about what she has learned from her counseling and to develop a plan of what she would like to continue doing when she no longer comes in for counseling. In attending to the various aspects of termination, I draw from both the cognitive behavioral and experiential approaches in assisting Ruth to move in this new direction in her life. This consolidation process will help Ruth put a new perspective on what she is taking away from her therapy experience, and it will continue to guide her work once therapy sessions have ended.

Working Toward Redecisions With Stan

See Session 11 (Solution-Focused Brief Therapy) and Session 12
(Narrative Therapy) on the *DVD for Theory and Practice*
of Counseling and Psychotherapy: The Case of Stan and Lecturettes.

In both of these sessions I focus Stan's attention on messages he incorporated
as a child and on the decisions he made. I assist him in thinking about the reasons he made certain early decisions. Finally, I support Stan in looking at these
decisions about life, about himself, and about others and in making necessary
revisions that can lead him to creating a life of his own choosing.

Solution-Focused Techniques   In Session 11 I invite Stan to experiment
with several *solution-focused techniques* as a way to gain clarity on past decisions
and to consider new decisions. Stan explains how he is always down on himself,
how he feels hopeless most of the time, and how he lacks self-confidence. This
gives me an opportunity to implement the *exception technique.* Exceptions are
times and situations in which Stan's presenting problem is absent or less notice-
able. As we explore the conditions under which these exceptions occurred, I encourage Stan to replicate those situations in the future. I ask Stan to tell me about
any time that he did not feel "down on himself" or hopeless. He describes a few
exceptions to how he typically feels, which opens a new line of questioning that
Stan and I explore: "Was there a time when anxiety did not get the best of you?"
"What did you do differently when you felt even somewhat hopeful?" "How did
you shift your mood from feeling hopeless to more optimistic?" "What steps did
you take to feel even slightly more self-confident in a social situation?" "What
did you actually do to make things different?" I enlist Stan in identifying specific
steps he took to overcome a problem, and Stan decides on other small steps he
can take to change the way he thinks, feels, and acts.

Other solution-focused therapy techniques that I implement with Stan are
the miracle question and scaling questions. As a way to elicit new goals from
Stan and invite him to consider new ways of being, I use the miracle question:
"Suppose a miracle happened while you are sleeping tonight and your problems completely vanished. What would be different about the next day?" If
Stan identifies feeling very confident with others as his miracle, I can then explore with him all the ways his life would be different if he were self-confident.
What could he do to move more in this direction? Scaling questions are then
used to identify new goals. I ask Stan: "On a scale of 0 to 10, where 10 is 'the best
it can be' and zero is 'the worst,' where would you rate your confidence level
with your friends right now? What would the next highest number look like?
What can you do to move up the scale?"

Narrative Therapy   In Session 12 our focus is on applying a technique of
narrative therapy that involves creating an alternative life story. I propose that
Stan think of his life as a book that he might want to revise. This technique
did not seem to work well with Stan, and I appreciated the fact that Stan let me
know that he could not relate to this idea. This is a reminder that every technique is a means to an end and not the end itself. It would be a mistake for me to

become attached to a particular idea or technique or to try to impose it on Stan. I then shifted to another metaphor, that of remodeling a house, which was in line with Stan's interests in construction. I wanted to get Stan thinking about ways that he might "remodel" his life. Much of Stan's life has been characterized by a problem-saturated story, and we explore ways that he can separate his problems from his identity. Stan begins to see that some of his early decisions about his identity no longer serve him well, and he is open to considering a range of new possibilities. He shares a vision of how his life might be different if his concerns did not dominate his life. By detaching himself from his problem-saturated story, he opens the way to construct a new life story.

Stan has only a couple of sessions remaining before our final session. I choose a technique often used by narrative therapists, the therapist letter, to provide Stan with a summary of our work together. I encourage him to read it at home and to bring any of his reactions into our following session. I want Stan to know that I appreciate his hard work both in and outside of his therapy sessions, and I provide this feedback in my letter:

> Dear Stan:
>
> I respect your willingness to struggle out loud, to challenge yourself, and to challenge me when you are uncomfortable with me. You never cease to surprise me by what you do in your therapy sessions. You have so often let me know that you were reluctant to talk, but then you nudged yourself and explored what made it difficult for you to talk with me. You mentioned many times how anxious you felt in our relationship, but you consistently were willing to talk about your anxiety. I have been impressed with the ways you push yourself out of your comfort zone and how you have been willing to take many risks. You did many things to bring about the safety and trust that you said you felt in here. When you did not feel trusting, you let me know. When you were not satisfied with our relationship, you brought this up. A number of times you said to me that I must be frustrated with you because of your slow pace. Well, you went at your own pace, and you took an active stance in working toward your goals. You continue to make strides, and I like the way that you are not willing to settle for a comfortable existence. I look forward to reviewing the journey we have taken together in our final two sessions, and I am excited to hear the ideas you have for continuing on your new journey.

Concluding Comments

Once clients understand the context of their early decisions, they are in a position to modify them if they decide these decisions are no longer working for them. Redecision therapy provides a framework for understanding how early childhood experiences play out in adulthood. A major part of therapy consists of creating new beginnings to modify some of our early decisions.

Spend a few minutes thinking and imagining the person you want to be. Let yourself identify specific characteristics you would have if you actually were the person you are striving to become. Try this homework assignment:

Pick some week that you would be willing to act as *if* you are this person in a setting, such as home, school, or work. At the end of the week, ask yourself what is stopping you from becoming the person you want to be.

I hope you will reflect on some of your early decisions and how they extend into your current functioning. Here are some questions to ask yourself as you think about the issues addressed in this chapter.

- Is there anything you can do to make the changes you most want to make?
- Are there any early decisions you made that you would like to examine more fully?
- Is there a decision about your life that you are willing to revise?
- What are some of the ways that the injunctions you received and the decisions you made based on these injunctions tend to work for you? Against you?
- How did your family of origin influence the kinds of messages that you heard in growing up?
- How did your family of origin influence some of the most central decisions you have made in your life to date?

CHAPTER THIRTEEN

Evaluation and Termination

Introduction

Just as the initial session sets the tone for the therapeutic relationship, the ending phase enables clients to maximize the benefits from the relationship and decide how they can continue the change process. The process of termination begins with planning for the eventual end of the relationship during the early phases of therapy. This preparation for termination is ongoing as you and your client collaboratively monitor progress over time (Davis & Younggren, 2009). As a counselor, your goal is to work with clients in such a way that they can terminate the professional relationship with you as soon as possible and continue to make changes on their own. From your first contact with clients, it is important to convey the idea that your intention is to assist them to function effectively without you. It is not helpful to clients if their therapy continues indefinitely.

Toward the end of the therapy experience, the therapist functions as a consultant and assists the client in consolidating gains and identifying potential future problem areas. *Termination* is the process of taking clinically and ethically appropriate steps to bring closure to the therapeutic relationship (Davis & Younggren, 2009). Terminating therapy can be viewed as a positive step, for it means that clients have reached a point where they can use their newly acquired skills to deal with challenges they may face. The tasks of termination include helping clients assess what they have accomplished in therapy, summarizing the counseling experience, dealing with feelings regarding ending the relationship, setting goals for the future, and exploring their strategies for dealing with future problems or setbacks.

For a useful discussion of termination issues, see Kramer (1990) *Positive Endings in Psychotherapy: Bringing Meaningful Closure to Therapeutic Relationships.*

Guidelines for Effective Termination

I find the action-oriented approaches (reality therapy, behavior therapy, cognitive behavior therapy, and solution-focused brief therapy) especially useful in providing methods for consolidating learning and transferring what was learned in therapy to daily living. Here are some guidelines for you to consider in effectively accomplishing the tasks of therapeutic endings:

• It is a good practice to discuss the termination process early and to remind clients of the approaching end of the therapy relationship with you. Ask clients what they'd most like to talk about in the final two meetings with you. At a session prior to the last one you could ask, "If this were our last meeting, how would that be for you?"

• If you are not limited to a specified number of sessions, and both you and your client determine that termination is appropriate, one option is to space out the final few sessions. Instead of meeting weekly, your client might come in every three weeks. This schedule allows more opportunity to practice new behaviors and to prepare for termination.

• Review the course of treatment. What lessons did clients learn, how did they learn them, and what do they intend to do with what they have learned? What did they find most helpful in the sessions with you? How do they evaluate their own participation in this process? It is good for clients to take the lead in addressing these questions. This review process involves both cognitive and emotional aspects. It should also include a discussion of ways to maintain treatment gains and ways to continue their work after termination.

• Encourage clients to talk about their feelings of separation and loss. Just as clients may have had fears about seeking help, they may have anxieties or concerns about terminating the counseling relationship.

• Be clear about your own feelings about endings. You may be ambivalent about letting go of certain clients. Reflect on the degree to which you may need your clients more than they need you. Monitor any signs of countertransference so that your needs do not make closure difficult for your clients. Talk to a supervisor or a trusted colleague about these feelings.

• A guiding principle of counseling is helping clients achieve self-directed behavior. Pay attention to clues your clients give about ending the client–counselor relationship and be willing to discuss this at appropriate times. Respect the client's decision regarding termination, but be willing to talk with the client about any reservations about the timing of termination you may have.

• Remember that if you are an effective counselor you'll eventually put yourself out of business—at least with your current clients. Your task is to get them moving on their own, not to keep them coming to you for advice. Give clients the tools to become their own counselors, which is a form of empowerment. Even though you may feel some sadness when terminating with some clients, realize that you have done a good job in your role of creating self-reliance in your client.

• Realize that a counseling experience is not aimed at resolving all of a client's problems. Counseling is an ongoing and evolutionary process. At a later period of development, clients may be ready to deal with new problems or concerns in ways they are not ready to do upon termination.

• Let your clients know of your availability at a future time. Encourage clients to return at a later time should they feel a need for further learning. Clients may need only a session or a few sessions to get refocused. Be sure clients know that asking for help in the future is not a sign of failure but an indication of new levels of strength.

• Assist clients in translating their learning into action programs. If clients have been successful, the ending stage is a *commencement*; they now have some new directions to follow in dealing with problems as they arise. Furthermore, clients acquire some needed tools and resources for continuing the process of personal growth. For this reason, discussing available programs and making referrals are especially timely tasks toward the end of your work with clients. In this way, termination of the professional relationship can lead to new beginnings in a client's personal relationships.

These guidelines are a good start in bringing about a successful ending to counseling. What other topics would you want to raise with your clients at the final phase of therapy? What goals are essential for an effective and positive ending of a counseling relationship? What are some techniques for closure you would use?

Becoming the Client: Taking Credit for Your Changes

You have become the client in all aspects of this book. Now, as this book is coming to an end, ask you to think about what it might be like for you as the client to end a therapeutic relationship. The final phase of your counseling may be a difficult time, and I want to give you an opportunity to fully express your feelings. Consider concepts and techniques that would be useful to bring closure to your experience if you were the client. What do you need to do to summarize your experience, cement your gains, and terminate effectively?

Positive endings include discussing your thoughts and feelings about your experience in the therapeutic journey. If you are like some clients, you may be concerned that you won't be able to carry into your everyday life some of the central things you learned in therapy. Understand what *you* did to make your therapy experience meaningful. Take credit for what you did to accomplish your goals in therapy.

During our final session, I ask you to imagine your life in some ideal future circumstance, a technique that is used by both Gestalt and psychodrama approaches. I might suggest to you any of the following:

• Imagine that you are coming in for a follow-up session five years from now and that we are meeting to discuss how your life has changed. What do you most want to be able to say to me?

• Let yourself think about all the ways in which you want to be different in your everyday life once you leave formal therapy. Close your eyes and carry on a silent dialogue between yourself and the people who are most special to you. What are you telling them? What are they replying?

• Imagine that a year has passed since you ended your counseling and nothing has changed in your life—that you have continued the way you have always been. Try to picture how you would feel.

During the final phase of therapy, I suggest that you continue keeping a journal—writing down the problems you are encountering, describing how you feel about yourself in specific situations, and listing your successes and difficulties in following through with your contracts. Because I believe that an appropriate book read at the right time could be a powerful catalyst in making changes, I encourage you to read as a way of continuing to work on yourself. I suggest that you formulate a contract that will spell out what you will do to maintain your gains and accomplish new goals you are setting for yourself. To implement your contract, I ask you to continue giving yourself homework assignments.

Narrative therapists sometimes write letters to clients between sessions to provide feedback and to reinforce changes clients are making. These letters can promote and empower progress by keeping the conversation alive between sessions. I might say any of the following to you in a brief letter: "I am impressed by your willingness to take risks." "I am wondering how you are doing with the homework that we agreed upon at our last session." "I hope that you will continue writing in your journal and bringing that into our sessions." "I appreciate your determination in creating an action plan and making a commitment to following through with your plan." Before we have our termination session, I might write a more detailed letter summarizing some of my observations about the changes I have seen in you since you began therapy.

During our final session, I am likely to give you an existential message to take with you: "I hope you have become aware of your role in bringing about change in your life. You can assume power by focusing on changing yourself rather than trying to get others to be different. You have become aware of the choices that are open to you; thus, you can now reflect on the decisions you will make. Even if you decide to remain largely as you are, you are now aware that you can choose differently. Although choosing for yourself can provoke anxiety, it does give you a sense that your life is yours and that you have the power to shape your own future."

Finally, I want you to know that you are welcome to call for follow-up sessions if the need arises. Although bringing closure to our work together is essential, I want you to feel welcome to call for future contacts if this is in your best interest.

Evaluating Ruth's Therapy Experience

See Session 13 (Evaluation and Termination) on the *DVD for Integrative Counseling: The Case of Ruth and Lecturettes.*

Throughout the 13 counseling sessions, Ruth and I discuss her progress in therapy. We especially look at the degree to which she is getting what she wants from counseling (and from me). If for some reason she is not successfully meeting her objectives, we explore possible factors that might be getting in the way of her progress. At our initial session I made clear to Ruth that a main aim of our relationship is to help her to function without me as her counselor. In our journey together we have been working toward the ultimate goal of Ruth becoming her own counselor.

When is it time for Ruth to terminate therapy? Termination of therapy is as important as the initial phase, for now the main task is to put into practice what she has learned in the sessions by applying new skills and attitudes to daily social situations. During the previous session, she brings up a desire to "go it alone." When she indicates this desire, I am thinking that this signifies major progress. We talk about her readiness to end therapy and her reasons for considering termination.

Ultimately, I see termination of Ruth's therapy as her choice. Once she attains a degree of increased self-awareness, has succeeded in making some cognitive shifts, and has acquired some specific behavioral skills in meeting present and future problems, I expect she will begin thinking of ending formal therapy. To keep Ruth in therapy after she has made significant changes on many levels could result in needlessly fostering her dependence on me, which certainly would not lead to her empowerment.

In our final sessions Ruth spends considerable time talking about what she learned in her counseling sessions, how she learned these lessons, and what she wants to do with what she has learned now that she will be terminating counseling. This is a good time to talk about where she has been and where she can go from here. Together we develop an action plan and talk about how she can best maintain her new learning. I also share with her my perceptions of the directions I have seen her take.

The final sessions address specific changes Ruth has made over the course of her therapy and what she considers to be the most helpful aspects of her therapy. She indicates that the focus of our work shifted at different times. Sometimes the emphasis was on Ruth's thoughts, other times on her feelings, and other times on insights she was gaining. At times she needed to simply experience and express her feelings, other times she needed to take action, and other times she needed to reflect on her beliefs, thoughts, and decisions. From her vantage point, she has gained a new appreciation for herself as a thinking, feeling, and doing individual.

We also talk about steps she can take to involve herself in other growth programs. She could find support in a variety of social networks. Getting involved in some form of social action program, or finding ways she can involve herself to benefit others, could be a most important way to maximize the benefits of her therapy. In essence, she can continue to challenge herself by doing things that are difficult for her yet at the same time broaden her range of choices. For example, she could get involved in an exercise class that she has previously avoided out of a fear of how others would look at her body. It is important that she express a willingness to deal with her feelings as they arise in new situations.

One of Ruth's core struggles was with her husband and members of her family, and referral to a couples therapist or a family therapist may be in order. She might decide to invite her husband and children to be part of a few family therapy sessions. Certainly her changes have not been easy for her husband, her children, and herself. Her changes have implications for others in her family. Even a session or two with the entire family could be instrumental in renegotiating some shifts in roles and expectations. If Ruth does not succeed in bringing about a family session, she can still continue to behave in different ways with each member of her family. Instead of placing the emphasis on changing others in her family, she can focus on herself and relate differently to her husband and children. Indeed, if she presents herself in new ways and keeps the focus on herself, others may be affected by her new way of being.

Before she entered counseling, Ruth was unaware of some patterns of her life that were not serving her well. Now she has a greater appreciation that she has the resources within her to become the expert in her own life. Once Ruth leaves formal therapy, I expect that she will continue to increase her awareness of times when she is thinking, feeling, and acting in ways that are not serving her well. When she catches herself in these patterns, Ruth now knows how to make a shift and do something different. When she hears her internal critic carping away at her, she can become aware of this negative voice and shift to a new dialogue. When she experiences depression or anxiety, she will notice this and remain for less time in these states. When she behaves in apologetic ways, she will realize that she does not have to apologize for her existence. The process of catching herself at those times when she becomes ensnared in self-defeating patterns enables her to become her own counselor.

To empower Ruth on her continuing journey, together we explore possible stumbling blocks and ways to cope with them. Ruth is likely to experience setbacks once formal therapy ends, and the goal of relapse prevention is to help her maintain the gains she has made by using what she has learned in therapy when she needs it in the future (Marlatt & Donovan, 2005). At times, it is inevitable that Ruth will revert to old patterns and experience self-defeating thoughts and behaviors. The point is not that she never experiences setbacks, but that she learns to catch herself when she slips into old familiar patterns. I hope Ruth will avoid slipping into discouragement and will focus on how she can get back on track.

Evaluating Stan's Therapy Experience

See Session 13 (An Integrative Approach) on the *DVD for Theory and Practice of Counseling and Psychotherapy: The Case of Stan and Lecturettes.*

What Stan will do once his therapy formally ends is as important as the sessions in the office. Therefore, together we spend considerable time talking about what he deems most significant in his therapy and what he will do with what he has learned once he no longer comes to counseling sessions. I am especially interested in hearing about Stan's perceptions regarding any changes in his life. I listen to what the counseling experience has meant to him and take my lead from his comments.

I ask Stan at the final session to review specific insights he had throughout the course of his personal work. My experience has taught me that many clients forget key lessons learned and discount the value of what they did in their therapy. I want to help Stan retain whatever he has learned about others, about human struggling, about life, and about himself. Unless he is able to articulate what he has learned through his counseling, and how he learned it, he may not recall key lessons when he is faced with future problems. I also ask Stan what he might do when he experiences setbacks or unexpected difficulties. I inquire about how he might more creatively cope with future problems as they arise. We talk about obstacles to further personal growth and how he can view any stumbling blocks as opportunities for continued growth. Stan and I rehearse and practice in a collaborative fashion various ways of applying the skills he has learned in his therapy.

In Adlerian terms, we are in the reorientation phase. At this time the central task is to encourage Stan to translate his insights into acting in new and more effective ways. We explore his perception of his future, and he establishes revised goals. Where does he want to go from here? What are some concrete plans he can put into action? What are some contracts he can establish as a way to provide himself with a useful direction? A number of options are open to him, some of which we explore during the final sessions.

Evaluating the process and outcomes of therapy is a part of our work during the final few sessions. It is of paramount importance that Stan be able to recognize what he actually did, both in the therapy sessions and in his life outside, to bring about the changes he is experiencing in his life. His growth is not due to magic on my part, for I am only instrumental in facilitating his changes. By recognizing his part in the success of his therapy, Stan will be able to continue making positive strides. Here are a few questions I ask Stan to help him appraise the meaning of his experience in counseling:

- What did you learn that you consider especially valuable?
- What can you do now to keep practicing new behaviors that work better for you?
- What will you do when you experience setbacks?
- How can you continue implementing in your life what was begun in counseling?
- Where do you want to go from here? Do you have any specific future plans?

Stan and I talk about how he can be different with others in his life, even if they are not different with him. We also explore ways he can deal with problems differently, and I ask Stan about changes he would like to see in his life one year hence. We explore his future goals and identify specific steps he can continue taking to achieve these new goals.

Once Stan decides what direction he wants to move toward, he will need to develop a practical plan of action and make a commitment to carry out his plan. Referrals and suggestions for continued growth are particularly useful at this time. For example, now that Stan's therapy is ending, he may want to consider joining a therapy group. I bring this up to him because much of his therapy has been centered on his social relationships and learning skills that will enhance his ability to meet new friends. In a group setting he can continue working on interpersonal concerns and can increasingly recognize the value of including others in his life. I then brainstorm with Stan about other ways he can continue building on the changes he has made in his therapy. He is able to come up with a wide range of options, which we then discuss.

Concluding Comments

The Future of Psychotherapy Integration

What is the future of psychotherapy integration? It may be reassuring to you to know that there is no one "right" approach to the integration of counseling practice. Integrative counseling is best viewed as an evolving framework rather than as a fixed approach. Gold and Stricker (2006) claim that "psychotherapy integration has moved from the fringes of psychotherapeutic activity and thinking to a much more prominent and central place" (p. 13). They observe that therapists with various orientations seem to be talking more freely about approaches other than their own and demonstrate a greater willingness to experiment with new methods and integrative perspectives. Stricker (2010) reminds us that providing the best service possible to clients should be the ultimate goal of the psychotherapy integration movement. Stricker states that "psychotherapy integration is a creative endeavor and promises to continue to contribute in a realistic and flexible manner to the development of the psychotherapeutic enterprise" (p. 109).

The Role of Research in Developing an Integrative Perspective

Both theory and research need to be considered in developing your way of working with clients. Become familiar with the research literature in the psychotherapy field and consider how you can apply research findings in your practice. Today there is an increasing demand in most agencies for practitioners to use techniques that are supported by research. Accountability is being increasingly emphasized, but counseling is a more complex process than merely picking out techniques that are empirically validated. The therapy relationship, the therapist's personality and therapeutic style, the client, and environmental factors are all vital contributors to the success of treatment.

Evidence-based practice (EBP) tends to emphasize only one of these aspects—selecting interventions based on the best available research. Norcross, Hogan, and Koocher (2008) advocate for inclusive evidence-based practices that incorporate the three pillars of EBP: looking for the best available research, relying on the clinician's expertise, and taking into consideration the client's characteristics, culture, and preferences. It is important to keep in mind that the involvement of an active, informed client is crucial to the success of therapy services. Based on your clinical expertise, you will be expected to make judgments regarding particular interventions, yet these decisions need to be made in the context of considering your client's values and preferences.

For a more detailed treatment of evidence-based practice, see Norcross, Beutler, and Levant (2006), *Evidence-Based Practice in Mental Health: Debate and Dialogue on the Fundamental Questions,* and Norcross, Hogan, and Koocher (2008), *Clinician's Guide to Evidence-Based Practices in Mental Health.*

Designing Your Personal Integrative Approach

I want to leave you with a few summary remarks concerning your personal integrative orientation to counseling. Remember that designing your counseling approach does not have to be completed by the time you finish this book or this course. A good place to begin is by mastering a primary theory that will serve as a guide for what you do in the counseling process. Select a theory that comes closest to your beliefs about human nature and the change process. Look for ways to personalize the theory or theories of your choice to your own practice with clients.

Take the key concepts of several theories that have personal relevance for you and apply these ideas to your own life. Throughout this book you have "become a client" as I applied various interventions with you. By thinking of yourself as a client, you can continue studying these theories from a personal perspective. What aspects of the different theories would most help you as a client in understanding yourself? In addition, ask yourself what aspects of each theory would be most useful to you as a therapist in working with diverse client groups. What basic concepts are essential aspects of your theoretical orientation? What concepts would most help you make sense of the work you are doing with your clients? Try to answer these questions by experimenting within the parameters of one or more theories. I have described the concepts and techniques I employ in my integrative approach, both as I worked with you as a client and also with the cases of Ruth and Stan. Reflect on these case examples as a way to create your own counseling style.

Commit yourself to a reading program and consider attending a variety of professional workshops. Reading is a realistic and useful way to expand your knowledge base and to provide you with ideas on how to create, implement, and evaluate techniques. Take time to review the resources given throughout this book and also those listed in the *References and Suggested Readings* at the end of the book.

Attend workshops dealing with different aspects of the counseling process and as a way to learn about the implementation of techniques. Just about every theoretical system I've mentioned is associated with one or more professional organizations where you can get further training in the particular orientation. (Consult the Where to Go From Here sections in *Theory and Practice of Counseling and Psychotherapy* [Corey, 2013d] for places to contact for training and supervision of the various specific therapy approaches.)

As you attend workshops, be open to ideas that seem to have particular meaning for you and that fit the context of your work. Don't adopt ideas without first putting them through your personal filter. As you experiment with many different counseling techniques, avoid using techniques in a rigid or "cookbook" method. Techniques are merely tools to assist you in effectively reaching your clients. Personalize your techniques so they fit your style and the needs of your clients, and be open to feedback from your clients about how well your techniques are working for them.

As you practice, be open to supervision throughout your career. Talk with supervisors and colleagues about what you are doing. Discuss some of your interventions with other professionals and think of alternative approaches you could take with clients. Remain a life-long learner and continue thinking about alternative theoretical frameworks. Be open to borrowing techniques from various theories, yet do so in a systematic way. It is important that you think about your theoretical rationale for the techniques you employ.

Continue reflecting on what fits for you and what set of blueprints will be most useful in creating an emerging model for practice. Although you will have a solid foundation consisting of theoretical constructs, realize that the art of integrative counseling consists of personalizing your knowledge so that how you function as a counselor is an expression of your personality and life experiences. No prefabricated model will fit you perfectly. Customize your approach to fit your personality and the needs of your clients. Even with the same client, you may need to adapt your methods at different phases of therapy.

After reading this chapter on evaluation and termination, take time to reflect on the following questions as a way of clarifying your thoughts on evaluating client outcomes and termination of the therapeutic relationship.

- In what ways can termination of therapy be a positive step?
- What guidelines do you think are most important for the effective termination of a therapy relationship?
- What are some ways you might prepare your clients for ending the therapy relationship?
- What difficulties might you face because of your own issues over loss or experiences with endings when assisting clients in exploring termination issues?
- What are your thoughts about how to evaluate the meaning of a therapy experience?
- What are some steps you can take toward designing your personal integrative approach to counseling?
- If you favor an integrative approach, do you have a primary theory that you use as a foundation? If so, what is this theory? What are some of the reasons you have chosen this theory?

REFERENCES AND SUGGESTED READINGS

This reference list represents a carefully chosen group of books that I think will be useful as resources for designing a personal integrative approach to counseling. References marked with an asterisk are highly recommended for further reading.

ALTMAN, N. (2008). Psychoanalytic therapy. In J. Frew & M. D. Spiegler (Eds.), *Contemporary psychotherapies for a diverse world* (pp. 42–92). Boston: Lahaska Press.

ARKOWITZ, H., & MILLER, W. R. (2008). Learning, applying, and extending motivational interviewing. In H. Arkowitz, H. A. Westra, W. R. Miller, & S. Rollnick (Eds.), *Motivational interviewing in the treatment of psychological disorders* (pp. 1–25). New York: Guilford Press.

*BECK, A. T., & WEISHAAR, M. E. (2011). Cognitive therapy. In R. J. Corsini & D. Wedding (Eds.), *Current psychotherapies* (9th ed., pp. 276–309). Belmont, CA: Brooks/Cole, Cengage Learning.

*BECK, J. S. (2005). *Cognitive therapy for challenging problems.* New York: Guilford Press.

*BECK, J. S. (2011). *Cognitive behavior therapy: Basics and beyond* (2nd ed.). New York: Guilford Press.

BEITMAN, B. D., SOTH, A. M., & GOOD, G. E. (2006). Integrating the psychotherapies through their emphases on the future. In G. Stricker & J. Gold (Eds.), *A casebook of psychotherapy integration* (pp. 43–54). Washington, DC: American Psychological Association.

*BITTER, J. R. (2009). *Theory and practice of family therapy and counseling.* Belmont, CA: Brooks/Cole, Cengage Learning.

BLATNER, A. (1996). *Acting-in: Practical applications of psychodramatic methods* (3rd ed.). New York: Springer.

BLATNER, A. (2006). Current trends in psychodrama. *International Journal of Psychotherapy, 11*(3), 43–53.

*BOHART, A. C. (2006). The client as active self-healer. In G. Stricker & J. Gold (Eds.), *A casebook of psychotherapy integration* (pp. 241–251). Washington, DC: American Psychological Association.

*BOHART, A. C., & TALLMAN, K. (2010). Clients: The neglected common factor in psychotherapy. In B. L. Duncan, S. D. Miller, B. E. Wampold, & M. A. Hubble (Eds.), *The heart and soul of change: Delivering what works in therapy* (2nd ed., pp. 83–111). Washington, DC: American Psychological Association.

*BROWN, L. (2010). *Feminist therapy.* Washington, DC: American Psychological Association.

* CAIN, D. J. (2010). *Person-centered psychotherapies.* Washington, DC: American Psychological Association.

*CARLSON, J., WATTS, R. E., & MANIACCI, M. (2006). *Adlerian therapy: Theory and practice.* Washington DC: American Psychological Association.

*CASHWELL, C. S., & YOUNG, J. S. (2011). *Integrating spirituality and religion into counseling: A guide to competent practice* (2nd ed.). Alexandria, VA: American Counseling Association.

COREY, G. (2012). *Theory and practice of group counseling* (8th ed.) [and *Student Manual*]. Belmont, CA: Brooks/Cole, Cengage Learning.

*COREY, G. (2013a). *Case approach to counseling and psychotherapy* (8th ed). Belmont, CA: Brooks/Cole, Cengage Learning.

*COREY, G. (with Haynes, R.). (2013b). *DVD for integrative counseling: The case of Ruth and lecturettes*. Belmont, CA: Brooks/Cole, Cengage Learning.

COREY, G. (2013c). *DVD for Theory and practice of counseling and psychotherapy: The case of Stan and lecturettes*. Belmont, CA: Brooks/Cole, Cengage Learning.

*COREY, G. (2013d). *Theory and practice of counseling and psychotherapy* (9th ed.) [and *Student Manual*]. Belmont, CA: Brooks/Cole, Cengage Learning.

CORSINI, R. J., & WEDDING, D. (Eds.). (2011). *Current psychotherapies* (9th ed.). Belmont, CA: Brooks/Cole, Cengage Learning.

*CRASKE, M. G. (2010). *Cognitive-behavioral therapy*. Washington, DC: American Psychological Association.

DAVIS, D., & YOUNGGREN, J. N. (2009). Ethical competence in psychotherapy termination. *Professional Psychology: Research and Practice, 40*(6), 572–578.

DeSHAZER, S. (1985). *Keys to solutions in brief therapy*. New York: Norton.

DeSHAZER, S. (1988). *Clues: Investigating solutions in brief therapy*. New York: Norton.

DeSHAZER, S. (1991). *Putting difference to work*. New York: Norton.

*DeSHAZER, S., & DOLAN, Y. M. (with Korman, H., Trepper, T., McCullom, E., & Berg, I. K.). (2007). *More than miracles: The state of the art of solution-focused brief therapy*. New York: Haworth Press.

DEURZEN, E. van. (2002). *Existential counselling and psychotherapy* (2nd ed.). London: Sage.

*DEURZEN, E. van. (2010). *Everyday mysteries: A handbook of existential psychotherapy* (2nd ed.). London: Routledge.

*DUNCAN, B. L., MILLER, S. D., & SPARKS, J. A. (2004). *The heroic client: A revolutionary way to improve effectiveness through client-directed, outcome-informed therapy*. San Francisco: Jossey-Bass.

*DUNCAN, B. L., MILLER, S. D., WAMPOLD, B. E., & HUBBLE, M. A. (Eds.). (2010). *The heart and soul of change: Delivering what works in therapy* (2nd ed.). Washington DC: American Psychological Association.

*ELKINS, D. N. (2009). *Humanistic psychology: A clinical manifesto*. Colorado Springs, CO: University of the Rockies Press.

ELLIOTT, R., BOHART, A. C., WATSON, J. C., & GREENBERG, L. S. (2011). Empathy. In J. C. Norcross (Ed.), *Psychotherapy relationships that work: Evidence-based responsiveness* (2nd ed., pp. 132–152). New York: Oxford University Press.

ELLIS, A. (1999). *How to make yourself happy and remarkably less disturbable*. Atascadero, CA: Impact Publishers.

*ELLIS, A. (2001a). *Feeling better, getting better, and staying better*. Atascadero, CA: Impact Publishers.

*ELLIS, A. (2001b). *Overcoming destructive beliefs, feelings, and behaviors*. Amherst, NY: Prometheus Books.

ELLIS, A., & MacLAREN, C. (2005). *Rational emotive behavior therapy: A therapist's guide* (2nd ed.). San Luis Obispo, CA: Impact Publishers.

FARBER, B. A., & DOOLIN, E. M. (2011). Positive regard and affirmation. In J. C. Norcross (Ed.), *Psychotherapy relationships that work: Evidence-based responsiveness* (2nd ed., pp. 168–186). New York: Oxford University Press.

*FREW, J., & SPIEGLER, M. D. (2008). *Contemporary psychotherapies for a diverse world*. Boston: Lahaska Press.

*GELLER, J. D., NORCROSS, J. C., & ORLINSKY, D. E. (Eds.). (2005). *The psychotherapist's own psychotherapy: Patient and clinician perspectives.* New York: Oxford University Press.

*GERMER, C. K., SIEGEL, R. D., & FULTON, P. R. (Eds.). (2005). *Mindfulness and psychotherapy.* New York: Guilford Press.

GLASSER, W. (1998). *Choice theory: A new psychology of personal freedom.* New York: HarperCollins.

*GLASSER, W. (2001). *Counseling with choice theory: The new reality therapy.* New York: HarperCollins.

GOLD, J., & STRICKER, G. (2006). Introduction: An overview of psychotherapy integration. In G. Stricker & J. Gold (Eds.), *A casebook of psychotherapy integration* (pp. 3–16). Washington, DC: American Psychological Association.

GOULDING, M., & GOULDING, R. (1979). *Changing lives through redecision therapy.* New York: Brunner/Mazel.

GREASON, D.P.B. (2011). Mindfulness. In C. S. Cashwell & J. S. Young (Eds.), *Integrating spirituality and religion into counseling: A guide to competent practice* (2nd ed., pp. 183–208). Alexandria, VA: American Counseling Association.

GREENBERG, L. S. (2011). *Emotion-focused therapy.* Washington, DC: American Psychological Association.

*GREENBERG, L. S., RICE, L. N., & ELLIOTT, R. (1993). *Facilitating emotional change: The moment-by-moment process.* New York: Guilford Press.

HAGEDORN, W. B., & MOORHEAD, H.J.H. (2011). Counselor self-awareness: Exploring attitudes, beliefs, and values. In C. S. Cashwell & J. S. Young (Eds.), *Integrating spirituality and religion into counseling: A guide to competent practice* (2nd ed., pp. 71–96). Alexandria, VA: American Counseling Association.

HAYES, J. A., GELSO, C. J., & HUMMEL, A. M. (2011). Management of countertransference. In J. C. Norcross (Ed.), *Psychotherapy relationships that work: Evidence-based responsiveness* (2nd ed.). New York: Oxford University Press.

*HORVATIN, T., & SCHREIBER, E. (Eds.). (2006). *The quintessential Zerka: Writings by Zerka Toeman Moreno on psychodrama, sociometry and group psychotherapy.* New York: Routledge (Taylor & Francis).

*HUBBLE, M. A., DUNCAN, B. L., MILLER, S. D., & WAMPOLD, B. E. (2010). Introduction. In B. L. Duncan, S. D. Miller, B. E. Wampold, & M. A. Hubble (Eds.), *The heart and soul of change: Delivering what works in therapy* (2nd ed., pp. 23–46). Washington DC: American Psychological Association.

*IVEY, A. E., & BROOKS-HARRIS, J. E. (2005). Integrative psychotherapy with culturally diverse clients. In J. C. Norcross & M. R. Goldfried (Eds.), *Handbook of psychotherapy integration* (2nd ed., pp. 321–339). New York: Oxford University Press.

*KABAT-ZINN, J. (1990). *Full catastrophe living: Using the wisdom of your body and mind to face stress, pain, and illness.* New York: Dell.

KERNBERG, O. F. (1997). Convergences and divergences in contemporary psychoanalytic technique and psychoanalytic psychotherapy. In J. K. Zeig (Ed.), *The evolution of psychotherapy: The third conference* (pp. 3–22). New York: Brunner/Mazel.

KRAMER, S. A. (1990). *Positive endings in psychotherapy: Bringing meaningful closure to therapeutic relationships.* San Francisco: Jossey-Bass.

LAMBERT, M. J. (2011). Psychotherapy research and its achievements. In J. C. Norcross, G. R. Vandenbos, & D. K. Freedheim (Eds.), *History of psychotherapy* (2nd ed., pp. 299–332). Washington, DC: American Psychological Association.

LAZARUS, A. A. (1997a). *Brief but comprehensive psychotherapy: The multimodal way.* New York: Springer.

LAZARUS, A. A. (1997b). Can psychotherapy be brief, focused, solution-oriented, and yet comprehensive? A personal evolutionary perspective. In J. K. Zeig (Ed.),

The evolution of psychotherapy: The third conference (pp. 83–94). New York: Brunner/ Mazel.

*LAZARUS, A. A. (2005). Multimodal therapy. In J. C. Norcross & M. R. Goldfried (Eds.), *Handbook of psychotherapy integration* (2nd ed., pp. 105–120). New York: Oxford University Press.

LAZARUS, A. A. (2006). Multimodal therapy: A seven-point integration. In G. Stricker & J. Gold (Eds.), *A casebook of psychotherapy integration* (pp. 17–28). Washington, DC: American Psychological Association.

*LAZARUS, A. A. (2008). Multimodal therapy. In R. J. Corsini & D. Wedding (Eds.), *Current psychotherapies* (8th ed., pp. 368–401). Belmont, CA: Brooks/Cole.

*LEDLEY, D. R., MARX, B. P., & HEIMBERG, R. G. (2010). *Making cognitive-behavioral therapy work: Clinical processes for new practitioners* (2nd ed.). New York: Guilford Press.

LEVENSKY, E. R., KERSH, B. C., CAVASOS, L. L., & BROOKS, J. A. (2008). Motivational interviewing. In W. O'Donohue, & J. E. Fisher (Eds.), *Cognitive behavior therapy: Applying empirically supported techniques in your practice* (2nd ed., pp. 357–366). Hoboken, NJ: Wiley.

*LEVENSON, H. (2010). *Brief dynamic therapy*. Washington, DC: American Psychological Association.

LUM, D. (2011). *Culturally competent practice: A framework for understanding diverse groups and justice issues* (4th ed.). Belmont, CA: Brooks/Cole, Cengage Learning.

MARLATT, G. A., & DONOVAN, D. M. (Eds.). (2005). *Relapse prevention: Maintenance strategies in the treatment of addictive behaviors* (2nd ed.). New York: Guilford Press.

*MEICHENBAUM, D. (1977). *Cognitive behavior modification: An integrative approach.* New York: Plenum Press.

MEICHENBAUM, D. (2007). Stress inoculation training: A preventive and treatment approach. In P. M. Lehrer, R. L. Woolfolk, & W. Sime (Eds.), *Principles and practices of stress management* (3rd ed., pp. 497–518). New York: Guilford Press.

*MEICHENBAUM, D. (2008). Stress inoculation training. In W. O'Donohue, & J. E. Fisher (Eds.), *Cognitive behavior therapy: Applying empirically supported techniques in your practice* (2nd ed., pp. 529–532). Hoboken, NJ: Wiley.

*MILLER, S. D., HUBBLE, M. A., DUNCAN, B. L., & WAMPOLD, B. E. (2010). Delivering what works. In B. L. Duncan, S. D. Miller, B. E. Wampold, & M. A. Hubble (Eds.), *The heart and soul of change: Delivering what works in therapy* (2nd ed., pp. 421–429). Washington, DC: American Psychological Association.

*MILLER, W. R., & ROLLNICK, S. (2002). *Motivational interviewing: Preparing people for change* (2nd ed.). New York: Guilford Press.

*MORENO, Z. T., BLOMKVIST, L. D., & RUTZEL, T. (2000). *Psychodrama, surplus reality and the art of healing*. Philadelphia: Routledge (Taylor & Francis).

*MURPHY, J. J. (2008). *Solution-focused counseling in schools* (2nd ed.). Alexandria, VA: American Counseling Association.

NEUKRUG, E. (2011). *Counseling theory and practice*. Belmont, CA: Brooks/Cole, Cengage Learning.

NEWRING, K.A.B., LOVERICH, T. M., HARRIS, C. D., & WHEELER, J. (2008). In W. O'Donohue, & J. E. Fisher (Eds.), *Cognitive behavior therapy: Applying empirically supported techniques in your practice* (2nd ed., pp. 422–433). Hoboken, NJ: Wiley.

*NORCROSS, J. C. (2005). A primer on psychotherapy integration. In J. C. Norcross & M. R. Goldfried (Eds.), *Handbook of psychotherapy integration* (2nd ed., pp. 3–23). New York: Oxford University Press.

NORCROSS, J. C. (2010). The therapeutic relationship. In B. L. Duncan, S. D. Miller, B. E. Wampold, & M. A. Hubble (Eds.), *The heart and soul of change: Delivering what works in therapy* (2nd ed., pp. 113–141). Washington DC: American Psychological Association.

*NORCROSS, J. C (Ed.). (2011). *Psychotherapy relationships that work* (2nd ed.). New York: Oxford University Press.

NORCROSS, J. C., & BEUTLER, L. E. (2011). Integrative psychotherapies. In R. J. Corsini & D. Wedding (Eds.), *Current psychotherapies* (9th ed., pp. 502–535). Belmont, CA: Brooks/Cole, Cengage Learning.

*NORCROSS, J. C., BEUTLER, L. E., & LEVANT, R. F. (Eds.). (2006). *Evidence-based practice in mental health: Debate and dialogue on the fundamental questions.* Washington, DC: American Psychological Association.

*NORCROSS, J. C., & GOLDFRIED, M. R. (Eds.). (2005). *Handbook of psychotherapy integration* (2nd ed.). New York: Oxford University Press.

*NORCROSS, J. C., & GUY, J. D. (2007). *Leaving it at the office: A guide to psychotherapist self-care.* New York: Guilford Press.

*NORCROSS, J. C., HOGAN, T. P., & KOOCHER, G. P. (2008). *Clinician's guide to evidence-based practices in mental health.* New York: Oxford University Press.

*NORCROSS, J. C., KARPIAK, C. P., & LISTER, K. M. (2005). What's an integrationist? A study of self-identified integrative and (occasionally) eclectic psychologists. *Journal of Clinical Psychology, 61,* 1587–1594.

NORCROSS, J. C., KREBS, P. M., & PROCHASKA, J. O. (2011). Stages of change. *Journal of Clinical Psychology: In Session, 67*(2), 143–154.

NORCROSS, J. C., & LAMBERT, M. J. (2011). Evidence-based therapy relationships. In J. C. Norcross (Ed.), *Psychotherapy relationships that work: Evidence-based responsiveness* (2nd ed., pp. 3–21). New York: Oxford University Press.

NORCROSS, J. C., & WAMPOLD, B. E. (2011a). Evidence-based therapy relationships: Research conclusions and clinical practices. In J. C. Norcross (Ed.), *Psychotherapy relationships that work: Evidence-based responsiveness* (2nd ed., pp. 423–430). New York: Oxford University Press.

NORCROSS, J. C., & WAMPOLD, J. C. (2011b). What works for whom: Tailoring psychotherapy to the person. *Journal of Clinical Psychology, 67*(2), 127–132.

O'DONOHUE, W., & FISHER, J. E. (Eds.). (2008). *Cognitive behavior therapy: Applying empirically supported techniques in your practice* (2nd ed.). Hoboken, NJ: Wiley.

PAUL, G. L. (1967). Outcome research in psychotherapy. *Journal of Consulting Psychology, 31,* 109–188.

PEDERSEN, P. B. (2008). Ethics, competence, and professional issues in cross-cultural counseling. In P. B. Pedersen, J. G. Draguns, W. E. Lonner, & J. E. Trimble (Eds.), *Counseling across cultures* (6th ed., pp. 5–20). Thousand Oaks, CA: Sage.

POLSTER, E. (1987). Escape from the present: Transition and storyline. In J. K. Zeig (Ed.), *The evolution of psychotherapy* (pp. 326–340). New York: Brunner/Mazel.

PROCHASKA, J. O., & DiCLEMENTE, C. C. (2005). The transtheoretical approach. In J. C. Norcross & M. R. Goldfried (Eds.), *Handbook of psychotherapy integration* (2nd ed., pp. 147–171). New York: Oxford University Press.

*PROCHASKA, J. O., & NORCROSS, J. C. (2010). *Systems of psychotherapy: A transtheoretical analysis* (7th ed.). Belmont, CA: Brooks/Cole, Cengage Learning.

ROBERTSON, L. A., & YOUNG, M. E. (2011). The revised ASERVIC spiritual competencies. In C. S. Cashwell & J. S. Young (Eds.), *Integrating spirituality and religion into counseling: A guide to competent practice* (2nd ed., pp. 25–42). Alexandria, VA: American Counseling Association.

ROGERS, C. (1957). The necessary and sufficient conditions of therapeutic personality change. *Journal of Consulting Psychology, 21,* 95–103.

ROGERS, C. (1961). *On becoming a person.* Boston: Houghton Mifflin.

ROGERS, C. (1980). *A way of being.* Boston: Houghton Mifflin.

*SCHNEIDER, K. J. (Ed.). (2008). *Existential-integrative psychotherapy: Guideposts to the core of practice.* New York: Routledge.

*SCHNEIDER, K. J., & KRUG, O. T. (2010). *Existential-humanistic therapy.* Washington, DC: American Psychological Association.

*SHARF, R. S. (2012). *Theories of psychotherapy and counseling: Concepts and cases* (5th ed.). Belmont, CA: Brooks/Cole, Cengage Learning.

SOLLOD, R. N. (2005). Integrating spirituality with psychotherapy. In J. C. Norcross & M. R. Goldfried (Eds.), *Handbook of psychotherapy integration* (2nd ed., pp. 403–416). New York: Oxford University Press.

*STEBNICKI, M. A. (2008). *Empathy fatigue: Healing the mind, body, and spirit of professional counselors.* New York: Springer.

*STRICKER, G. (2010). *Psychotherapy integration.* Washington, DC: American Psychological Association.

*STRICKER, G., & GOLD, J. (Eds.). (2006). *A casebook of psychotherapy integration.* Washington, DC: American Psychological Association.

*SUE, D. W., & SUE, D. (2008). *Counseling the culturally diverse: Theory and practice* (5th ed.). New York: Wiley.

*TEYBER, E., & McCLURE, F. H. (2011). *Interpersonal process in therapy: An integrative model* (2nd ed.). Belmont, CA: Brooks/Cole, Cengage Learning.

VONTRESS, C. E. (2008). Existential therapy. In J. Frew & M. D. Spiegler (Eds.), *Contemporary psychotherapies for a diverse world* (pp. 141–176). Boston: Lahaska Press.

*WAMPOLD, B. E. (2001). *The great psychotherapy debate: Models, methods, and findings.* Mahwah, NJ: Erlbaum.

WAMPOLD, B. E. (2010). *The basics of psychotherapy: An introduction to theory and practice.* Washington, DC: American Psychological Association.

WEITEN, W., DUNN, D. S., & HAMMER, E. Y. (2012). *Psychology applied to modern life: Adjustment in the 21st century* (10th ed.). Belmont, CA: Wadsworth, Cengage Learning.

*WOLDT, A., & TOMAN, S. (Eds.). (2005). *Gestalt therapy: History, theory, and practice.* Thousand Oaks, CA: Sage.

WUBBOLDING, R. E. (2000). *Reality therapy for the 21st century.* Muncie, IN: Accelerated Development (Taylor & Francis Group).

*WUBBOLDING, R. (2011). *Reality therapy.* Washington, DC: American Psychological Association.

YOUNG, J. S., & CASHWELL, C. S. (2011a). Integrating spirituality and religion into counseling: An introduction. In C. S. Cashwell & J. S. Young (Eds.), *Integrating spirituality and religion into counseling: A guide to competent practice* (2nd ed., pp. 1–24). Alexandria, VA: American Counseling Association.

YOUNG, J. S., & CASHWELL, C. S. (2011b). Where do we go from here? In C. S. Cashwell & J. S. Young (Eds.), *Integrating spirituality and religion into counseling: A guide to competent practice* (2nd ed., pp. 279–289). Alexandria, VA: American Counseling Association.

TO THE OWNER OF THIS BOOK:

I hope that you have found *The Art of Integrative Counseling*, Third Edition useful. So that this book can be improved in a future edition, would you take the time to complete this sheet and return it? Thank you.

School and address: _____

_____

Department:_____

Instructor's name:_____

1. What I like most about this book is:_____

_____

_____

2. What I like least about this book is:_____

_____

_____

3. My general reaction to this book is:_____

_____

_____

4. The name of the course in which I used this book is:_____

_____

5. Were all of the chapters of the book assigned for you to read?_____

   If not, which ones weren't? _____

6. In the space below, or on a separate sheet of paper, please write specific suggestions for improving this book and anything else you'd care to share about your experience in using this book.

_____

_____

DO NOT STAPLE. PLEASE SEAL WITH TAPE.

FOLD HERE

BROOKS/COLE
CENGAGE Learning

NO POSTAGE
NECESSARY
IF MAILED
IN THE
UNITED STATES

BUSINESS REPLY MAIL
FIRST-CLASS MAIL   PERMIT NO. 34   BELMONT CA

POSTAGE WILL BE PAID BY ADDRESSEE

Attn: Counseling Editor

BrooksCole/Cengage Learning
20 Davis Drive
Belmont, CA   94002-9801

FOLD HERE

OPTIONAL:

Your name: _____ Date: _____

May we quote you, either in promotion for *The Art of Integrative Counseling*, Third Edition or in future publishing ventures?

Yes: _____   No: _____

Sincerely yours,

Gerald Corey